*Alexander the Corrector*

# Alexander the Corrector

### The Tormented Genius Whose
### Cruden's Concordance *Unwrote the Bible*

## JULIA KEAY

THE OVERLOOK PRESS
Woodstock & New York

This edition first published in the United States in 2005 by
The Overlook Press, Peter Mayer Publishers, Inc.
Woodstock & New York

WOODSTOCK:
One Overlook Drive
Woodstock, NY 12498
www.overlookpress.com
[for individual orders, bulk and special sales, contact our Woodstock office]

NEW YORK:
141 Wooster Street
New York, NY 10012

∞ The paper used in this book meets the requirements for paper
permanence as described in the ANSI Z39.48-1992 standard.

Library of Congress Cataloging-in-Publication Data

Keay, Julia.
Alexander the Corrector : the tormented genius whose Cruden's
concordance unwrote the Bible / Julia Keay.
1. Cruden, Alexander, 1701-1770. 2. Biblical scholars—Great Britain—
Biography. I. Title.
BS501.C78 K43 2005      220/.092 B 22      2005040606

Printed in the United States of America
ISBN 1-58567-690-X
2 4 6 8 9 7 5 3 1

*For Anna*

# Contents

| | | |
|---|---|---|
| *List of Illustrations* | | ix |
| *Acknowledgements* | | xv |
| *Preface* | | xvii |
| 1 | A Singular Addiction | 1 |
| 2 | The South Part of this Island | 22 |
| 3 | Monsieur Whatever-You-Please | 37 |
| 4 | Oh, for an 'Orlando'! | 56 |
| 5 | No Ordinary Queen | 70 |
| 6 | Receptacles of Misery | 96 |
| 7 | A Hundred Hairs to Hang by | 120 |
| 8 | *Coup de Grâce* | 136 |
| 9 | Too Much Religion | 164 |
| 10 | The Hundredth Hair | 182 |
| 11 | 'That which Men call MADNESSE' | 202 |
| 12 | A Matter of Life and Death | 219 |
| 13 | Much Personal Respect | 237 |
| | *Epilogue* | 245 |
| | *Notes* | 249 |
| | *Bibliography* | 255 |
| | *Index* | 261 |

# Illustrations

The modest plaque commemorating the birth of Alexander
Cruden in Aberdeen. *(Photograph by Nell Keay)*

A view of Netherkirkgate, Aberdeen, c.1750. *(Reproduced courtesy
of the University of Aberdeen)*

The Old Grammar School, Aberdeen. *(Reproduced courtesy of the
University of Aberdeen)*

Marischal College, Aberdeen, c.1780, from a drawing by James Skene
of Rubislaw, Fasti. *(Reproduced courtesy of Aberdeen City Archives)*

All that remains of the Aberdeen Tolbooth, scene of Cruden's first
incarceration. *(Photograph by Nell Keay)*

Reverend Thomas Blackwell, Professor of Divinity and Principal of
Marischal College. *(Reproduced courtesy of the University of
Aberdeen)*

Thomas Blackwell Junior, by Jonathan Richardson. *(Photograph ©
The Pierpont Morgan Library, New York)*

Jameson's House in Schoolhill, Aberdeen. *(Reproduced courtesy of
Aberdeen City Archives)*

John Strype's Plan of the City of London, c.1720. *(Photograph ©
Museum of London)*

James Stanley, 10th Earl of Derby. Engraving by Van der Gucht
from a painting by H. Winstanley. *(Reproduced courtesy of the
National Portrait Galley, London)*

Caroline of Anspach, wife of George II, c.1716, after Sir Godfrey Kneller, Bt. Cruden dedicated the first edition of his Concordance to the Queen. *(Reproduced courtesy of the National Portrait Galley, London)*

A page from Cruden's Complete Concordance to the Holy Scriptures. *(Photograph © The British Library, London)*

St James's Palace, by T. Bowles. *(Photograph © Guildhall Library/ Corporation of London)*

Elizabeth Blackwell. *(Photograph © Hulton/Archive)*

Illustrations from Elizabeth Blackwell's *Curious Herbal*. *(Photographs © Bridgeman Art Library, London)*

Alexander Cruden MA. Engraved by W.C. Edwards, c.1762.

Alexander Cruden MA. Engraved by T. Cook (unknown date). *(Reproduced courtesy of the Ashmolean Museum, Oxford)*

Alexander Cruden. Derived by Rex Whistler, c.1934.

Dr James Monro (1680–1752), by John Michael Williams, c.1747. *(Reproduced courtesy of the Royal College of Physicians of London)*

Dr John Monro (1715–1791), by Nathaniel Dance, c.1769. *(Reproduced courtesy of the Royal College of Physicians of London)*

'Scene in a Madhouse', from Hogarth's *Rake's Progress*. *(Photograph © Corbis)*

Lord Chief Justice Sir William Lee, KC, by C.F. Barker. *(Reproduced courtesy of the National Portrait Galley, London)*

Interior view of Westminster Hall, by Pugin and Rowlandson. *(Photograph © Guildhall Library/Corporation of London)*

Cruden's Index of Matters to Newton's edition of *Paradise Lost* (published in 1749). *(Photograph © The British Library, London)*

Spenser's *Faerie Queene* in the 1753 edition corrected by Cruden. *(Photograph © The British Library, London)*

Profile of Cruden in Camden Passage, Islington. (*In* From Camden Passage with Love *by John Payton, The Book Guild Ltd, Sussex)*

Cruden's profile and memorial plaque in Camden Passage were unveiled by the future Poet Laureate John Betjeman in 1965. (*In From Camden Passage with Love by John Payton, The Book Guild Ltd, Sussex*)

'I am somewhat of a disposition that if I had a hundred hairs to hang by and ninety nine should fail, I would endeavour to hang on by the hundredth, and if that should fail I then submit to the will of God.'

ALEXANDER CRUDEN

# Acknowledgements

I owe a great debt of gratitude to Judith Cripps, City Archivist at Aberdeen City Archives, and Michelle Gait of Aberdeen University Library Special Collections, who have been unfailingly generous with their time and their expertise. Fiona Watson, Archivist of the Northern Health Services Archive, Robin Myers, Hon. Archivist of the Worshipful Company of Stationers and Newspaper Makers, and Colin Gale, Archivist of Bethlem Royal Hospital, have provided me with invaluable background information on various stages of Cruden's life; and thanks, too, to the staffs of the National Library of Scotland, the British Library, the London Library, the Bodleian Library and Aberdeen City Library. I am also grateful to Elma McLaren for information on St Nicholas Kirk Aberdeen; to Susanah Mackay-James for research in London; to Paddy Forsyth and Ruth Johnston for research in Glasgow; to Charlie Gore for research in Sussex; to Bruce Madge for showing me his article on Elizabeth Blackwell; to Charlie Atkins for information on eighteenth century law courts; to Bikram Grewal and Alpana Khare for lending their house as the perfect 'writer's retreat' from a Scottish winter; and to my daughter Nell for taking photographs. Thanks, too, to Richard Johnson of HarperCollins for taking my word that Cruden's was a great story, to Robert Lacey, also of HarperCollins, for most perceptive editing, and to my agent, Bruce Hunter, for championing the project with such enthusiasm. The seeds of this book were sown by my daughter Anna when she asked me if I knew anything about Alexander Cruden (the answer, then, was 'no'); that it reached fruition is thanks to my husband John, who sets me the best of examples and who has nurtured it, and me, throughout.

# Preface

Alexander Cruden was solely and entirely responsible for 'a work which will live as long as the English language'; he undertook 'a labour which has seldom been equalled and cannot be exceeded'; he produced a book, first published in 1737, which has gone through countless editions, which has never been superseded, and which has never, in more than 250 years, been out of print. Yet if he is remembered at all, it is not for this. Alexander Cruden is remembered because, according to everyone who has ever written about him, he was mad.

'We have here at present a very extraordinary man, Mr Cruden,' wrote a Cambridge don to a London antiquary in 1755. 'The poor man (I pity him heartily) is supposed not to be quite in his right mind.' The *Biographia Britannica* of 1789 stated that 'such decided symptoms of insanity appeared in his conduct as rendered confinement necessary'. In 1836 the Reverend Samuel Blackburn went further – and was more poetic: 'He had a mind in which reason tottered, if she were not entirely dethroned'; ten years later William Youngman decided his fellow cleric had not been poetic enough: 'Alexander Cruden was one of those "or craz'd by care, or crossed by hopeless love", who trod the path of life on the verge of that awful abyss, where the hopes and happiness of so many great minds have been ingulfed.'

A pattern was emerging: each successive account made Cruden's madness sound more dramatic than the last. The pattern continued. He was 'a man of weak intellect' (Plomer's *Dictionary of Booksellers*, 1850). 'His mind became unhinged' (*DNB*, 1888). He was 'a confused and pious wretch . . . a man of diseased mind' (Dr S.M. Parrish, Professor of English at Cornell University, in an after-dinner speech in 1969). He was 'the perfect fool' (Roy Porter, *A Social History of Madness*, 1987). He 'became insane' (*Concise DNB*, 1992).

So, obviously, Alexander Cruden was mad. Why, though, had each writer on Cruden's life decided that his predecessor had understated the extent of his madness? What was the 'disappointment in love of an especially sad nature' that had resulted in this devoutly religious man being 'three times confined in a lunatic asylum'? And, most mysterious of all, how could a work of such monumental and meticulous scholarship as Cruden's Concordance have been the product of a mind 'in which reason tottered, if she were not entirely dethroned'?

# 1

# A Singular Addiction

When English soldier and angler Richard Franck made a tour of Scotland in 1656 he was so disgusted by the state of the road leading to Aberdeen that he almost gave up before he got there. 'The cawses [roadways] are uncartable,' he grumbled, 'pointed with rocky stumpy stones, and dawb'd all over with dingy dirt, that makes it impassible; and the fields are ten times worse because o'erspread with miry clay and incumbred with bogs that will bury a horse.' But he persevered – and was rewarded. (Maybe the weather improved.) 'Heaven,' he was soon eulogising, 'certainly has bless'd Aberdeen.' Every aspect of the city and its surroundings came under his scrutiny, and met with his approval: the fine buildings, the cleanly swept streets, the sun-drenched harbour, even 'the generous breasts of the ocean, from whence both mariner and merchant accumulate treasure dragged forth from the solid deeps of the sea'. And, the Cromwellian soldier was pleased to discover, its citizens were every bit as praiseworthy: 'here is no complaint of poverty, nor luxurious superfluities; the houses are fill'd with hospitality, not with profaneness'.

Into this paragon of Scottish cities, forty years later, Alexander Cruden was born, the second child – and second son – of Baillie William Cruden and his wife Isobel, *née* Pyper. The Crudens were worthy citizens, hard-working, sober, even a little dour as befitted good Calvinists, but not without aspirations. William Cruden was a Town Councillor as well as a baillie (magistrate or alderman), and had inherited from his merchant father a modest fortune and a stylish house in the centre of a surprisingly stylish town. As another Englishman, Daniel Defoe, would remark in 1706, just because Aberdeen was remote from other centres of population, this did not mean it was in any way inferior.

> *The great marketplace is very beautiful and spacious, and the Streets adjoining are very handsome and well-built, the Houses lofty and high; built not so high as to be inconvenient, as in Edinburgh, or low, to be contemptible, as in most other places. The generality of the citizens' Houses are built of Stone, four storeys high, with handsome Sashwindows, and are very well furnished within, the citizens here being as gay and genteel, and perhaps, as rich, as in any city in Scotland.*

So surprised was Defoe to find elegance and refinement where he had expected bleak utility that he failed to notice (or forgot to mention) the many other houses in Aberdeen which, to the despair of the Town Council, were still 'built of wood, with lath and plaister chimneys, the roof covered with turf, heath or straw' – structures so combustible that entire rows of them could, and did, burn down in an afternoon.

There is no house now on the site of the house in which Alexander Cruden was born. There is instead, in the very heart of Aberdeen, a passage which leads to a staircase which leads to a carpark – a concrete corner on the way to somewhere else, so draughty that even the litter doesn't loiter for long. At one end of the railings at the top of the staircase, screwed to the wall just below waist height, is a brass plaque which reads:

ALEXANDER CRUDEN

*1699–1770*

MASTER OF ARTS, MARISCHAL COLLEGE
COMPILER OF THE CONCORDANCE
TO THE BIBLE
WAS BORN IN A HOUSE IN CRUDEN'S COURT*
NEAR THIS SPOT

The house stood back from the street then, as now, called the Gallowgate. Just round the corner in one direction was Defoe's 'beautiful and spacious marketplace', the Castlegate, complete with elegant Mercat Cross and lowering Tolbooth or jail; just down the street in the other direction was the great St Nicholas Kirk, where the Cruden parents worshipped and where, on 8 June 1699, their second son Alexander was baptised. He was a puny baby, would remain small for his age throughout his childhood and felt his lack of inches even as an adult. But despite his supposed frailty and unlike several of his eventual ten siblings (six brothers and four sisters), he managed to survive both infancy and early childhood. At the age of eight wee Alexander Cruden, like his brother George before him, was enrolled as a pupil in Aberdeen Grammar School.

---

* 'Cruden's Court', although named after him, did not exist in Alexander Cruden's lifetime. The row, or 'court', of dwellings was constructed on the site of his birthplace sometime in the nineteenth century, and was itself demolished in the twentieth century.

Every morning the brothers left the house with the 'handsome Sash-windows', crossed the cobblestoned Gallowgate and plunged into the labyrinth of alleys that skulked behind the turreted grandeur of the Provost's Lodging. Dodging the fully-laden farm wagons that creaked along Flourmill Lane and skirting the high walls of St Nicholas' churchyard, they trudged – or, if they were late, no doubt they sprinted – up School Hill and into the Grammar School to be educated. (Between 1794 and 1798 the future poet George (Lord) Byron would make the same daily journey when he, too, was living just off the Gallowgate and attending Aberdeen Grammar School.)

A good Presbyterian education has been likened to a good Islamic education: intense, rigid, repetitive, solemn; discouraging any individuality or imagination, requiring unquestioning dedication from its students and demanding their complete devotion to one Book, and acceptance of that Book as the incontrovertible Word of God. Such, exactly, was Alexander Cruden's education at Aberdeen Grammar School. Pupils (all boys) were allowed only twelve days' holiday a year (three days at the start of every quarter); classes lasted for eight hours a day, six days a week (most of the seventh day, Sunday, was spent in church); the students were expected to learn passages of the Bible by heart every day; they were catechised by the presiding minister every day – with a master standing by to administer painful punishment with the dreaded leather 'tawse' if they faltered; and, apart from Bible Study, every class on every day was conducted in Latin. When he entered the Grammar School at the age of eight Cruden was presented with a copy of his first Latin primer, the redoubtable *Ruddiman's Rudiments*; by the time he left five years later he had worked his way through Caesar and Sallust, Livy and Cicero, Virgil and Horace – heavy-duty works of Latin literature that he had not only read, but studied and scanned and translated and committed in huge chunks to memory. And he was still only thirteen years old.

Luckily for wee Alexander, he liked Latin. Its rigid logic appealed to his methodical mind. It followed rules. It held no surprises to disturb his sense of order, its structures were consistent, each word had a clear-cut meaning, and its irregular forms were sufficiently unusual to be memorised. It demanded attention to detail, an ability to concentrate and an excellent memory, qualities Cruden had in abundance. His memory, in particular, was prodigious. So he was good at Latin. He did not shine, but then it was not in his nature to shine. His elder brother George was the star not just of the Cruden family but of the whole of Aberdeen Grammar School. And when George entered Marischal College as an undergraduate at thirteen (the standard age for entry to university), he became a star pupil there too. Alexander was content just to trundle along in the pale gleam cast by his brother's brilliance.

Marischal College (pronounced 'Marshall') was the younger of Aberdeen's two universities. The older, King's College, had been founded in 1495 by William Elphinstone, a remarkable churchman originally from Glasgow, who was 'promoted' to the Bishopric of Aberdeen after a spell as James IV's ambassador to France. Horrified to discover that the inhabitants of his new diocese were 'rude, ignorant and almost savage', Elphinstone had applied to the Pope (Alexander VI, a member of the dreaded Borgia family and father of the infamous Lucrezia) for permission to establish a college in this most northerly of Scottish towns to bring the light of learning into what he, as a Glaswegian, saw as its chilly darkness. The resulting establishment was named St Mary's College in honour of the Blessed Virgin (but as soon as Pope Alexander died in 1503 Elphinstone renamed it King's College in honour of his old patron King James).

Aberdeen's second university was founded in 1593 by an

alumnus of its first.* One of the richest of Scotland's earls, who was said to be able to travel the length of Scotland and never miss a night in his own castle, George Keith, 5th Earl Marischal, had graduated from King's in about 1570. To complete his education he went on a prolonged Grand Tour of Europe, during which he spent several years studying in Calvinist Geneva, and after which he returned home to found Marischal College as a Protestant rival to his Catholic *alma mater*. In 1641 there was an attempt to amalgamate the two universities when the Scots Parliament, by this time itself under Presbyterian control, passed an Act 'to uneit and erect the tue colledgeis of Aberdeen, viz. the old colledge thairof and the new callit Marischellis Colledge, in ane joynt universitie . . .'.[1] King's, which the Reformation had sent into sad decline, was enthusiastic about the plan; Marischal, which was thriving, refused to have anything to do with it; in 1661 all the legislation of the Scots Parliament during the Civil War and Protectorate was repealed anyway, and the 'ane joynt universitie' did not materialise for another two hundred years.

Although post-Reformation King's had long ceased to be a Catholic institution, the whiff of popery drifting through its precincts was still strong enough to put sceptical Presbyterians off their studies. Besides, Marischal College was, like so much else in Aberdeen, just along the street from the Cruden home, whereas King's was a mile or so to the north in the leafy burgh of Kirkton of Aberdon (also, and still, known as 'Old Aberdeen'). So the Cruden brothers attended Marischal College, where their life was as regulated and rigorous as it had been at the Grammar School. Prayers and Bible Reading at

---

* Although the first university in Aberdeen, King's College was only the third in Scotland after St Andrews (founded 1412) and Glasgow (founded 1451). Edinburgh University (founded 1583) was the fourth and Marischal (1593) the fifth. The oldest universities in England, Oxford and Cambridge, date from the thirteenth century.

6 a.m. (6.30 in winter) were followed by classes, lectures and tutorials all the way through to a final Reading of the Scriptures at 8 p.m. The curriculum, however, was considerably broader. The brothers studied Greek and French as well as Latin, they studied history and geography, philosophy and theology, physiology and mathematics. The brilliant George topped the class in every subject, particularly Greek, at which he excelled even by his own high standards. The studious Alexander got by. Latin he was good at; Greek he could manage; French – by working hard and applying his talent for learning by rote – he could manage as well. He had little interest in geography, physiology or mathematics; but for one subject he developed a deep and lasting passion. Like William Tyndale before him, Alexander Cruden became 'singularly addicted to the study of the Scriptures'.*

In most households in early eighteenth century Scotland the only book, if there were any books at all, was the Bible. It was regarded with great reverence as the source of wisdom on all matters. In the absence of any other form of reading material – no literature, no history, no novels, no newspapers – it also served as a complete library in miniature. It provided inspiration as well as enlightenment, contained as many songs and stories as it did homilies and sermons, told tales of far-away places and long-ago people, of romance and endeavour, of death and disaster, of mortal sin, holy redemption and eternal salvation; it provided nourishment for the imagination as well as sustenance for the immortal soul. But for Calvinists the Bible did far more than that. As the Quran to Muslims, so the Bible to Calvinists: it was quite simply the Word of God.

---

* The story of William Tyndale (c.1494–1536), the first person to translate the Bible into English, is well told in *The Making of the English Bible* by Benson Bobrick.

Blessed with a literal mind as well as a Calvinist upbringing, Alexander Cruden had sat through the daily family Bible readings as a small child, paralysed by the solemnity of actually listening to the Word of God. At the Grammar School he applied himself to Bible Study with such diligence that he could quote from the Holy Scriptures at even greater length than he could quote from Virgil. He took to carrying a Bible around with him as if it were a guide-book or an instruction manual (both of which, to him, it clearly was); and at Marischal College he finally saw how he could put his passion to good use. Brother George was destined for an academic career – he would go into the Church.

When George graduated at the age of seventeen, he was, as expected, awarded a place as one of Marischal College's Regents, junior lecturers who might one day become professors. But before Alexander could take any further steps along the road to his own destiny, the brothers were forced to take an unexpected break from their studies.

Aberdeen being the most civic-minded of Scottish burghs, and their father being a Burgess and a Town Councillor, local politics had always been an important part of Cruden family life. But the Crudens, like most of their fellow Aberdonians, had never felt very involved in national politics. The death of a sovereign, whether far away in Edinburgh or (since the 1603 Union of the Crowns had sent James VI of Scotland hurtling south to become James I of Great Britain) even further away in London, was marked in Aberdeen with respect and solemnity. 'The Sunday subsequent to the event . . . was appointed for humiliation and public mourning, the churches and cross were hung with black and the bells were muffled, and tolled during the interval of sermons.' On the Monday the accession of the new sovereign (whoever he or she might be) was greeted with 'unbounded demonstrations of joy by all ranks of the people'; there were 'bonfires on the streets and ringing the bells; the cross was decorated with tapestry, and the citizens accompanied the magistrates in a procession through the streets manifesting in psalmody their joy on the happy occasion'.[2] And on the Tuesday the citizens of Aberdeen forgot all about who was on the throne and went back to the serious business of running their burgh and making a living. But the events of 1714–15 brought Aberdeen directly, if briefly, into the centre of national affairs.

With the death of Queen Anne in 1714 the thrones of England and Scotland passed to her distant cousin, Hanoverian (and Protestant) George. This was sufficiently unpopular both north and south of the border for Anne's Catholic half-brother, James Francis Edward Stewart, the Old Pretender, to be encouraged to make a bid for the crowns he thought rightfully his. The first serious Jacobite* Rising started on 6 September 1715 when the Earl of Mar raised the standard of rebellion in Braemar, and it arrived in Aberdeen two weeks later when the young Earl Marischal, whose mother was a Catholic, rode into the city at the head of a band of like-minded nobles and country gentlemen and proclaimed 'King James VIII'† at the Mercat Cross.

'In Aberdeen,' according to historian Alexander Keith, 'fanaticism in religion was of late growth; Episcopalian and Presbyterian in the seventeenth century regarded one another with far greater venom than ever poisoned the relationship of Catholic and Reformer in the sixteenth century.'[3] By the early years of the eighteenth century the two-pronged antidote of geographical isolation and civic pride was beginning to repair the damage (not for nothing had King Robert the Bruce given

---

* From *Jacobus*, the Latin for 'James'.

† Scots consider the Kings James should be numbered according to their place in the Scottish succession. Thus the King who also became James I of England remains, to Scots, James VI, and James II is still sometimes referred to as James VII.

the city its motto, '*Bon Accord*'); but the 1715 Jacobite Rising threatened new disharmony.

Support for the Jacobites, always strong in the Scottish Highlands, was strongest of all in the rich, castle-strewn hinterland of Aberdeen. The largest landowners and most powerful nobles (the Gordon Earls of Huntly, the Hay Earls of Errol, the Mackenzie Earls of Seaforth, the Erskine Earls of Mar) were eager champions of the Jacobite cause. So, seemingly, were a majority of Aberdeen's Town Council – perhaps even a majority of Aberdonians. But many, including the Crudens, were not. The Cruden family sat tight-lipped while the Incorporated Trades fêted the Earl Marischal and his proclamation; they listened impassively to news of the inconclusive Battle of Sheriffmuir (near Perth) fought between Jacobites and Hanoverians in November; and if they were among the crowd of excited citizens who lined the streets when the Old Pretender rode into Aberdeen in December 1715, it would have been to glower their disapproval rather than to rejoice. Feelings ran so high between the different factions in the crowd that what James Francis Edward had hoped would be a welcoming party turned into a brawl and then a riot. Running battles broke out along the Gallowgate, stones were thrown, precious glass windows were smashed (including, according to Alexander, all those in the Cruden house) and not a few heads were broken in the affray. For a while after the Old Pretender's arrival in Aberdeen, Baillie William even had to submit to having Stewart soldiers billeted in his house, an episode which served only to intensify Alexander's hatred of Jacobites, far stronger than mere political preference, which would endure till his dying day.

This first Jacobite adventure fizzled out through a combination of bad management and lack of support, and in February the Old Pretender scuttled off back to the Continent with the Earl of Mar, leaving his followers to the mercies of the

Hanoverian government. Although romantic legend would have it otherwise, those mercies were in fact reasonably tender. The Jacobite members of Aberdeen Town Council were forced to stand down and their speedily elected replacements 'took the first opportunitie of congratulating the wisest and best of Kings [George I] on the late great and happie turn of affairs in these northern parts'; the 10th, and last, Earl Marischal was dispossessed of his title and estates but managed to flee the country before he was caught; all but one of the professors at Marischal College were dismissed for supporting their disgraced patron, and the University was forced to close its doors.

Radical changes were required before those doors could be reopened. The one remaining professor was promoted to Principal. Replacements were found for the departed Professors of Greek and mathematics. A chair of medicine was inaugurated, and the young, brilliant and safely anti-Jacobite George Cruden was re-engaged as Regent together with two newcomers. These changes were all minutely scrutinised before being approved by the Hanoverian government, and by the beginning of 1717 the College had reopened for business and Alexander Cruden had resumed his studies.

Not many months later the replacement Professor of Greek fell ill and George Cruden was chosen to succeed him. At the tender age of twenty he became a fully-fledged Professor, and the Cruden parents William and Isobel (who had recently given birth to their tenth child) must have glowed with pride at this confirmation of the brilliance of their first-born. But their second-born soon had an achievement to report too. Beavering away almost unnoticed in George's shadow, Alexander graduated MA and was accepted by the Marischal College Professor of Divinity to study for the Presbyterian ministry.

Reverend Thomas Blackwell DD was not just Professor of Divinity at Marischal College. The sole survivor of the

University's previous regime, Blackwell was now also its Principal and, accordingly, one of the most powerful men in Aberdeen. His influence would govern not just the remainder of Alexander Cruden's university career; it would dictate the course of his entire life.

The Blackwell and Cruden families had much in common. The parents were exact contemporaries, would each have a great many children and would lose several of them in infancy, and their sons were fellow students both at the Grammar School and at Marischal College. But, unlike the Crudens, the 'great and pious' Reverend Thomas Blackwell and his genteel wife Christian were connected by blood or marriage to some of Aberdeen's – even Scotland's – most reputable and learned families, and they contrived to keep the relationship between themselves and the humbler Crudens formal and distant. In their mutual support for the Hanoverian government during the 1715 Jacobite Rising the socially ambitious William Cruden discerned a very definite brotherhood between himself and the Reverend Thomas. By the time George had been awarded his professorship at Marischal College, and Alexander had been accepted as one of Principal Blackwell's students of Divinity, William Cruden was well on the way to considering Thomas Blackwell his social equal. The Reverend did not reciprocate.

Thomas Blackwell was a churchman long before he was an academic. Originally from Glasgow, he had been ordained in Paisley in 1693 and called to the ministry of St Nicholas in Aberdeen in 1700. Here he served his congregation well, preaching impressive sermons, baptising countless infants – including, to date, eleven of his own and several of the Crudens' – and officiating at many of their sad little burials. During his time as Professor of Divinity at Marischal College he published three lengthy works of theology – *Ratio Sacra, or an Appeal Unto the Rational World about the Reasonableness* *of Revealed Religion directed against the Three Prevailing Errors of Atheism, Deism and Bourignonism** (1710), *Schema Sacrum,* which had an equally catchy subtitle – *A Sacred Scheme of Natural and Revealed Religion, making a Scriptural-Rational Account of Creation, Divine Predestination and the Wise Divine Procedure* (1711), and *Methodus Evangelica* (1712). When, in 1717, Blackwell was invited to become Principal of Marischal College he accepted graciously, considering the honour to be no more than he deserved.

Alexander Cruden shared none of his father's aspirations, and did not think of himself as the equal, either socially or intellectually, of any of the Blackwells. He had spent his school years being bullied and intimidated by the eldest Blackwell son, Thomas Junior, and was so much in awe of the Principal himself that during their first few tutorials he hardly dared speak. But he kept his head down and concentrated on his studies, and gradually the lofty Reverend became aware of his timid student's diligence.

Neither at this nor at any other time in his life did Alexander Cruden aspire to be an original thinker. He knew he would never be a great theologian, or even a truly great scholar. His strength lay in his familiarity with the Bible, and his close attention to every word it contained as unquestionably the Word of God. The more thoroughly he came to know his Bible, the more strength he derived from it. 'The meek shall inherit the earth', it told him, 'blessed are the poor in spirit for theirs is the kingdom of heaven', and 'whosoever exalteth himself shall be abased, and he that humbleth himself shall

---

* Antoinette Bourignon (1616–80) was a French religious 'fanatic' who believed that religion should be more to do with inward emotions than with knowledge or practice. Her ideas, anathema to Presbyterians, were currently attracting considerable interest in Scotland. So dangerous did they seem to the ecclesiastical authorities that until 1889 a solemn renunciation of them was required of every candidate for the ministry.

be exalted' (this last was particularly comforting when the likes of Thomas Blackwell Junior and his cronies mocked Alexander's slight stature or his tendency to stammer under stress); and the more he studied, the more clearly he understood his own place in the *Schema Sacrum*. As a minister of the Gospel it would be his duty to bring the Word of God to those poor unfortunate souls who could not, or would not, read it for themselves. It was an awesome prospect.

With his exemplary brother George prodding him on one side, the Reverend Thomas Blackwell stooping from his august heights to beckon him on from the other, and a copy of the Holy Scriptures clasped tightly in his hand, Cruden's confidence slowly grew. Had he kept his mind on his studies for just a few months longer the Presbyterian Church in Aberdeen would have gained one more minister – and the world might never have had the benefit of Cruden's Concordance. But at the age of twenty, shortly before he was due to be ordained, Alexander's attention wandered, he looked up from his books, he saw a girl, and he fell in love.

First loves are traditionally ill-fated, wreathed in sighs and throbbing with heartbreak as one or other party turns out to be unsuitable, unwilling, or otherwise unsatisfactory. Mercifully few have consequences as calamitous as Alexander Cruden's.

The full story of what happened in Aberdeen in that autumn of 1720 remains a mystery. At the time the only thing anyone knew for certain was that all of a sudden Baillie William Cruden's second son Alexander, the timid little theology student, had gone mad and had had to be locked away in the Tolbooth. Since there was no history of madness in the Cruden family and the young man himself had shown no previous signs of lunacy, opinion in the town was divided: some were convinced that he must have been bitten by a rabid dog;

others thought it much more likely that he had suffered a disappointment in love. The former theory was eventually discounted because 'nothing can be gathered from the history of that dreadful distemper which favours this opinion'; the latter gained ground – and was embellished: the disappointment in love was 'of an especially sad nature, but it is doubtful whether this operated as a cause or a consequence'. In other words, no one was sure whether Alexander's love affair had foundered because he had gone mad, or whether he had gone mad because his love affair had foundered.

Though the Crudens were respectable, and respected, citizens of Aberdeen, they were not of sufficient consequence for their domestic misfortunes to remain a hot topic for long. No new titbits of information were forthcoming, public attention was doubtless soon diverted by some other drama, and the story faded from view. Not until Alexander Cruden was old and famous did anyone think it worth revisiting; not until he and most of the other main players were dead did anyone publish an account of it, and even then, to avoid embarrassment to 'those relations of the parties still living', no names (apart from Cruden's) were ever mentioned.

The first account was published in *Biographia Britannica* in 1789. It was written by Alexander Chalmers (one of a confusing surfeit of Alexanders to feature in the story of Alexander Cruden), whose father had known Cruden well and who had himself, as a small boy, met Cruden when the latter returned to Aberdeen in his old age to give a series of lectures. When he was commissioned to write an article on Cruden for the *Biographia Britannica* Chalmers found himself torn between his duty as a writer to tell the truth, his loyalty to his fellow Aberdonians and his high regard for Cruden. In the end he decided on a compromise, telling some of the truth but by no means all of it.

At the age of twenty, Chalmers confirmed, Alexander

Cruden had indeed fallen in love; the object of his affections had been 'the daughter of a clergyman from Aberdeen'; and his attentions to her had been rejected 'in terms not the most gentle'. This painful snub had caused the young suitor 'to use such outrageous attempts to obtain an interview with the object of his affections that obliged his friends to send him to a place of confinement'. So far so good, Chalmers must have thought; now for the difficult bit. 'Shortly after he was placed under restraint,' Chalmers continued (and one can almost see him having to force the words from his pen), 'it was revealed that a criminal intercourse had subsisted between her and her own brother, by whom she was actually pregnant.'*

Because he was the first biographer to write about Cruden, and because he would do so in one form or another for various dictionaries of biography and as the preface to several editions of Cruden's Concordance over a period of nearly thirty years, Chalmers became the accepted authority on the life of Alexander Cruden. But Chalmers was a sensitive man. He went through such elaborate contortions to avoid hurting anyone's feelings, his later versions contained so many inconsistencies, and elements of the story were until quite recently still so shocking, that it is hardly surprising subsequent writers either got into a muddle or decided not to delve any deeper than they had to into such murky waters. Now that too much time has elapsed for anyone's feelings still to be vulnerable, and now that few things are considered too shocking to explore, it is possible to pursue the questions raised by Chalmers' various versions without fear of what might be revealed.

On some facts Chalmers is consistent: Alexander Cruden had fallen in love, had been rejected, had taken this disappointment badly, had reacted outrageously and had ended up in a

---

* 'As there are some relations of the parties yet living' (Chalmers added in a footnote) 'the names are omitted.'

lunatic asylum. On other details, such as who was responsible for having Cruden locked away, he contradicts himself, initially asserting that it was 'his friends', then that it was 'her friends', before eventually settling for 'his or her friends'. (A later biographer would decide, on unspecified grounds, that it was his parents.[4]) The first question that leaps to mind is what could possibly constitute such an outrageous attempt to obtain an interview with someone that the perpetrator had to be sent to a place of confinement because of it? Whatever did Cruden do? Shin up a drainpipe and break in through her bedroom window? That would, in eighteenth century Aberdeen, have been startling behaviour indeed, and if in the heat of the moment he did go to that extreme, then he might well have been arrested and thrown in jail until he had cooled down. But why not just jail? Why a lunatic asylum?

In fact in 1720 there was no lunatic asylum in Aberdeen; the city's Tolbooth, a forbidding stronghold not half a mile from Cruden's home, served both purposes. But Chalmers makes it very clear that Cruden was confined in the Tolbooth not as a delinquent or a criminal, but as a lunatic. If he had shinned up a drainpipe and broken in through the girl's bedroom window, and if as a result he had been arrested and thrown in jail until he had cooled down, why did Chalmers not come straight out and say so? He must have known that Cruden's reputation would be much less damaged by the revelation of such an adolescent indiscretion than by the far darker implications of what he (and others) did say. Besides, such an extreme reaction even to 'rejection in terms not the most gentle' seems totally out of character in a man who in later life, in far crueller adversity, would barely lose his temper, let alone cause a public disturbance.

Perhaps Cruden suffered some kind of a breakdown as a result of his rejection. But could even the most painful rebuff have been sufficient (in the words of a later biographer,

William Youngman) to 'blast his fondest hopes, darken his fairest prospects and cast him upon the world with a shattered and distracted mind'? Could it have been enough to send him insane?

According to Professor R.A. Houston's *Madness and Society in Eighteenth Century Scotland,* this was certainly possible. 'Unrequited love was presented as a cause and symptom of derangement or melancholy for both men and women. A third of Robert Burton's 1621 *Anatomy of Melancholy* was devoted to "love melancholy" though Burton conceived this as a masculine condition.' (Women, particularly Irish women, were said in a later study to have been more likely to be driven mad by lust.[5])

'Love melancholy' therefore seems a distinct possibility. But there were others. Alexander Chalmers' revelation that the young lady had not only been having 'a criminal intercourse' with her own brother, but that she was expecting a baby from this incestuous relationship, explains his reluctance to name names. Might the shock of discovering such a scandal have had something to do with Cruden's supposed madness? Did he even know about it? Since Chalmers vouchsafed no opinion on this point, later biographers have made up their own minds, some deciding that Cruden's madness was the result of finding out that the girl he loved was pregnant by her own brother, others that he had gone mad and been locked away before the story broke, and therefore never knew anything about it. (William Youngman was much comforted by the idea that 'the covert of the asylum sheltered him from a greater calamity'.) The Tolbooth registers for the period in question have not survived, so there is no official record of Cruden's admission, far less any information on the reasons for it. The only reference Cruden himself would ever make to the episode is cryptic. Writing many years later, and going into the minimum of detail, he merely remarks darkly that 'In the year 1720

[I was] in a treacherous Manner decoy'd into the publick prison at Aberdeen by the Advice of a conceited Man.'* This raises far more questions than it answers – but at least it confirms that he was there.

The only prison for the combined burghs of Aberdeen, Arbroath, Montrose, Brechin and Bervie (i.e. most of the north-east of Scotland), Aberdeen Tolbooth was bleak, dark and severely overcrowded. The walls glistened with damp, the straw scattered on the floors had long been trampled to a slime, and the windows, barred but not glazed, let in icy draughts straight off the North Sea. Into this cold and noxious gloom the prisoners were packed, according to a contemporary magistrate, 'like salmon in a barrel'. Those under sentence of death and awaiting public execution – 'rebellis denuncit for slauchter, murther and exercising beistlie cruellties upon thair nichtbouris' and other similar villains – were held in chains, their fetters clamped to iron bars set into the walls of the condemned cell. Lesser criminals were dumped in the malodorous stew of the communal cells below, where beggars and poachers and 'persons apprehended for carrying unlicensed arms' wrestled for elbow-room with debtors, drunkards and perpetrators of other unspecified 'outrages'. That this mêlée also included several genuine lunatics is beyond doubt, for not only was there no lunatic asylum in Aberdeen, there was no asylum or hospital anywhere in Scotland for the safe housing of the insane.

To a delicate young man reared in an atmosphere of obedience, restraint, study and prayer, and in surroundings of the utmost respectability, being locked in the squalor of the Tolbooth among the rabble of Aberdeen must have been more than misery – it was just the kind of ordeal that could well

---

* In contemporary parlance, according to the *OED*, 'conceited' was used to describe 'one who conceives as a design'. In other words, a plotter.

have driven Alexander Cruden out of his mind. Crammed into an overcrowded cell in this 'sink of vice and debauchery', forced to fight his brutish companions for every inch of space and every morsel of food, to suffer their pitiless taunts, and probably their physical assaults, at his lack of size, his neat clothes, his educated speech and – most cruelly of all – his own supposed insanity; that he survived all that without even the comfort of a Bible (which, if he had had one with him when he arrived, would surely have been torn from his grasp and gleefully shredded before his eyes), would suggest not that Cruden was insane but, quite the contrary, that he was possessed of formidable strength of mind. Maybe the question of whether he had really gone mad had not been satisfactorily answered after all.

The next question, clearly, is who was the girl? Biographer Chalmers must have known exactly who she was (otherwise how could he have known whether any of her relations were still alive in 1789), but all he was prepared to say was that she was 'the daughter of a clergyman from Aberdeen', and that once it was discovered that she was pregnant by her brother she 'was immediately sent out of the country and never returned'.

There were dozens of clergymen in Aberdeen in 1720 and, in those days of enormous families, each of them could easily have had half a dozen daughters, so 'the daughter of a clergyman from Aberdeen' is not a great deal to go on. Aberdeen's first newspaper was not launched until 1747, so in 1720 there were no gossip columnists or investigative journalists to splash such a scandal over the headlines; there are no surviving contemporary (and relevant) diaries and little social correspondence. Either from an excess of tact or an excess of prudishness – surely not from a lack of curiosity – subsequent writers seem to have made no effort to identify her; and since this was a story that would have been energetically suppressed by everyone involved, the mysterious young lady seemed destined to remain nameless.

There is no record of how long Cruden spent in the Tolbooth – it was probably weeks, possibly months, but not years. What is certain is that his reputed madness, his spell in prison, and the fact that he had not completed his training had put paid to his hopes of ever becoming a minister of the Church. In the spring of 1724 he sailed from Aberdeen on a ship named the *Phoenix*, and would not return to the city of his birth and the scene of his unexplained disgrace for forty-five years.

# 2

# The South Part of this Island

The *Phoenix* docked at Woolwich near London on 2 April 1724 and, according to Cruden's contemporary and fellow Aberdonian William Simpson, 'in June of that year, by the recommendation of his constant friend the great Dr Calamy, [Cruden] became tutor to the only son of the valuable Henry Coltman at Elm Hall at Southgate'.

Edmund Calamy (the third of that name, his son would be the fourth) was a celebrated English Presbyterian minister who had visited Aberdeen in 1709 and had received an honorary Doctorate of Divinity at Marischal College. During that visit he had become well acquainted with the current Professor of Divinity, the Reverend Thomas Blackwell, and it seems that Blackwell had now put this friendship to good use on behalf of his unfortunate former pupil. Possibly it was Blackwell, too, who had suggested that since Cruden would never be able to become a minister, maybe he should think about becoming a teacher instead. As a Latin and Greek scholar with a good knowledge of French, he had all the right qualifications, and the Reverend's friend Dr Calamy was just the man to point him in the direction of a good position. It meant Cruden leaving Aberdeen, but in the circumstances would that not be the best thing for him to do anyway? In England, where no one knew him or anything about his unhappy past, he would be free to make a completely fresh start.

The Scottish education system was held in such high esteem in England that graduates of any of the Scottish universities were in great demand both as teachers and as private tutors who could coach the sons of gentlemen for entrance to university. Nothing is known of Henry Coltman (apart from the fact that to someone he was 'valuable'), but he would surely have leapt at the chance of employing a graduate of Aberdeen's Marischal College as tutor to his only son. Southgate is now part of London (two stops short of Cockfosters at the northern end of the Piccadilly Line). In 1724 it was a separate village occupying the high ground between the Lea and Barnet valleys, with a scatter of large country houses, like Elm Hall, in the well-wooded vicinity. Elm Hall must have provided Cruden with just the tranquil environment he needed in which to gather together the scattered pieces of his life. Here were no curious stares or mocking glances, no powerful professors or disappointed parents, no glowering Tolbooth to remind him every time he looked out of the window of the horrors he had endured within its walls. Here instead was the gentle, unfamiliar English countryside and the kindly Coltman family who welcomed him into their home, quickly befriended him and were full of admiration for his learning. There was reassurance, too, in finding that he had a talent for teaching and that he could earn his own living. His only grumble was with the minister in the local church; he had 'heard the Gospel preached more fully and agreeably by the ministers [in Aberdeen] than ever I had the happiness to hear it from the ministers of the south part of this island'.

He would keep in touch with his friends the Coltmans and

correspond with his pupil long after he had left their employ, and in later years Mrs Coltman would come unhesitatingly to his assistance in his many moments of need. But for now, when Coltman junior was crammed sufficiently full of Latin and Greek by his little Scottish tutor to pass his entrance exams and go off to university, Cruden moved on too; first to another position as tutor near Ware in Hertfordshire and then to a third, on the Isle of Man.

Although he would write at great and vociferous length about his later spells of 'confinement', Cruden would only once be constrained to mention his sojourn in Aberdeen's Tolbooth. Even when he did refer to it he would go into so little detail that it is impossible to tell whether he knew exactly what had happened and why, or if he was utterly bewildered by the whole experience and at a loss to understand how he had ended up so far from both his roots and his dreams. Either way, he put up with his enforced if comfortable rustication for two years – and then he started to fret.

None of the families he worked for and lived amongst had found any cause to question the state of his mind; but neither had any of them given him any scope to use his real talent – which was hardly surprising, since none of them knew what it was. To have mentioned his training for the ministry would have been to invite questions about his failure to complete it. So, as far as they were aware, theology was just one of the subjects Cruden had studied for his MA in Aberdeen. He had taken it in turns with the rest of the household to say grace before meals, and he had been allowed to regale the families with occasional readings from the Holy Scriptures, but that was no longer enough. At the age of seventeen he had taken the decision to dedicate his life to the service of God, and that decision was irrevocable. Events had conspired to make it impossible for him to become a minister of the Gospel, but there were other ways he could serve the Almighty. And he had the first inklings of an idea of what one of those things might be.

The idea was so ambitious that for a while after he first thought of it he had waved it aside as being far beyond his capabilities. But it stayed with him, and the more time he spent pondering it, the more strongly it took hold of his mind. When his Manx student left for university in the autumn of 1726, Alexander Cruden packed his bags and went back to London.

Of the plethora of Alexanders that feature in the story of Alexander Cruden, none would turn out to be more remarkable than Alexander Blackwell, the fourth son of Cruden's former tutor the Reverend Thomas Blackwell. Nine years younger than Cruden, Alexander Blackwell had also been born in Aberdeen and baptised in St Nicholas Kirk, and he had followed his namesake through Aberdeen Grammar School and on to Marischal College. If their backgrounds and their education were strikingly similar, however, the characters of these two Alexanders could hardly have been more different. Confident where Cruden was timid, capricious where Cruden was single-minded, and as eye-catching as Cruden was inconspicuous, Alexander Blackwell courted controversy from a very early age. So carefully would he cover his tracks, and so many and varied would be the rumours and inventions surrounding him, that no single account has ever told the whole story of Alexander Blackwell's life.

'This unhappy man,' according to an article in *The Gentleman's Magazine* of September 1747, 'so far answered the hopes and expectations of his father [the Reverend Thomas Blackwell] that before he was fifteen he had acquired an extraordinary knowledge of Latin and Greek; and was greatly distinguished for his understanding of the classics and other useful learning.' Presumably to the great disappointment of his Reverend father, however, 'Alexander Blackwell's mind ran upon seeing the world and so strong was his desire that he left [Marischal College] before he had taken any degree and went away so privately that his friends knew not what was become of him till after his arrival in London.'

Alexander Blackwell's arrival in London, apparently after an interval spent studying medicine in Leiden, coincided almost exactly with Alexander Cruden's return to the city in the autumn of 1726. And by another coincidence the two Alexanders then went into the very same business: Blackwell became 'corrector of the press to Mr Wilkins, an eminent printer', while Cruden 'was employed by Mr Watson as corrector of the press'. But it would be several years before the erstwhile schoolfellows came face to face.

A 'corrector of the press' was a proof-reader. In information-hungry London an enormous weight of printed material was clattering off the city's presses every day – newspapers, journals, pamphlets, periodicals, tracts, books – and before it could go forward for printing every block of every page of every item had to be closely perused and vetted for typesetting errors. 'Correctors of the press' were in great demand. It was not Cruden's first choice of employment – he worked initially for a variety of different publishers as a translator of Latin, Greek and French texts – but it turned out to be exactly the sort of painstaking, meticulous work for which he was ideally suited. It was also regular, full-time work, which was crucial. On his only previous visit to London he had stayed with Dr Calamy, and in his various teaching posts around the country his living expenses had been covered by his employers. Now he had to support himself entirely, and London, he soon found out, was an expensive place to live.

If his one-room lodging above a noisy inn (the Rose & Crown in Little Britain, hard by Smithfield cattle market) was a far cry from the guest room in Dr Calamy's comfortable home in Westminster, London was an even further cry from the only other city of which Cruden had any experience, Aberdeen. Its population of half a million (more than twenty times that of Aberdeen*) lived at close and crowded quarters in an area barely three miles by two, stretching from St James's Park in the west to Whitechapel in the east, and from Sadler's Wells in the north to the Thames in the south, with London Bridge the only crossing over the river. It was a city of elegance and culture, of gracious living and enlightened thinking, of drawing-rooms, gentlemen's clubs, theatres, coffee-houses and leisurely carriage-rides in the park. But beneath its stylish veneer London was also a city of drunkenness, filth and squalor, of brothels, ale-houses, prostitutes, pickpockets, rampant crime and blatant godlessness. In his series of contemporary engravings, *A Rake's Progress,* William Hogarth would depict a wealthy young Englishman moving up to London from the provinces and making the transition from rustic swain to urban dandy; corrupted by depraved parsons and fleeced by obsequious tradesmen along the way, the now dissolute Rake leaves his path strewn with abandoned sweethearts, diseased prostitutes and fatherless children as he squanders his riches and ruins his health before dying a squalid death in Bedlam. When Cruden arrived in London towards the end of 1726, London-born Hogarth was beginning to make his name as an engraver, and the scandalous conduct of his fellow citizens was providing copious and very profitable material for the young artist's pen. Had the scholarly Aberdonian been faced with this kaleidoscope of vice and virtue straight from the shelter of his remote academic cloisters, he would have found it as distracting as it was shocking. But although he was a sensitive soul, and vice would always make him sad, Cruden

---

\* Aberdeen's population was estimated in 1755 at about twenty-two thousand.

had witnessed far worse horrors in the Tolbooth in Aberdeen than anything he would see in the streets of London; besides, he had something important to do. So he settled easily into his new life in the capital and started to concentrate on his great idea.

At the end of every long day spent poring over reams of typeset pages for his employer, Cruden scuttled back to his lodging above the Rose & Crown. There he laboured far into the night over his project, and soon his cramped little room was overflowing with piles and stacks and sheaves of bits of paper covered with his slightly untidy handwriting. He lived in constant fear of someone opening the door so suddenly that the draught would blow his candles over and set fire to his precious papers. He had not even begun to calculate how long it would take him to carry his project through; indeed he was by no means certain that he *could* carry it through, and he knew he could hope for no income from it until it was completed. He just knew he had to try, because this would be his Great Work for the Lord.

Even those who would doubt his sanity would never doubt the immensity of the task he had set himself, nor the almost unimaginable logistical problems that it involved. William Youngman, Cruden's later biographer, who firmly believed that his subject was deranged, decided that it was only because his lunacy was interrupted by occasional spells of lucidity that he was able to take on such a work. 'Few would imagine,' wrote Youngman in 1840, 'that a man who could confine himself to such an employment could be the subject of that waywardness of mind which frequently attends the higher powers of genius. What would have been to others intolerable drudgery, was a sedative to his agitated mind; and the labour which would have wasted the energies of a happier man, was the balm of his wounded spirit.' For Alexander Cruden had embarked on what was surely the most ambitious task of compilation ever undertaken by one man, a work more lasting than Johnson's *Dictionary*, more wordy than Roget's *Thesaurus* and three times the length of the Complete Works of Shakespeare – the compilation of a new and comprehensive Concordance to the Holy Bible.

'A Concordance,' Cruden would patiently explain to anyone who didn't know, 'is a Dictionary, or an Index to the Bible, wherein all the words used through the Inspired Writings are arranged alphabetically, and the various places where they occur are referred to, to assist us in finding out passages, and comparing the several significations [meanings] of the same word.' This modest description does not even begin to convey the scale of Cruden's Concordance. The immediate reaction of anyone encountering the book for the first time (with the possible exception of a clergyman rushing to complete his sermon) is to ask 'How on earth did he do it?'

The Authorised King James Version of the Bible is (apparently) 774,746 words long.[1] Cruden's Concordance, at roughly 2,370,000 words, is much, much longer (and by the time he had finished it he was probably one of the few people – if not the only person – in the world to have worked out how many *different* words the Bible contains). He does not list every single occurrence of every different word (omitting 'a', 'of', 'to', 'the' and 'with' altogether, and restricting such words as 'and', 'from' and 'but' to only a few references each); neither does he limit himself merely to nouns such as 'honey' (for which there are thirty-five references and an explanation of what honey is and where it comes from) or 'wine' (for which there are ninety-four direct references, separate entries for 'wine-bibber', 'wine-bottle', 'wine-cellars', 'wine-fat', 'wine-press', 'wine-presses' and 'wines', as well as a long discussion on the origins, properties and Biblical significance of this 'useful and agreeable liquor'). In order to make his Concordance as easy as possible to use, Cruden divides the references to the word 'all', for example, into 'all', 'above all', 'according to all', 'after all', 'at all', 'before all', 'for all', 'from all', 'in all', 'of all', 'upon all', 'over all', 'all these', 'all this', 'all that', 'unto all', 'with all', 'all the while' and 'all ye'. For each of these references he then includes enough of the contextual sentence to show the searcher which is the reference he needs, and gives Chapter and Verse to the exact place or places in the Bible where it occurs:

### With ALL

*Num*.16.30. *with a.* that appertain to them

*Deut*.6.5. thou shalt love the Lord *with a.* thy

heart, *with a.* thy soul, 11.13. *Mat.* 22.37

2 *Chron.* 25.7. *with a.* the children of Ephraim

*Prov*.4.7. *with a.* thy getting, get understanding

*Acts*.10.2. that feared God *with a.* his house, 16.34.

1 *Cor*.1.2. *with a.* that in every place call on Jesus

*Phil*.1.25. I shall abide and continue *with* you *a.*

2.17. If offered, I joy and rejoice *with* you *a.*

### ALL the while

1 *Sam*.22.4. *a. the while* David was in the hold

25.7. nothing missing *a. the while* they were in Carmel

27.11. so will be his manner *a. the while* he dwelleth

*Job*.27.3. *a. the while* my breath is in me

### ALL ye

*Isa*.48.14. *a. ye* assemble yourselves, and hear

50.11. behold *a. ye* that kindle a fire, that compass

66.10. be glad with her, *a. ye* that love her

*Jer*.29.20 hear the word, *a. ye* of the captivity

*Lam*.1.12. is it nothing to you, *a. ye* that pass by?

etc.

Not content with listing the occurrences of each word, Cruden 'leads the Reader into the meaning of many passages of Scripture' by explaining any word with which he fears the Reader may not be familiar, taking particular care with words relating to Jewish customs and ceremonies, a clear understanding of which he thought vital to a true understanding of the Bible. The entry for the word 'Synagogue' for example, in addition to its fifty-plus individual references, starts with a four-thousand-word article covering the history of synagogues and their structure, layout and decoration as well as the rules and observances of synagogue services. As biographer Chalmers said, 'Cruden's Concordance appears so vast a performance for one man that one cannot cease to wonder by what means it was procured.' 'To gratify this curiosity,' he continues, 'the author collected from the surviving friends of Mr Cruden some memoirs ...' Frustratingly, after this promising start, Chalmers goes on to say nothing at all about Cruden's working methods.

Intimate knowledge of the 'Inspired Writings' would have given Cruden the best possible foundation on which to build, but he would still have been faced with the problem of how to organise such a mass of material. His Concordance is divided into three main parts, or 'alphabets' as he called them. The first alphabet, much the longest, is to the 'Holy Scriptures' – i.e. the Old and New Testaments. The second alphabet is to the proper names in the Old and New Testaments, explains who each person or where each place was, and gives Chapter and Verse for each time they are mentioned. The third alphabet is 'to the Books called Apocrypha'. (Since the books of the Apocrypha were 'not of Divine Inspiration ... and are of no authority in the church of God', Cruden was reluctant to include them, and only did so in order that no one could accuse his Concordance of being 'deficient in any thing'.) These three 'alphabets' are followed by 'A Brief Account of the History and Excellency of the Scriptures', and the book ends with a 'Compendium to the Holy Bible wherein the Contents of Each Chapter Are Given'.

Computers (which threaten finally to eclipse Cruden's Concordance) have made the compilation of such works comparatively easy. But Cruden had only pen and ink and reams of paper. So how did he do it? One of his biographers suggested that he made lists on 'long strips of paper'. Did he make just one list of all the words in all the 'alphabets' to which he intended to include references, including proper names? He so disliked the Apocrypha that it is hard to imagine him including its words in lists of the words from the Divine Oracles. So did he make three different lists, one for each 'alphabet'? Did he put the words in the lists in alphabetical order as he went along, or did that step come later? In the alphabet to the Old and New Testaments alone there are 1019 header-words that start with the letter 'C', of which 153 start with 'Ca'. Using just pen and paper, how long does it take to put 153 words into their correct alphabetical order, let alone 1019 words? It would be impossible to get it absolutely right first time, and each time he made a mistake he would have had to write the list out all over again, because until he had a clear, correctly alphabetised list it would be impossible to find the right place to put the references.

Suppose, then, that instead of 'long strips of paper', he had a card-index. Even given that the letter 'C' probably has more than the average number of header-words, Cruden's complete list of header-words – and therefore his total number of cards – would have run to something like twenty thousand. For each reference he would have had to hunt through twenty thousand cards to find the right place to put it; each reference also probably contained several 'material' words that needed to be cross-referenced, so for a short phrase like '. . . behold <u>all ye</u> that <u>kindle</u> a <u>fire</u> . . .' he would have had to hunt *four times* through twenty thousand cards to find the right place for each of the four cross-references. Once he started writing the references onto his pieces of paper or into his card-index, each letter of the alphabet would have very soon contained enough material to fill a reasonable-length book. One can only agree with Alexander Chalmers that 'the bare inspection of the work before us will afford a stupendous proof of patience and per-severance'.

There had, as Cruden freely admitted, been Concordances to the Bible before. A Dominican Friar by the name of Hugo de St Charo (later a Cardinal) had compiled the first as long ago as the thirteenth century. Cardinal Hugo's Concordance was in Latin, the language into which the Bible had been translated by St Jerome in the fourth century from the original Hebrew, Greek and Aramaic, and which, for nearly a thousand years, would remain the only permitted language for the (Christian) Holy Scriptures. To underline the magnitude of his own task, Cruden was at pains to point out that Cardinal Hugo's was 'a great and laborious work, for the successful completion of which he employed *five hundred* monks of his order to assist him'. The first Hebrew Concordance appeared some two hundred years after Cardinal Hugo's and was a comparable labour involving almost as many assistants: 'Rabbi Mordecai Nathan began it in the year 1438 and completed it in 1448,' said Cruden, 'being no less than ten years in finish-ing it; and . . . was obliged to employ a great many writers in this work.' Although Rabbi Nathan could copy the pattern of Cardinal Hugo's work, he had to start his compilation from scratch because Latin and Hebrew had neither script nor alphabet in common.

Cruden's was not even the first Biblical Concordance in English. That honour goes to John Marbeck, organist at Windsor Chapel, who produced a Concordance in 1550 and was immediately arrested on the orders of Queen Mary (the obsessively Catholic and excessively bloodthirsty daughter of Henry VIII) and sentenced to be burnt at the stake for heresy. (He was reprieved.) Marbeck's Concordance was very much shorter than Cruden's and, because the chapters of the Bible were not divided into verses until 1545 and the new system was not available until Marbeck's Concordance was more or less finished, it refers the reader only to the relevant chapter of the relevant Book of the Bible ('Exodus III', 'Deuteronomy XIV' etc.). There were later English Concordances too, including the Cambridge Concordance and several abstracts or small Concordances. But even the Cambridge Concordance fell well short of Cruden's ideal, being neither thorough enough, comprehensive enough nor accurate enough to meet his meticulous standards. As Alexander Chalmers pointed out, 'a comparison of Cruden's work with those of his predecessors must convince every reader how far he went beyond them and in truth how little he could avail himself of their labours since, in order to make a correct Concordance, one for the accuracy of which he himself would be held responsible, it was absolutely necessary for him to begin as if no such work had ever preceded; and this he did with uncommon zeal'.

So he toiled away both day and night with uncommon zeal, allowing himself time off only on Sundays to go to church. But progress was agonisingly slow, and the difficulties mounted. His room was far too small, his growing piles of paper constantly threatened to escape his efforts to keep them under control, and his work as a proof-corrector was so demanding of his time and concentration that when he sat down at the end of each long working day to start work again on his Concordance he found it increasingly hard to focus on yet more acres of words. It was no life for a young man still in his twenties, but he had no thought of giving up. Indeed he had two very compelling reasons to persevere. Not only would his Concordance be his great labour for the Lord, it would be a way of proving to himself, to his family in Aberdeen, and to all those people who had been so ready to believe that 'poor wee Alexander Cruden was out of his head, what a shame', that he was nothing of the sort. Cruden's Concordance would be incontrovertible proof of Cruden's sanity.

But his great labour was proving more laborious than he had anticipated, and not until he had worked himself almost to a standstill did salvation fall, apparently out of the blue, into his lap.

Every Sunday Cruden walked the mile or so from Little Britain to Great St Helen's Church to attend the services and enjoy the sermons of the Reverend Dr Guise. One Sunday in 1729, when he had been in London for more than two years, and just a few weeks before his thirtieth birthday, Dr Guise introduced Cruden to a friend of his, another clerical gentleman, the Reverend Dr Maddox. Dr Maddox was currently chaplain to the Bishop of Chichester and he was in London on an errand. Just outside Chichester on the edge of the Sussex Downs was the little hamlet of Halnaker where James Stanley, 10th Earl of Derby, had a country seat. It had come to Dr Maddox's attention that Lord Derby was looking for a French reader, and he had volunteered to come to London to find someone to fill the post. His friend Dr Guise had mentioned that he had in his congregation a young and studious Scotsman who had worked as both translator and corrector of French texts. Was there any chance, Dr Maddox now enquired, that Mr Cruden might be interested in the position of French reader to Lord Derby?

Cruden was euphoric. What clearer sign could there be that God wanted him to complete his Great Work? An Earl could hardly want his French reader to spend more than a couple of hours a day reading to him from the latest French newspapers, periodicals or books; this would mean that he, Cruden, would have the rest of every day free to work on his Concordance.

Since the country seat of an Earl would presumably be spacious, he would also surely have all the room he could possibly need in which to spread out and organise his papers. No more proof-correcting, no more living in a cramped and noisy room with foul smells from the kitchens or the gutters wafting in through the window, no more rummaging under the bed for his clothes because every spare table, shelf and inch of floorboard was piled high with pieces of paper. There could not have been a more perfect answer to his prayers.

Unaware that in his excitement he had overlooked one important detail, Cruden waited only until Dr Maddox had confirmed that his employment with the Earl would be for a minimum of one year before accepting his proposal, handing in his resignation to Mr Watson, and packing his bags for Sussex.

# 3

# Monsieur Whatever-You-Please

There is a dreadful inevitability about Cruden's fate at Halnaker. He was too delighted by his appointment; too quick to flourish it as proof of his triumph over disaster. Something had to go wrong.

He arrived at Halnaker in early June 1729. Although Lord Derby was apparently at home, he did not immediately send for his new French reader, so Cruden had time to settle in and find his way about. Set amidst gracious acres of parkland complete with obligatory herd of deer, Halnaker* was more a venerable mansion than a truly stately home, but it boasted a medieval great hall with ornate panelling and stained glass windows, a long picture gallery, a sizeable chapel, a wonderful library and quite enough space and splendour to live up to his expectations. It also boasted a large household ruled by the lofty Mr Clayton, the Earl's chamberlain, and the not quite so lofty Mr Frederick, his steward. Cruden was given to understand that as French reader to the Earl, his position in

---

* Now in ruins.

the domestic hierarchy would be below Mr Clayton, more or less on a level with Mr Frederick and the Earl's chaplain Mr Ball, and comfortably above the butlers, footmen, valets, housekeepers, cooks and their assorted underlings. Since this corresponded almost exactly with his position as tutor in previous households, he was quite content. But when he discovered that, in addition to his own room, he would have the use of a book-lined sitting-room where meals would be served to him by the younger servants, he knew that his prayers had indeed been answered. As soon as he had unpacked his belongings, been introduced to such members of the household as were deemed worthy of his acquaintance, and been taken on a tour of the grounds by the amiable Mr Ball, he sat down to spread the news.

He wrote letters to his friends 'in and about London who with great encouragement had advised me to embrace the business', telling them that 'things were in a very promising way'. He wrote to his parents informing them that although their son might not yet have reached quite the exalted heights they had once anticipated, he was well on his way; his position at Halnaker, as French reader to a 'Noble Lord', was most 'honourable and pleasant', was assured for a full year, and they could look for even greater achievements to follow. But his letter to one of his former pupils revealed that the important detail which had previously slipped his mind had at last forced itself on his attention: 'I wrote to my pupil Mr Coltman that my not pronouncing French exactly was giving me some uneasiness.'

Cruden managed to brush aside his uneasiness – French pronunciation was only a matter of practice, and he would soon have plenty of opportunity for that. So he spent his time reading his Bible, conversing with Mr Ball and contemplating his good fortune. Mr Frederick appeared friendly enough, but he was less sure about Mr Clayton. Soon after his arrival at

Halnaker the chamberlain paid him a visit in his sitting-room and engaged him in conversation. Cruden told him he had worked for about three years as a corrector of the press in London, where his professional reputation 'had been rather on the growing than declining hand'; he spoke of his home in Aberdeen, his family, his religious convictions, his politics, and his vehement support for the Protestant succession 'that had been the security through the love of God of these nations from popery and slavery'. As the conversation delved deeper into politics and religion Cruden began to feel uncomfortable; he was getting the distinct impression that the chamberlain shared none of his views. But this uneasiness, too, he managed to brush aside, consoling himself with the thought that although he might have spoken more freely than was wise, 'he had behaved himself with all moderation imaginable and had declared himself an enemy to bigotry and persecution'.

His introduction to his new employer came when he was invited to join Lord Derby for a morning ride around the estate. James Stanley, 10th Earl of Derby and Lord Lieutenant of Lancaster, was a former soldier who had fought in Flanders with the then Prince of Orange and had achieved the rank of colonel before leaving the army to serve as a Whig MP under Queen Anne. Now aged sixty-five, he had retired from public life to spend his time indulging his love of books and works of art and improving his estates at Halnaker and at Knowsley near Liverpool. As large and indolent as his thirty-year-old French reader was small and industrious, the Earl can have found nothing to criticise in Cruden's demeanour – the young Scotsman was neatly dressed, polite without being familiar, and full of praise for the beauties of the Sussex countryside. Everything seemed to go very smoothly on what Cruden described as 'a most agreeable outing'.

After this initial meeting another week elapsed before the Earl finally decided it was time to put his French reader to work. There is no evidence that Cruden used this delay to start work again on his Concordance. Maybe he decided that since he had a whole year ahead of him there was no hurry; maybe he thought it best to get Lord Derby's permission before spending time on a project that had nothing to do with his employment. The summons eventually came one evening when Cruden had just finished his meal. Making sure that his wig was straight and his cravat neatly tied (he was always very meticulous about his appearance), Cruden followed the footman to the library. The Earl spoke French well, but his eyesight had recently failed to the point where he found it difficult to read, particularly in the evenings and by candlelight – thus his need for a French reader and the evening summons.

The Earl first asked Cruden to read to him from the latest newssheet which had just been delivered from London. Cruden obliged – and since the newssheet was in English both parties were quite happy with the result. The Earl then passed Cruden a French book and asked him to start reading from that. Cruden had studied French at Marischal College, had translated several works from French into English, and had since proof-corrected many more for Mr Watson, so his spelling, his grammar and his comprehension were faultless; but he had never, in all that time, heard the language spoken out loud. He had no idea how it should be pronounced. He read French as he would have read Latin, pronouncing each word phonetically, and his reading for the Earl was utterly incomprehensible.

At the end of what was probably quite a short session the Earl, who was either too polite or too indolent to comment on Cruden's performance, suggested merely that he had had enough and that Cruden could retire, which, with some relief, he did. But when, a week later, Lord Derby left Halnaker for Knowsley without having called on the services of his French reader again, Cruden must have realised that something was wrong. He was not kept in suspense for very long.

*My noble and dear Lord,* [starts a distraught letter dated 'Halnaker, July 7 1729',] *I am very sensibly affected with the account Mr Frederick has given me this morning that your Lordship has been pleased to discharge me from your service.*

The notebook in which Cruden drafted his letters to Lord Derby (or, it has been suggested, into which he copied them) has somehow survived intact, and is held in Oxford's Bodleian Library.[1] It is a poignant little volume. In contrast to other of his letters which have also survived and which are models of elegant penmanship, his handwriting in these letters vividly illustrates his distress: in some it is large and loopy, in others it is small and cramped, and the pages are littered with ink-blots and crossings out (which suggests they are more likely to be drafts). They reveal, too, that his real anxiety was less for his career or for his Concordance than for his reputation.

*When I came down to Halnaker I concluded from what I saw and heard that things were in a very promising way and accordingly I writ to my parents a very encouraging letter and also to some friends in England so that my leaving your Lordship's service will be a mighty surprise to them and, I doubt not, will create a bad opinion of me in the minds of my acquaintances.*

He had looked on his appointment at Halnaker as further proof that despite the time he had spent in Aberdeen Tolbooth, he was no more insane than the next man; it had seemed to close the door on his calamitous past and offer him the prospect of a serene and respectable future. He now bitterly regretted having so hastily shared this prospect with everyone he knew. His abrupt dismissal, after less than a month in the Earl's employ, proved that the door to his past was not closed at all, and he was staring into a future shrouded in the dark clouds of failure. The humiliation was too painful to bear, or to share.

Two days after Mr Frederick broke the news of his dismissal, a tearful Cruden left Halnaker for London. He announced neither his departure from Sussex nor his return to the capital to anyone, because he was hoping that both would only be temporary. He had thought of a way to recover his position.

'My plan,' he wrote to Lord Derby, 'is to fly to London and for some time to be under a good French master, and when he can attest my reading the French and my fitness for your Lordship's service in that respect, I will wait on your Lordship at Knowsley.'

Going incognito (which involved wearing his travelling wig instead of his everyday wig and advertising neither his name nor his presence in the capital), he found lodgings in Soho, a part of town where he was unlikely to be recognised and which was home to a large number of Huguenot refugees who had fled from persecution in France at the end of the seventeenth century.

*London July 15 1729*
*Providence has brought me to a French house of good religious people where I have good opportunity to talk and read French, and a French master comes every day to teach me and says that I may depend upon it I shall be able to read French in a week's time perfectly well. If your Lordship will be pleased to honour me with your commands, a letter directed to Monsieur whatever-you-please* à la maison du Mme Boulanger vis à vis la Couronne et la Chèvre près de l'Eglise des Grêques, rue de la Couronne, Soho, *will come safe to my hand.*

Forgoing even the pleasure of attending Great St Helen's Church and seeing his old friend Dr Guise, Cruden lay low in the depths of Soho and concentrated on his French conversation; he found a French eating house where he could talk French with the staff and his fellow diners, and he waited. But his Lordship was not pleased to honour Cruden with his commands or with any other form of communication, and no letters came safe to his hand. As far as Lord Derby was concerned, his French reader had been dismissed and that was the end of the story. Cruden refused to admit defeat. He wrote again and again to Lord Derby, assuring him that his French was now impeccable (and writing partly in French as if to prove it), and pleading with him to change his mind.

*Aôut 11 1729*

*Je vous supplie trés humblement de me permettre de l'assurer de la continuation de mes profonds respects, voyant que je suis encore privé de Bonheur et l'Honneur vous rendre personellement mes trés-humbles services. Heureux et mille fois heureux si pouvoir vous persuader d'avoir compassion sur celui qui est sans réserve votre trés devoté serviteur. Mon exile me parait fort long et j'espère que le heureux moment approche quand j'aurai l'honneur et felicité d'être avec vous et vous servir.*

(I humbly beg your permission to present you with my profound respects, since I am still deprived of the happiness and the honour of offering you my most humble services. [I would be] a thousand times happy could I persuade you to have compassion on one who is without reservation your very devoted servant. My exile seems very long, and I hope that the happy moment draws near when I will have the honour and joy to be with you and to serve you.)

He heard nothing. His French pronunciation was as good as it could get, he had no other work and very little money, he was too distraught even to think about his Concordance, and he still could not bring himself to get in touch with any of his friends because that would have meant allowing his failure to become public knowledge. There was only one thing for it – he would have to go to Knowsley and speak to the Earl in person.

In 1729 the two-hundred-mile journey from London to Knowsley was not one to be undertaken lightly. The state of the roads was something of a national scandal which was only slowly being addressed; even the main highways were little more than poorly-maintained tracks which could be rendered impassable by a night of heavy rain. Those fleetest of all messengers, the postboys, took an average of six days to travel from London to Edinburgh, while even on a fine summer day a good coach-and-four allowed twelve hours to cover the fifty-three miles from London to Cambridge. There were other dangers, too, than the risk of sinking your cart up to its axles in a rut or your horse up to its belly in a bog. 'Highwaymen lurked in the unfelled thickets and unenclosed heaths and were in league with many of the keepers of inns along the way.' 'In Scotland,' according to English historian G.M. Trevelyan, 'the highwayman was unknown; he would have wearied of waiting for the rare passengers, and would have been little richer after their plunder than before. But in England no one began a journey wholly free from the fear of such encounters.'

Too preoccupied to worry overmuch about highwaymen, Cruden left London for Knowsley in early September. He was travelling on horseback and, since he could not afford to pay for a change of mount, he rode the same black mare the whole way. When horse and rider reached Knowsley after six days on the road they were both in a state of collapse. To a man unused to strenuous physical exercise, this journey had involved a supreme effort; an effort which he prayed would be rewarded.

Lord Derby was indeed at home, Cruden was informed, as was Mr Clayton his chamberlain. But when he sent a message to the Earl via one of the footmen asking for an interview, the request was flatly denied. Unable to believe that the Earl who had shown him such kindness at Halnaker was capable of such heartlessness now, Cruden suspected Mr Clayton's pernicious influence in this blunt refusal. His customary docility deserted him and he treated the housekeeper, the cook, the footman and any other servants who were within earshot to a bitter diatribe against the chamberlain. But his rage evaporated before he had finished speaking, and he offered his listeners such an anguished apology for his lapse in manners that they were soon vying with each other to ease his distress.

The footman who had answered the door brought him a small beer, the housekeeper took pity on his exhaustion and gave him something to eat, and when he then fell fast asleep at the table, she arranged for him to be put to bed in a spare room in the servants' quarters. He woke the following morning with not the least idea where he was, with every limb and muscle aching and with hardly the strength to get out of bed. No sooner had the events of the previous day come back to him than the door opened and Mr Whitwell, steward here as Mr Frederick had been at Halnaker, entered with the news that he had been instructed by the Earl to ask Mr Cruden to leave Knowsley directly. With only the meekest of protests that he never travelled on a Sunday, and that his horse was too tired to carry him anyway, Cruden got dressed, accepted breakfast from the housekeeper and the offer of the loan of a horse from the stables from Mr Whitwell, said his farewells and rode sadly away.

But he did not go far. The prospect of another gruelling six-day journey so soon after the last was more than he could contemplate. So he rode only the twelve miles to Liverpool, found himself a lodging, and went back to bed. Whether he then became too ill to travel or whether he just could not bring himself to return to London is hard to tell, but he stayed in Liverpool for the best part of a month. The notebook in the Bodleian Library contains copies of the letters he apparently wrote to Lord Derby from Liverpool. They are interspersed with jottings (in French as well as English), references to the Bible, practice signatures and the occasional doodle; the whole thing reads as much like a diary as correspondence, so it is possible he never actually sent any of the letters, but was just writing to relieve his feelings.

> *If your Lordship will not allow justice to be done in restoring me to your service, which God forbid, how great an injury will be done me? Upon this melancholy supposition I should be quite out of business, which would be a very great injury done me, and to my sensible loss, as my reputation will also suffer among my friends in and about London who have hitherto shown a considerable regard for me. O! will your Lordship be immovable to all the arguments I have proposed for you?*

He wrote about Mr Clayton, too, remembering conversations he had had at Halnaker which had confirmed the chamberlain's prejudice against his religious views.

> *Mr Ball told me there was an unguarded expression Mr Clayton spoke of me in presence of your Lordship 'And besides he is a rank Presbyterian'. I replied to Mr Ball that I did not desire to be deemed of any party or denomination but was a lover of all really good and religious people. I likewise told Dr Maddox that I took Mr Clayton for my enemy and pushed it so far that he was forced to give me this answer. 'You know Mr Clayton is not of your principles.' I answered 'My principles, what does that signify to him? I*

*give nobody disturbance with my principles.' Mr Cruden*
[suddenly referring to himself in the third person] *was
never ashamed to own his principles for he sets up for an
enemy to all Hypocrisy and Dissimulation and has a mighty
regard for Veracity and Plain-dealing which he judges to
be two amiable qualities. O my Lord, is it justice that I
should be made a sacrifice to any person filled with enmity?*

At one point he complained of being 'confin'd this week to
my chamber by reason of a defluxion or humour in the sole
of my foot which is the effect of my being bled with leeches,
and have been in great pain night and day'. In another letter
he described how 'I am left destitute of all business whereas
I had been several years in a very creditable way of living;
moreover my father has a numerous family of sons and daughters, providence hitherto provided for me not to be a charge
on him since I left the place of my nativity. If they knew my
present situation and my affairs I am afraid it would make
too deep an impression, and perhaps be a means of hastening
him to his grave.'

Eventually, though, he accepted that none of these arguments was going to make Lord Derby change his mind; the
episode was over; there was nothing for him here. He would
have to swallow his pride and return to his old life in London.

Cruden had resigned himself to obloquy; he found none. His
friends in London were pleased to see him, Mr Watson
immediately re-engaged him as a proof-corrector, and within
weeks his room – still in the vicinity of Little Britain – was
once again filling up with pieces of paper. By the beginning
of 1730 he was back at work on his Concordance.

Cruden's Concordance is not just remarkable for its size.
It is remarkable because, unlike other Biblical Concordances,
and unlike such comparable works as Samuel Johnson's

*Dictionary of the English Language,* it was entirely the work of one man. The earliest Concordances, as Cruden himself was always quick to point out, had involved teams of compilers sometimes several hundred strong. Dr Johnson (who was born ten years after Cruden and who would not start work on his *Dictionary* until 1746), would famously employ six amanuenses for 'the mechanical part' of his 'arduous and important work'. James Boswell recorded a conversation between Dr Johnson and Dr Adams in which the latter protested that 'the French Academy, which consists of forty members, took forty years to compile their Dictionary', so how could Johnson possibly hope to produce his in three? Johnson replied, 'Sir, thus it is. Let me see, forty times forty is sixteen hundred. As three to sixteen hundred, so is the proportion of an Englishman to a Frenchman. I have no doubt that I can do it in three years.'[2] (He did not, as far as anyone knows, make similar computations involving Scotsmen, perhaps because five of his six assistants came from north of the border.)

Cruden, however, was not just one man doing the work of six (or even sixteen hundred). He was doing it in whatever time he had left over from his full-time job as a proof-corrector, and he was receiving no financial support from anyone. According to G.M. Trevelyan, 'the reading public [in the early eighteenth century] was so small that authors could not live by their sales alone. Patronage was still necessary for authors to subsist, and it could be courted in a number of ways. The aspirant might present copies, or dedicate editions of his works, to "a person of quality", who might reward him with a bag of guineas, or haply with a living or with a post in public or private service.' Samuel Johnson would be famously disappointed in his expectations of a 'bag of guineas' in return for dedicating the first edition of his *Dictionary* to the tight-fisted Earl of Chesterfield, but he would sell the copyright to his publishers for £1575, of which half was paid in advance. Although the total was the equivalent of over £100,000 today, it had to cover the wages of his amanuenses as well as all the printing costs of the *Dictionary*, and these would have been considerable; even so, what was left would have been more than enough to provide Johnson with a comfortable living had the great man not been so careless about money. Cruden had hoped that his post with the Earl of Derby at Halnaker would provide him if not with a comfortable living, at least with a subsistence. That dream had now faded, and he was faced with the prospect of compiling his Concordance without patronage, without bags of guineas or a public or private post, and with only such money to live on as he could earn from his proof-correcting.

Far from convincing the world of his sanity, as he intended, Cruden's resolve to persist in the near-impossible task of compiling his Concordance single-handed has been used as yet another pointer to his madness. Taken in isolation, and disregarding what had gone before (and what would come after), his tenacity certainly proves that he was determined. It might even suggest that he was more than a little obsessive. But mad?

In 1828 John Connolly, Professor of the Nature and Treatment of Diseases at the (new) University of London, would come to the conclusion that 'the very confinement is admitted as the strongest of all proofs that a man must be mad'. And this, exactly, was Cruden's problem. The interpretation put, then and since, on everything he said or did was informed by the fact that as a young man he had been locked up as a lunatic. Casual comments such as 'He must be mad!' or 'What a crazy thing to do!' take on a far deeper significance when applied to one who would repeatedly be so confined.

Alexander Cruden was a deeply religious man whose only desire was to serve his Lord. He would clearly have made an excellent minister of the Church, and any quirks in his behaviour are indicative more of intense frustration that this role was denied him than of any form of madness. Since it *was* denied him, he put his heart and soul into his Concordance. Although he did expect that he would one day see some financial return for all his effort, money was far from being his main objective. 'My great aim and design in this Work,' he would write in his Preface to the First Edition, 'is to render the study of the holy Scriptures more easy to all Christians, whether private Christians or Ministers of the Gospel who make the Scripture the standard of their preaching.' In the Preface to the Second Edition he would add that he intended his Concordance to be 'the means of propagating among my countrymen, and through all the British dominions, the knowledge of God'. If he could never be a minister himself, at least he could facilitate the labours of those who had the good fortune to be ministers. So earnestly did he wish to make the study of the Scriptures easy for his readers that he sometimes got carried away with his 'significations'. Any word he thought might be unfamiliar to his countrymen he defined in energetic, if not always very accurate, detail.

### QUAIL
*Birds somewhat less than pigeons and larger than sparrows . . . and we are told that their flesh is very delicious and agreeable. Some authors confirm that in eastern and southern countries Quails are innumerable . . . and that sometimes they fly so thick over the sea, that being weary they fall into ships, sometimes in such numbers that they sink them with their weight.*

### SCORPION
*A venomous reptile somewhat like a small lobster that has a bladder full of dangerous poison . . . They say that the dam brings forth eleven young ones which are small round worms that after she has sat on them and hatched them then they kill the mother. They are more mischievous to women than men, and more to girls than women.*

## SERPENT

*It is said of the serpent that when he is old he has the secret of growing young again, and of stripping off his old skin by squeezing himself between two rocks. He assaults a man if he has his clothes on, but flees if he finds him naked. When he goes to drink at a fountain he first vomits up all his poison for fear of poisoning himself as he is drinking. He stops up his ears that he may not hear the voice of the charmer or enchanter. He applies one of his ears hard to the ground and stops up the other with his tail.*

## SWALLOW

*It appears in spring and summer and goes away in autumn. It is thought that it passes the sea and withdraws into hotter climates, where it either hides itself in holes in the earth or even in marshes, and under the water, wherein sometimes great lumps of swallows have been fished up fixed to one another by the claws and beak, and when they are laid in a warm place they move and recover, though before they seemed to be dead.*

## TORTOISE

*In Hebrew* Choled *which the Septuagint translate by* land crocodile, *others by* green frog. *This* land crocodile *is a sort of lizard which feeds upon the sweetest flowers it can find; this makes its entrails to be very much valued for their agreeable smell.*

## WHALE

*Is the greatest of fishes that we know of. Profane authors have given extravagant accounts of the bigness of this creature; some say that whales have been seen of six hundred feet long, and three hundred and sixty feet thick. In Scripture there is mention made of the whale. But the Hebrew word* Thannim *is generally used for all large fishes, whether of rivers or of the sea. The Leviathan mentioned in Job 41.1. is thought by a great many interpreters to be the whale, though others think it is the crocodile.*

These examples, and others, give the impression that Cruden was really enjoying himself (it is interesting to note that Dr Johnson too would have strange notions about the behaviour of swallows). The future, though, was beginning to worry him. Although he knew that 'poor sinful man can do nothing absolutely perfect and complete', he wanted his Concordance to be as near perfect as human effort could make it. Since he himself was a mere proof-corrector, he also knew that he would at some stage have to hand it over to others – to printers, publishers and booksellers – to complete its preparation for sale. In 1734, when the great work was finally nearing completion, he decided that he was not prepared to hand it over to anyone. He was going to give up his work as a proof-corrector, become a publisher and a bookseller, and oversee every stage of the Concordance's production himself. It was at this moment that a young acquaintance, recently arrived from Aberdeen to study the printing trade in London, and to whom Cruden had mentioned his plans, offered to introduce him to someone who might be in a position to help.

James Chalmers, the apprentice printer, can only have been about twenty years old when he arrived in London. He would later be the father of Cruden's biographer, Alexander Chalmers, and when reminiscing in his old age would tell his son how his innocent offer of assistance had caused Cruden nothing but pain. Alexander Chalmers, in his turn, would tell the story in his 1824 *Life of Alexander Cruden*, prefixed to the Eighth Edition of Cruden's Concordance.

James Chalmers and Alexander Cruden had walked from Cruden's lodgings in Little Britain towards the Royal Exchange, through that part of the city which had been reduced to ashes by the Great Fire of 1666 and which had since been, and in some cases was still being, rebuilt. As they picked their way through the horse-drawn traffic that crowded the streets, and dodged the droves of cattle skittering over the cobbles on their way to Smithfield, Cruden no doubt pointed out some of the sights to his young Aberdonian companion: the fine dome of the new St Paul's Cathedral, rebuilt after the Great Fire by Sir Christopher Wren and completed less than forty years before; the imposing trade halls of Cheapside or the about-to-be-opened Bank of England building on Threadneedle Street. The Royal Exchange itself had also been destroyed in the Great Fire and since rebuilt, and now once again thronged with bankers and brokers, booksellers and printers, traders and merchants of all descriptions. When they arrived at their destination, the house near the Royal Exchange to which James Chalmers was taking Cruden, their minds were surely filled with London rather than Aberdeen and with the present rather than the past; they were both blithely unaware of the shock that lay in store.

*An incident happened* [would write Biographer Chalmers] *which we shall relate because Mr Cruden often mentioned it as one of the most remarkable occurrences of his life. The house was occupied by a near relation of the young lady* [the girl with whom Cruden had so totally fallen in love back in Aberdeen] *and when they knocked at the door of the house it was opened by the young lady herself, who, unknown to Mr Cruden or his friend, had found an asylum here.*

   *Mr Cruden started back with visible signs of wonder and agony, and grasping his friend's hand, exclaimed wildly 'Ah! She still has her fine black eyes.' His friend* [Chalmers Senior] *was at this time equally ignorant of the lady's asylum, or perhaps of her crime,* [he] *being not above four years old when the shocking affair happened.*

Poor Cruden. The past came flooding back. Ten years after leaving Aberdeen, and fourteen years after he had been so ignominiously imprisoned in the Tolbooth, he must have thought he had left all that trauma and tragedy far behind him. Yet here he was once again face to face with the mystery girl who, wittingly or unwittingly, had been the cause of all his troubles and who was 'probably the only woman with whom he was ever genuinely in love'.[3]

An incident that Cruden himself described as 'one of the most remarkable occurrences of his life' demands the closest possible scrutiny. Evidently it was 'remarkable' because it was such a coincidence; and the coincidence was the lady herself. So who on earth was she? If the story of Cruden's life was to be fully told and understood, it was imperative that the young lady be identified.

Biographer Chalmers was still being super-cautious, and his account of the incident gave nothing away. William Young-man's version of the story, written some twenty or so years after Chalmers', proves marginally more informative: 'the door to which [Cruden] had been accidentally led', said Youngman, 'was that of the lady's younger brother'.

So Cruden's mysterious love was now living in London with her younger brother; and that younger brother was in a position to be of use to someone who was about to become a bookseller; *ergo* he probably had some connection with the book trade. But that is the only information to be squeezed out of Chalmers or Youngman, and as 'members of the book trade in London' were even more numerous than 'daughters of clergymen from Aberdeen', the trail seemed to be going cold before it had even been picked up.

It is commonly not until long after a fruitless struggle to find an appropriate phrase has been abandoned that the wanted words suddenly materialise out of nowhere; so it is not until the seeker of an elusive clue has moved on to other things that it sneaks up and taps him or her on the shoulder.

It was, appropriately enough, Alexander Cruden's own Last Will and Testament that eventually yielded the first clue to the identity of the mystery girl.

Dated April 1770, just a few months before he died, the Will runs to four folio pages written in an elaborate longhand which is not easy to read. It opens with a few prayers and some sermonising, and continues with a series of bequests to various members of his family. Then there is a long section listing sacks of coal to be handed round the indigent of Aberdeen, leather-bound Bibles to be presented to devout citizens, copies of improving works to diligent schoolboys, and so on. In the middle of this section – at the bottom of the third page, with not even a complete sentence to itself – is another bequest leaving £10 to someone whose name is almost illegible but who, over the page, is described as 'daughter of the great and pious minister of the gospel, the Rev'd Thomas Blackwell'. The name of this particular 'daughter of a clergyman from Aberdeen' turned out, on closer examination, to be Christiana Blackwell.

# 4

# Oh, for an 'Orlando'!

The discovery of a 'Christiana Blackwell' in Cruden's Will brought a sudden new significance to the Reverend Thomas Blackwell, hitherto relevant only as Cruden's tutor at Marischal College.

The *Dictionary of National Biography* finds several members of this particular Blackwell family worth mentioning, containing as it does entries for:

1. Alexander Blackwell *(1709–1747) adventurer, brother of Thomas Blackwell the younger*
2. Elizabeth Blackwell, *botanical delineator (fl.1737) wife of Alexander Blackwell*
3. Thomas Blackwell *the elder (1660?–1728) Scottish Divine, professor of divinity, Marischal College, Aberdeen*
4. Thomas Blackwell *the younger (1701–1757) classical scholar, son of Thomas Blackwell the elder*

Three of these, Cruden's professor (3), his childhood tormentor (4), and the colourful prodigy who had 'left university before he had taken any degree and went away so privately that his friends knew not what was become of him till after his arrival in London' and who had then, like Cruden, become a corrector of the press (1), have already featured in Cruden's story. The Register of Baptisms for St Nicholas Kirk in Aberdeen provides details of the rest of the family, confirming that the Reverend Thomas Blackwell and his wife Christian Johnston had half a dozen sons (including the *DNB*'s Thomas and Alexander) as well as the anticipated half-dozen daughters, who included another Elizabeth and not one but *two* Christianas.

The confusion over names was getting worse. There were already three Alexanders (Cruden, his biographer Chalmers and the prodigal Blackwell) and two Thomases (Blackwell father and eldest son). Now there were two Elizabeth Blackwells (wife-of-Alexander and daughter-of-Thomas) and two Christianas, who were sisters. This last is not as strange as it might seem. Names were often duplicated within a single family, usually when a child died young (as all too often happened) and the name was reused for a later child; Cruden himself had two brothers called William; the first, born in 1703, had died as a baby and the name had been used again for the second, born in 1711. The first Christiana Blackwell had obviously died young and the name had been used again for the second.

But any hopes that the Christiana Blackwell to whom Cruden would leave a legacy in 1770 might be the girl with whom he had fallen in love in 1720 were quickly dashed – the Register of Baptisms reveals that the surviving Christiana Blackwell was not born until 1721.

Despite this setback, the Blackwells were intriguing enough to warrant further investigation – particularly the adventurous Alexander. Having thus described him, the *Concise DNB* goes on to say that he 'practised as a printer, became bankrupt, was suspected of quackery and at the age of thirty-eight was arrested in Sweden, convicted of treason and beheaded'. The full 1888 *DNB* hints at more intrigue, stating that he was 'an adventurer whose career is for the most part enveloped in mystery and contradiction'. His wife Elizabeth was 'a botanical delineator' who 'relieved her husband when in embarrassed circumstances' and 'is positively asserted by James Bruce (*Lives of Eminent Men of Aberdeen*, 1841) to have been the daughter of a stocking merchant in Aberdeen and to have eloped with her husband to London before he found employment as a corrector of the press'. This is followed by an unusual caveat: 'No authority is given for these statements,' as if the writer of the *DNB* article was not convinced they were correct. And indeed, in his 1832 edition of *Lives of Eminent Men of Aberdeen* (nine years earlier than the edition quoted in the *DNB*) James Bruce had said something altogether different. According to his original version:

> *the first event in Elizabeth Blackwell's life which is known was her secret marriage with Alexander Blackwell and her elopement with him to London. It is probable from the name that Blackwell was her relative. Of the peculiar circumstances which prevented this affectionate pair from being publicly united we are in complete ignorance.*

Given the nature of the scandal that had either sent Cruden mad or had occurred during his madness, a haunting possibility was emerging.

Some things were known for sure. The girl with whom Cruden had fallen in love had been having an incestuous relationship with her brother, and this had resulted in her pregnancy. Sometime thereafter the girl had been sent away from Aberdeen. Also sometime thereafter Alexander Blackwell had unexpectedly left Aberdeen and had ended up in London. By 1734, at the time of Cruden's startling encounter with the girl, she was living in London with her younger brother.

Also known for sure were the facts that Alexander Blackwell was in the same business as Cruden – i.e. the book trade; that he had a sister, two years older than himself, called Elizabeth; that his wife's name was also Elizabeth, and that the couple had eloped. According to James Bruce, Alexander Blackwell's wife had been called Elizabeth Blackwell *before* they were married. In other words, Blackwell was her maiden name as well as her married name. Bruce thought it 'probable' that the two were somehow related, and he knew that 'peculiar circumstances' had prevented them from being 'publicly united'.

The possibility was too pressing to ignore: were Alexander and Elizabeth Blackwell the brother and sister who had indulged in 'a criminal intercourse' which had resulted in an incestuous baby? Could the 'peculiar circumstances' have been that the girl with whom Alexander Blackwell eloped was his sister? Could Cruden's mystery love, the 'daughter of a clergyman from Aberdeen', have been Elizabeth Blackwell?

Maybe that reliable authority Alexander Chalmers can shed more light on 'this affectionate pair'. In his enormous (thirty-two volume) *General Biographical Dictionary* (published between 1812 and 1817) Chalmers gives them a joint entry under the heading 'Alexander and Elizabeth Blackwell'. After giving some details of Alexander Blackwell's early life, he goes on to say: 'It would appear that his union to Elizabeth Blackwell, who was the daughter of a merchant in Aberdeen, took place under clandestine circumstances, and was a step which gave a direction to all his future fortunes: this was a secret elopement to London where he arrived before any of his friends knew where he was.' The section on Elizabeth, meanwhile, begins: 'Hitherto we hear nothing of his wife – and perhaps but for the misfortunes of the husband, the virtues of this noble woman might never have emerged into the light of public fame.'

So Chalmers, too, knowing as much about contemporary Aberdeen as anyone, confirmed the 'clandestine circumstances' of their marriage, and did not preclude husband and wife having the same surname. But was his assertion that she was 'the daughter of a merchant in Aberdeen' just an assumption? Or was it deliberate disinformation intended to protect 'the relations of the parties still living'? There is no record of any other Blackwells living in Aberdeen at the time (all the Reverend Thomas's relations came from, and remained in, Glasgow), or of any other Elizabeth Blackwell with whom Alexander Blackwell could have eloped. It is beginning to look as though, once again, Chalmers has decided to tell some of the truth, but by no means all of it. Either that, or he had found information on the Blackwells – particularly Elizabeth Blackwell – strangely hard to come by.

The only advance on Chalmers' 'daughter of a merchant in Aberdeen' would come with the second edition of James Bruce's *Lives of Eminent Men of Aberdeen*, published in 1841. Here, suddenly, and as quoted in the *DNB*, she becomes 'the daughter of a *stocking* merchant in Aberdeen'. And for more than a hundred years that was it.

Not until 1961 did anyone make an attempt to identify her. In an article on Elizabeth Blackwell entitled 'The Forgotten Herbalist' published in *The Scotsman* in September of that year, Aberdeen journalist Fenton Wyness stated that 'Alexander Blackwell eloped with, and married, his second cousin Elizabeth Blachrie, the sixth daughter of William Blachrie the stocking merchant.' But, as with the information supplied by James Bruce and used by the *DNB*, no authority was given for these statements.

The unexpected appearance of an 'Elizabeth Blachrie', as with every other development in what is becoming an impossibly tangled story, leads to yet another question. Why had marriage to his second cousin obliged Alexander Blackwell to elope? The answer to this one seemed likely to lie in Aberdeen parish records, and in a thorough search of the Blackwell, Blachrie and Cruden families, as well as the Fordyce family who were the link that made the Blackwells and the Blachries into cousins.

These families all turned out to be vast, having twelve, nine, eleven and sixteen children respectively, and names become a complete nightmare. In the total of fifty-six persons who made up the four families (including parents) there were four Alexanders, four Christian(a)s, five Elizabeths, five Isobells, five Thomases, five Georges and seven Williams, as well as three each of James, John and David. (As with the Crudens and the Blackwells, the Fordyces had reused names for their children; they had had three sons called Thomas, the first two of whom died as infants – and the third, somehow even more poignantly, as a three-year-old.) The families turned out to be almost inextricably entwined – they were each other's brothers-in-law, sisters-in-law, aunts, uncles, cousins, godfathers, ministers, tutors, students, schoolfellows, marriage witnesses, fellow councillors and so on. When the four family trees were written on a single page with lines drawn to show all the connections, the result looked like a demented spider's web.

The first relevant fact to emerge from the web was that Alexander Blackwell and Elizabeth Blachrie were related only because his cousin had married her uncle. It was stretching it a bit even to call them cousins, and they were certainly only cousins by marriage rather than by blood, a relationship that could not have prevented their own marriage on grounds of consanguinity. Since there had already been at least one marriage between members of the two families, family disapproval was not a plausible obstacle either. In fact their union would most likely have been welcomed by everyone concerned. There was no obvious reason why they would have felt compelled to elope.

Although almost nothing is known about the early life of 'Elizabeth Blackwell, wife of Alexander Blackwell', her later life is quite well documented. As Chalmers put it, 'the virtues of this noble woman did emerge into the light of public fame'. Maybe the light of public fame would illuminate the mystery of who she really was. Elizabeth Blackwell had a talent for drawing, and in 1737 she produced a series of 'botanical delineations' to illustrate a book of medicinal herbs. *A Curious Herbal* was published to great acclaim and, because it was the first book of its kind at a time when there was a tremendous market for scientific textbooks, it not only provided the pair with a much-needed income, it assured Elizabeth of a place in several dictionaries of biography, histories of women in science, works on botanical illustration and so on. Most of these obviously took their information on her life from Chalmers, Youngman and Bruce, so did nothing to further the search. But one of them[1] happens to mention that the second volume of her *Curious Herbal* contained a dedication to 'my uncle, John Johnston, with gratitude from his much obliged niece, Elizabeth Blackwell'.

John Johnston was Professor of Medicine at Glasgow University from 1714 to 1749; it was his sister Christian who had married the Reverend Thomas Blackwell and was the mother of Thomas, Alexander, Elizabeth *et al.* Professor Johnston *was not and never had been* Elizabeth Blachrie's uncle. He *was and always had been* Elizabeth Blackwell's uncle.

The illustrator of the *Curious Herbal* was indisputably the wife of Alexander Blackwell, son of the Reverend Thomas. This dedication provides clear evidence that she was Elizabeth Blackwell, daughter of the Reverend Thomas. Elizabeth-daughter-of-Thomas and Elizabeth-wife-of-Alexander were indeed one and the same person. Elizabeth Blachrie was a red herring. Alexander Blackwell had eloped with his sister.

But there is still a problem. When the incestuously conceived baby was born in Aberdeen in 1721, Alexander Blackwell was only twelve years old, which probably (but not definitely) made him too young to have been the father of Elizabeth's child. So what were the alternatives?

As already noted, the Reverend Thomas Blackwell and his wife Christian had six sons: Thomas (b.1701), John (1704), David (1707), Alexander (1709), George (1710) and Charles (1716). By 1728 the records of Marischal College teaching appointments were listing only three: Thomas, George and Charles. John and David had apparently died as infants, but Alexander was still very much alive in 1728. He was omitted from the list of Blackwell sons because, in Chalmers' revealing words, 'his parents were not very desirous of preserving his memory'. George and Charles were certainly too young to have fathered Elizabeth's child, so if the father was not Alexander, it had to be Cruden's childhood tormentor, the dreaded Thomas.

These discoveries put an entirely different complexion on everything that had happened to Alexander Cruden in Aberdeen. They also provide an explanation for Cruden's cryptic remark that 'In the year 1720 [I was] in a treacherous Manner decoy'd into the publick prison at Aberdeen by the Advice of a conceited Man.' The Blackwells (or at least some of them), who had been the grandees of the tale, possibly even Cruden's benefactors, were rapidly turning into the villains. No wonder Chalmers had found information on them hard to come by.

Few people, it transpired, have anything good to say about Thomas Blackwell Junior. Highly qualified and professionally successful (Professor of Greek and then, like his father, Principal of Marischal College), he was variously described as pedantic, pompous, dignified and self-important; according to *Fasti Academiae Mariscallanae Aberdonensis* his opinions were 'inclined to be heretical' and he 'brought on a consumptive habit by great abstemiousness', and according to Chalmers, while at home 'he chose only the conversation of persons of superior rank and fortune'.[2] His nickname among his students, tellingly, was *Ratio Profana*, a sly reference to his father's book *Ratio Sacra*. It indicated that his students at least suspected their learned professor of all kinds of skulduggery. But incest?

Incest is one of the few sexual relationships which is still taboo today. In eighteenth century Aberdeen it was even more shocking – and, probably, more common. With such large families to accommodate, living conditions even amongst the prosperous were cramped. Children slept three or four or five to a bed, and once the candles had been blown out, the search for warmth, comfort and sensation would have had predictable results. But to a family such as that of the Reverend Thomas Blackwell, even the taint of illegitimacy would have been disastrous. In his *Annals of Aberdeen from the Reign of King William the Lion to the End of the Year 1818*, William Kennedy quoted from old court records to show what happened to those citizens who, as he put it, 'persevered in their irregularities in defiance of the civil and ecclesiastical authorities'.

*1/7/1638 Jeills Paterson, who confessed fornication with Adam Dow, servant to Alexander Sutherland of Forres, within his ship, at the quay, was ordered to be carted from the cross to the quayside, where she was to be ducked* [in the sea], *thereafter to be confined in the correction house till Whitsunday next, and to be whipped every Monday during that period.*

*17/12/1660 George Mill, who had been whipped through the town for a trelapse* [third offence] *in fornication, was found to have been* heinously *guilty, and remitted to the presbytery as worthy of excommunication.*

Fornication even amongst Aberdeen's lowlier citizens was considered sinful enough to earn the culprits a public ducking followed by a whipping every Monday for the best part of a year. Any suggestion of straightforward fornication, let alone of incestuous fornication, in an eminent family like the Blackwells would have instantly destroyed the Reverend's illustrious career and reduced the family's reputation to ruins. As the historian of Aberdeen's universities has pointed out, when it came to university appointments 'there were standards of morality, conduct and manners which were seldom breached – scandalous professors no one wanted'.[3] But Thomas Blackwell was not just a professor, he was the Principal, as well as being a minister of the Church. It was doubly unthinkable that any murmur of scandal could be allowed to touch him.

Illegitimacy statistics for the north-east of Scotland in the eighteenth century could be taken to prove that the 'lower orders' were more promiscuous than their social superiors. (Of the sixty-seven unmarried mothers in one survey whose occupations were known, thirty-six were domestic servants, twenty-six were farm workers, two were agricultural labourers and two were farmers' daughters. The remaining one was described as 'idle' – presumably she was a 'lady of leisure'.[4]) But these statistics could just as well demonstrate that the 'higher orders' were less willing to admit to their promiscuity and/or in a better position to cover it up. In the days when families of eleven, twelve or even more children were unremarkable, and when the arrival and departure of infants caused as little comment as the changing of the seasons, it was the easiest thing in the world for the illegitimate child of a daughter to be passed off as the legitimate child of her mother. Close the doors, keep both mother and daughter out of sight for a few months, pay the household servants to keep their mouths shut, and who was to know where the child came from? Between 1701 and 1716 Elizabeth Blackwell's mother had given birth to eleven children. In 1721, just a few weeks after

Alexander Cruden was 'placed under restraint' in Aberdeen Tolbooth, she supposedly produced another. Christiana Blackwell was baptised in St Nicholas on 5 January 1721 and thereafter lived her life as 'the daughter of the great and pious minister of the Gospel, the Reverend Thomas Blackwell'. The scandal was averted.

Since so much was at stake, there was probably nothing the Reverend Thomas would not have done to safeguard the family secret. The unexpected arrival on the scene of a suitor for his wayward daughter had therefore presented a very real threat. A suitor might contrive an illicit meeting; he might get close enough or be sharp-eyed enough to guess the truth; Elizabeth might even be tempted to whisper the tale of her woes into his sympathetic ear. Whoever he was, and however drastic the method required, the suitor had to be removed from the scene; and just in case he knew, or even *suspected*, anything incriminating, everything he said had somehow to be discredited.

The Reverend Thomas Blackwell was a powerful man. The fact that Elizabeth's suitor was Alexander Cruden, already under his power on two counts (as his pupil and as the younger brother of one of his junior professors, the brilliant George), turned his power into omnipotence. It was just a question of a few words in the appropriate ear, and Alexander Cruden found himself locked in the Tolbooth.

From then on it would have been easy for the mighty Reverend. He could pay a gracious visit to Alexander's parents in their house in the Gallowgate; he could reassure them that he did not hold them responsible for their son's outrageous behaviour (which, destined to remain forever undefined, might only have amounted to his being in the wrong place at the wrong time). He could ask for their understanding, as parents of young daughters themselves, of his reluctance to say too much about a delicate matter that had been so upsetting to his own daughter that she had (been) withdrawn from public view; and he could give them his word that as Principal of Marischal College, and therefore the direct superior of their eldest son George, he would do everything in his power to see that George's flourishing academic career was not in any way damaged by Alexander's sad lapse into insanity.

The Cruden parents knew nothing of the dark Blackwell secret, so they had no reason to suspect the Reverend of foul play. On the contrary, they were probably grateful for his visit, acutely embarrassed to discover that their younger son had caused him so much trouble and, as Thomas Blackwell intended, horrified to think that George's career might suffer as a result of it. They took the hint. If the Reverend said that Alexander had lost his mind then he must, indeed, have lost his mind, and the last thing they were going to do was plague him with awkward questions.

There is, as has been noted, no record of how long Cruden spent in the Tolbooth. At the very least Thomas Blackwell would have made sure he was kept there, out of harm's way, until well after the baby was born and had been baptised as his daughter. Once she was safely accepted as such by everyone who mattered – his friends, his congregation and his professional patrons – the threat presented by Elizabeth's erstwhile suitor would be greatly diminished, because by then it would also have been accepted by everyone who mattered that Alexander Cruden was out of his head, and that nothing he said could be taken seriously.

As for Elizabeth herself, whichever of her brothers was the father of her child, it would have been an obvious move for her to leave home when the prodigal Alexander did. Maybe, since he had 'gone away so privately that even his friends knew not what was become of him', they had fled Aberdeen together. It was the perfect – indeed probably the only – opportunity for her to escape from the rigidly disapproving parents who had no doubt been keeping her locked in the attic for her sins (and, if Thomas was the father, to get away from the clutches of the elder brother who had abused her), and to make her home instead with the charismatic black sheep of the family who cared not a jot for propriety and to whom she was clearly very close.

Even after Alexander Cruden had been released, the Reverend had retained a strong hold over the Cruden family; a word out of place, even the faintest whisper of a rumour, and George Cruden would have found his tenure as Professor of Greek at Marischal College abruptly terminated. So Cruden had gone from being held in prison as a lunatic to being held at home as a hostage to his brother's career. It is devoutly to be hoped that during this extended ordeal he gained solace from his Bible, because there was precious little solace for him anywhere else. Even if he had somehow managed to hang onto his sanity, he must have been severely traumatised by his time in the Tolbooth; it can have done nothing for his already fragile confidence to know that his prospects were being sacrificed to those of his brother; and whatever else the future held for him, his cherished ambition to make a career for himself in the Church was now out of the question. He must have felt, like the sons of Korah, deserted by his Lord:

> *Thou hast laid me in the lowest pit, in darkness;*
> *thou hast put away mine acquaintance far from me;*
> *thou hast made me an abomination unto them;*
> *I am shut up and cannot come forth;*
> *Lord, why castest thou off my soul?*
>
> (Psalm 88)

Cruden would have known that the workings of his Lord were often mysterious, but even such a loyal servant as he must have wondered whether He could not have found a better way to answer his prayer. For in 1723 his twenty-six-year-old brother George contracted typhoid and died. The Reverend Thomas Blackwell's hold over the Crudens had been plucked from his grasp. His little game was over. He would have to find some other way of ensuring Alexander's silence, maybe by arranging for him to leave Aberdeen altogether. Perhaps his old friend Dr Calamy could help . . .

So it was that like a leaf snatched from its branch by an unseasonal storm, racked and battered and dropped back to earth only when it was many miles from its native tree, Alexander Cruden had found himself, in the spring of 1724, standing on the Westminster doorstep of the great Dr Calamy. And so, ten years later, on the doorstep of a house near London's Royal Exchange, he found himself once again face to face with Elizabeth Blackwell.

This chance encounter took him completely by surprise at a moment when, worn down by the relentless labour of preparing his Concordance and apprehensive about the future, he must have been at his most vulnerable. If anything would have brought on a new bout of insanity, it would surely have been this 'agonising' meeting. It did nothing of the sort. His mind, the mind that would be labelled 'diseased', 'confused', 'unhinged', was resilient enough to withstand this shock as it had withstood the shock of his being locked in Aberdeen Tolbooth. According to Chalmers, 'Cruden did not then, nor ever, enter the house, or court the acquaintance of its owner, who was indeed a younger brother of the lady. But he never again mentioned the name of the unhappy woman but with the bitterest grief and the most tender compassion.'

# 5

# No Ordinary Queen

In the minds of those who knew Elizabeth and Alexander Blackwell in London there was no question about their relationship. Everyone knew they were married. Since there would have been no objection to a brother and sister setting up home together, this can only have been because they announced themselves as man and wife and lived as such. According to the first edition of James Bruce's *Lives of Eminent Men of Aberdeen* (written when he was still in ignorance of what had gone before), they were clearly devoted to each other.

> We are bound, on reflecting on the virtuous life of Elizabeth Blackwell and her pious attachment to her husband, to believe that theirs was a most justifiable if not an absolutely necessary elopement. We think there must have been some unreasonable and as religious writers say 'inconvincible obstinacy' on the part of the old people to the wishes of their offspring which rendered it quite proper and highly becoming for the young folk to take the matter into their

*own hands. That it was a judicious elopement may indeed
be fairly inferred from the fact that their union was a most
affectionate one.*

Presumably by the time he produced his second edition Bruce
had realised why the 'old people' had been so 'unreasonably
obstinate'. But he had no idea how to deal with his discovery,
so he fudged the issue, cutting all reference to Elizabeth's
'virtue' and 'piety' and presenting her vaguely as 'the daughter
of a stocking merchant from Aberdeen'. Since there were probably almost as many stocking merchants in Aberdeen in the
early eighteenth century as there were ministers of the Church,
and given the Scots' lack of imagination when it came to
naming their children, he was confident that somewhere
among their multitudinous daughters there would be an
Elizabeth who would fit the bill; and he was right.

Chalmers referred to Elizabeth Blackwell as 'unhappy'
because he imagined a woman living with such a dark secret
had to be unhappy, not because he thought she shared any of
Cruden's regrets about their relationship (or lack of it). There
is nothing to suggest that she had ever reciprocated the tender
feelings of her ill-fated admirer, but his sudden appearance
on her doorstep must have been almost as great a shock for
her as it was for him. The roundabout route that she and her
brother Alexander had taken from Aberdeen to London via
Leiden, where he might or might not have studied medicine,
had thrown everyone off their scent, and they had established
themselves in London without any questions being asked.
Links between Aberdeen and London were as minimal as were
the chances of the couple coming across anyone in the capital
who knew anything about them, their past or their relationship
to each other. Yet here she was, standing face to face with
someone who definitely knew who they were and who possibly
knew much more. Although she probably never realised it,

Elizabeth Blackwell was lucky that her one-time suitor Alexander Cruden was a man of such discretion and devotion that he would never breathe a word about them to anyone. But her luck, and more particularly that of her husband/brother Alexander, was about to run out.

Chalmers calls Alexander Blackwell 'a man of mercurial and adventurous temperament', while John Nichols, in his *Literary Anecdotes of the Eighteenth Century,* thought him 'possessed of a good natural genius but somewhat flighty and a little conceited; his conversation was agreeable, and he might be considered on the whole as a well-bred accomplished gentleman'. Having been employed for a while as a proof-corrector when he first arrived in London, the flighty (but accomplished) gentleman had soon tired of such pedestrian work, and in 1730, knowing himself worthy and capable of higher things, he had acquired premises in the Strand and set up as a printer. His natural genius should have warned him that this was not a wise move. The printing trade in eighteenth century London was highly organised. Printers fiercely defended their rights and privileges, had strict rules about who was permitted to do what and when, and had ways of dealing with upstarts who styled themselves printers without first going through the requisite apprenticeship, however well-bred and agreeable they might be. Alexander Blackwell had served no apprenticeship at all and, sure enough, his rivals found numerous crafty and devious ways to damage his business. Contracts and commissions were hard to come by, his best compositors were lured away to work elsewhere, and by the time of Elizabeth's meeting with Cruden he was on the verge of bankruptcy. A few months later, at the end of 1734, he was arrested for non-payment of his debts and sentenced to two years in Highgate Prison.

Cruden was altogether more circumspect. He understood the rules of the printing trade and its inflexible hierarchy. He knew that things had changed since those early days when 'the printer was generally a publisher, and the publisher was generally a bookseller, who sold the books he printed'.[1] The trades were going their separate ways. Booksellers, who had no such regulations on apprenticeships, now held the copyright of books, commissioned printers to print them and supervised the printing (in effect being the precursors of modern publishers) as well as being responsible for selling the end product. There was no copyright on periodicals, and booksellers were not involved in their production or their retailing, so in that field the printer could still be king. But in the case of books the bookseller reigned supreme. The author, as always, was of little account. William Hogarth's father, who had also been imprisoned for debt, died in 1718 at the age of fifty-five while struggling to produce an enormous Latin dictionary. 'I had before my eyes the precarious state of authors and men of learning,' wrote his artistic son. 'I saw the difficulties my father went through whose dependence was chiefly on his pen, and the cruel treatment he met with from booksellers and printers.' Likewise the London bookseller John Dunton who, facing bankruptcy in the early years of the eighteenth century, declared that even *in extremis* he 'could not stoop so low as to turn author'. But Cruden was familiar with the cruel ways of printers and not the least bothered by the lowly status of authors. He just wanted his Concordance to find the widest possible readership. The best way to ensure that it did so was to become a bookseller, and the best place to become a bookseller was in the vicinity of the Royal Exchange.

Although the Royal Exchange was widely recognised as the commercial and financial heart of London, in Cruden's time it also vied with the area round St Paul's Cathedral (Fleet Street, Paternoster Row, etc.) as the most important centre of London's book trade. 'Evidence for the history of the book trade,' states the industry's historian Laurence Worms, 'to a large extent derives from surviving books and their imprints, and with addresses as diverse as Royal Exchange, Cornhill, Poultry, Threadneedle Street, Lombard Street, Sweetings' Rents or Pope's Head Alley, it is not immediately obvious that these places formed in effect a single site, a small and contiguous cluster of streets and passages dominated by the Exchange at its centre.'[2]

Giving a wide berth to Pope's Head Alley, Cruden rented premises at the more acceptably named 'sign of the Bible & Anchor under the Royal Exchange'. He did not intend to go into bookselling on any great scale. His premises probably consisted just of one small room; and since it would still be some years before his Concordance was published, for a while he sold few books. A stickler for professional propriety, he signed up (and paid up) to become a liveryman of the Stationers' Company; and he resigned all but one of his proof-correcting jobs in order to give himself more time. Then he installed himself at the Bible & Anchor and started the task, almost as massive as its compilation, of sorting out the Concordance's accumulated mounds of paper and preparing them for printing.

Although he was still 'labouring almost incessantly' and allowing himself no more than four or five hours' sleep a night, Cruden was not too preoccupied to notice the death, towards the end of 1734, of a bookseller named Robert Matthews. He was not personally acquainted with Matthews, but he did know, because he passed his shop every day and had seen the imposing sign above the door, that Matthews had been *Bookseller by Royal Warrant to Queen Caroline*.

There was no remuneration involved in being holder of a Royal Warrant. It was purely an honorary position. But Cruden could think of nothing more likely to enhance the reputation (and boost the sales) of his Concordance than to have it not only 'compiled by' but 'sold by' the *Bookseller by*

*Royal Warrant to the Queen,* particularly when the queen in question was Caroline of Anspach. At Matthews' death the title became vacant and, with characteristic single-mindedness, Cruden set off in pursuit of the very thing that would lend his Concordance the weight it deserved.

George II's Queen was no ordinary queen. She was, in Cruden's words, 'a Princess of noble virtues ... possessed of all those talents which make conversation either delightful or improving'. Not only was she a lover of literature and an eager student of science, she was cultured, philanthropic and devout. What Cruden called her 'heroic constancy' to the Protestant faith had given her the strength to reject a proposal of marriage from the Roman Catholic Archduke Charles (afterwards Holy Roman Emperor Charles VI). Later marrying the Protestant George Augustus, Prince of Hanover, she had determinedly, if discreetly, promoted the cause of the Hanoverian succession to the British throne. She was a queen after Cruden's own heart. To have such a paragon as the patron of his endeavours would not only be good for his Concordance, it would, although he would never have admitted it, be balm to his wounded pride. What better way to obliterate the still-painful snubs of an earl than to win the official approval of a queen?

The Queen received recommendations for Royal Warrant holders from the Prime Minister, Sir Robert Walpole, and the Prime Minister in turn relied on his advisers to suggest the most suitable candidate. So Cruden started lobbying. He haunted the coffee houses round the Royal Exchange, bending the ear of anyone he thought might have the slightest influence with Walpole. He mentions particularly having secured the endorsements of three doctors, Stewart, Mortimer and Monro, although he does not say why their approval should have furthered his cause. He also wrote letters to everyone he could think of – including Sir Hans Sloane, President of the Royal Society and physician to the royal family:

> *Royal Exchange December 21 1734*
> *Honourable Sir*
>
> *I reckon it a great honour and favour that you are pleased to allow me the Liberty of writing to you and of making you acquainted with the Situation of my affair relating to my being Her Majesty's bookseller . . . I obtained a particular recommendation from My Lord Mayor and the greatest part of Whig aldermen and some very considerable citizens known to Sir Robert Walpole . . . and last Tuesday I had the honour to wait upon Sir Robert at his Levy and to speak to him. He was so kind as to tell me that he would do me all the service he could, and that he was not engaged [i.e. committed to anyone else], and he was satisfied that my character was entire . . . The Favour Sir I would humbly beg of you, is that you would please to put Sir Robert in mind of my affair that he may be pleased to lay it before Her Majesty and bring it to a favourable determination for me, for tho' I am satisfied of his friendship, yet it is possible he may forget the affair for some time in his great multiplicity of business.[3]*

To this suitably deferential and typically dogged epistle Cruden attached a copy of his 'particular recommendation' from 'some very considerable citizens':

> *December eleventh 1734*
>
> *We are satisfied that Mr Alexander Cruden, Bookseller and Liveryman of the Stationers Company, is a person of good character and great integrity . . . and we believe him to be well qualified to serve Her Majesty in the character of bookseller.*

*Signed:*

> *James Colebrooke        John Salter*

| | |
|---|---|
| *William Billers* | *Robert Kendall* |
| *William Jenkins* | *John Eyles* |
| *Roger Mainwaring* | *Robert Baylis* |
| *John Jacob* | *Henry Hankey* |
| *Edward Bellamy* | *Richard Hopkin* |
| *John Thomson* | *Gerard Conyers* |

The fact that so many 'considerable citizens' were willing to support his candidacy for the Royal Warrant suggests that, even if the Great Work itself was still lying in heaps all over his floor, the existence of Cruden's Concordance was already well-known and its appearance eagerly anticipated. Their support, combined with his tenacity, did the trick. In April 1735, wee Alexander Cruden from the Gallowgate in Aberdeen was appointed *Bookseller by Royal Warrant to Queen Caroline*. Balm indeed.

Quite by chance, Cruden was not the only Aberdonian to be appealing to Sir Hans Sloane for help in that winter of 1734–35. When her brother/husband Alexander was sent to Highgate Prison, Elizabeth Blackwell was left not only penniless but burdened by his debts. There may also have been children of this unconventional union. A son and daughter of an Alexander Blackwell, William and Blanche Christian, are recorded as having died in London in 1736 and 1738 respectively, but as there were definitely other Blackwells living in London in that period it is impossible to know whether the bereaved father and the imprisoned bankrupt were one and the same. James Bruce says that at the time of Alexander Blackwell's execution in Sweden in 1747 'Elizabeth was making arrangements to leave England with her only child, and join her husband'. So it is possible that they had had two children or even three. Yet no other account makes any mention of either of them having any children at all. As with so many details of their private lives, the truth has been erased by the passage of time and by dissimulation on the part of everyone concerned. But whether she was on her own, dandling a baby on her knee, or surrounded by toddlers, there is no doubt that the twenty-eight-year-old Elizabeth Blackwell was in serious trouble. According to Chalmers, she rose to the occasion:

> *Like the flower which blooms mostly by night, the better quality of woman's nature is chiefly developed under the cloud of sorrow; and it is only when the powers of man have been prostrated, or found of no avail, that her weakness shines forth in its real character – latent strength. Elizabeth Blackwell happened to possess a taste for drawing flowers* [or, in James Bruce's patronising words, 'She had in her girlish days practised the drawing and colouring of flowers – a suitable and amiable accomplishment for her sex']; *a taste then so very rare, that there was hardly any engraved work in existence containing representations of this interesting department of creation. The acknowledged want of a good herbal occurred to her as affording the means of exerting this gift in a useful way.*

So Elizabeth started drawing flowers. And when she had accumulated a sufficient portfolio she took it to Sir Hans Sloane and asked for his advice. Sir Hans Sloane was not just a physician; like many medical men of his day he was also a noted botanist. A Fellow of the Royal Society by the time he was twenty-five, he had spent a year in Jamaica in 1685, had returned with eight hundred botanical specimens and later had written a much admired *Natural History of Jamaica*. He had become President of the Royal Society in 1727 (having previously spent thirty years as its Secretary), and was a generous and supportive patron of young scientists of all disciplines.* Elizabeth was sure he would agree that there was a need for an illustrated medicinal herbal; now she wanted to know if he thought her drawings were good enough, and whether he would be able to advise her about how to proceed with the project.

Elizabeth Blackwell's botanical drawings have been sniffily dismissed as 'wanting accuracy in delineating the more minute parts',[4] and more recently and even more sniffily as 'not worthy of their reputation ... the work of an industrious amateur, showing no touch of genius'.[5] To the uneducated eye this seems unnecessarily harsh criticism (see plates section); they were certainly 'sufficiently distinctive of their subject' to impress Sir Hans Sloane, if for no other reason than that hers was the first proposal to illustrate a book for which he did agree there was a pressing need. So, probably at about the same time as he was agreeing to (or at least raising no objection to) Cruden's request for his support in the matter of the Royal Warrant, Sloane agreed to help Elizabeth with her herbal. He introduced her to Dr Richard Mead, FRS, a physician so eminent that he has been described as 'the leader of his profession ... who rode about London in a gilt carriage drawn by six horses and accompanied by two running footmen',[6] and to Isaac Rand, a member of the Society of Apothecaries and curator of the physic garden at Chelsea. On Rand's advice she moved out of the house near the Royal Exchange (scene of the startling meeting with Cruden) and into lodgings in Swan Walk, close to the physic garden, 'where she was supplied with plants, which she depicted with extreme skill and delicacy'.† In a story littered with strange coincidences, it

---

* He is commemorated in London's Chelsea not just by Sloane Square, Street, Avenue, etc., but also by Hans Street, Place, Crescent, etc.
† The 1888 *DNB* was less sniffy about Elizabeth's talents.

thus so happened that the erstwhile suitor and the erstwhile object of his admiration spent the next two years toiling away at their respective books less than three miles away from each other.

Elizabeth Blackwell's *Herbal*, as an invaluable aid to physicians and apothecaries, was very much a book of its time, of the Enlightenment, a nourishing draught for a world with a huge and insatiable thirst for knowledge. In that Cruden's Concordance subjected the Bible to the sort of scrutiny, analysis and categorisation which Elizabeth Blackwell was applying to the botanical flora, it too was a work of the Age of Enlightenment – although, paradoxically, Cruden himself viewed the Enlightenment with a jaundiced eye. Like a shipwrecked sailor hanging on for dear life to scriptural certainty, he watched others launch themselves towards an unknown shore with nothing to sustain them except their own ability. He did not condemn them for going, but he was desperately fearful that they would not make it. His Concordance was in the nature of a dogged rearguard action mounted against the stampede for practical and scientific knowledge that seemed likely to trample underfoot all the virtues he cherished – humility, penitence, abstinence and, above all, a complete and utter belief in the Word of God. Cruden saw his Concordance as a much-needed lifeline. Elizabeth Blackwell saw her *Herbal* as the key to Highgate Prison.

Elizabeth had help with her *Herbal*, in a way that Cruden never had. The patronage of Sir Hans Sloane encouraged others to support her project; a document, attesting their satisfaction with Mrs Blackwell's specimens, and recommending her contemplated work to public attention, was signed by six eminent physicians, including Dr Mead, and dated 1 October 1735. Dr Mead advised her on which plants she should include, Isaac Rand placed the resources of the Chelsea Physic Garden at her disposal and ensured that she had fresh specimens of flowers and plants to draw, while her husband/brother Alexander 'lent her all the aid in his power' from his prison cell. 'The share her husband took in the work was to attach the Latin names of the plants, together with a short account of their principal characters and uses, chiefly taken, by permission, from Philip Miller's [unillustrated] *Botanicum Officinale*.'[7] The rest of the work was Elizabeth's. 'After finishing the drawings, she engraved them on copper herself, and then coloured the prints with her own hands.'

Elizabeth Blackwell's book was published just ahead of Cruden's Concordance. The first volume of *A Curious Herbal* appeared in 1737 in large folio, containing 252 plates, each of which is occupied by one distinct flower or plant. Accompanied by laudatory certificates from the College of Physicians and the College of Surgeons and dedicated to Dr Mead – '. . . give me leave to tell the readers how much they are in your debt for this work, and to acknowledge the honour of your friendship . . .' – it was encouragingly well-received. Alexander Chalmers, writing in c.1813, would remark that 'although the style of the engravings is what would now be called hard, it is fully on a level with the prevailing taste of the age; and as a piece of labour executed, it would appear, in the space of four years, by the hands of one *woman* [his italics], the whole work is entitled alike to our wonder and admiration'. Its success meant that Elizabeth was soon able to pay off some of the most pressing of Alexander's creditors and start work on her second volume, which would bring the total number of plants covered to five hundred.

Meanwhile Cruden was still struggling to contain his monumental work between two covers. 'My intention', he declared in his introduction to the First Edition, 'had been to produce an octavo volume' small enough to be carried around by those for whom he intended it to be an indispensable *vade mecum*. But having had one section printed up in the smallest typeface available, he realised that not only was the text so tiny that it would have been impossible for all but the most eagle-eyed of clergymen to read, there was still far too much material to fit into one octavo volume. 'So I found it necessary to alter my scheme, and to compile one to be printed in this large [quarto] volume, in order to make those improvements which now render it preferable to any other.' He experimented with layouts, with typefaces, with paper, with the use of italics and with putting his 'alphabets' in different orders. He checked and rechecked his references although by now he knew the Bible inside out. He had pages printed with two columns of text and then with three; and he prayed for guidance and strength, until finally he was satisfied. But even then he was far from finished.

Setting more than a thousand pages of three-columned text in what was still a very small typeface took the compositors many months. A nightmare task even for the most expert proof-corrector, the entire two-and-a-half-million-word text had next to be checked for errors. (An appendix to the original transcripts of Shakespeare's plays excused any imperfections by pointing out that 'Only the most unrelaxing vigilance and supervision can arrest the brood of error that haunt the printing-house and the copyists' desk alike.') Then all the corrections had to be incorporated. Then it had to be printed. And Cruden either executed or supervised every single stage of the whole process himself. What was beginning to worry him almost as much as the effort involved, though, was the expenditure. In his *Printing in England* (1960), P.M. Handover details the costs of producing the first edition of Edward Gibbon's *The Decline and Fall of the Roman Empire* in 1776:

| | |
|---|---|
| *Printing 90 sheets at £1.6s with notes at the bottom of the page* | £117 0s 0d |
| *180 reams of paper at 19s.* | £171 0s 0d |
| *Paid the Corrector, extra care* | £ 5 5s 0d |

| *Advertisements and incidental expenses* | £ 16 15s 0d |
|---|---|
| | £310 0s 0d |

Adjusting the figure to allow for differences in the value of the pound forty years ahead of Gibbon, for the fact that the Concordance had three times the number of pages of *The Decline and Fall* and therefore three times as many sheets to be printed on three times the amount of paper, for the fact that small type cost more to compose, and deducting the corrector's charge (did correctors get paid more for taking 'extra care'?), which he would presumably have waived, the production of Cruden's Concordance must have cost something in the region of £500.*

Frugal by nature, and having been gainfully employed for most of the past ten years, Cruden thought he had managed to put enough money by to cover all the costs of producing the Concordance. But his savings ran out. Although he had always been reluctant to involve anyone in the project who might try to influence his method, he realised that if the Concordance was ever to appear he had to find some subscribers willing to put money into it.

In the end this was not as difficult as he had feared. His gentle modesty had won him many friends in the printing and publishing world: 'In private life Mr Cruden was courteous and affable, ready to assist all that came within his reach. To booksellers and printers he rendered himself useful in every employment where the talents of a scholar and the scrupulous eye of a corrector were requisite. His manners were extremely simple and inoffensive; he was always to be trusted, always industrious.'[8] When the courteous and affable Mr Cruden put the word out that he was looking for subscribers, there was no shortage of takers.

---

* At today's rate, the equivalent of about £34,000.

The final list of subscribers to Cruden's Concordance was 'D. Midwinter, A. Bettesworth and C. Hitch, J. and J. Pemberton, R. Ware, C. Rivington, R. Ford, F. Clay, A. Ward, J. and P. Knapton, J. Clarke, T. Longman, R. Hett, J. Oswald, J. Wood, A. Cruden, and J. Davidson.' All these gentlemen were publishers, who presumably knew a good investment when they saw one: Charles Rivington was the leading theological publisher of the day (and father of John Rivington, who would later become publisher to the Society for the Propagation of Christian Knowledge), John Oswald had been Cruden's landlord in Little Britain, and five of the others, Arthur Bettesworth and his son-in-law Charles Hitch, Mr Longman and the two Messrs Knapton would also, twenty years later, be among the first subscribers to Dr Johnson's *Dictionary of the English Language.* Their subscription to such books entitled them to reduced-price copies which they could then sell at full price in their own bookshops. But Cruden was no longer worried about keeping a monopoly on the sales of his Concordance – for now it was enough that it should see the light of day.

He was still working part-time as a proof-corrector and, in conformity with the Royal Warrant, he was now also selling books and had taken on a young assistant, John Scott. But no matter how busy he was, or how wrapped up in his own problems, he must have known about the launch of Elizabeth Blackwell's *Herbal.* The coffee-houses round the Royal Exchange hummed with literary gossip as little groups of writers or booksellers or printers picked over new books with admiration or envy or disdain, discussed each other's publications, compared notes and prices and techniques. Word of such an innovative and well-patronised book would have reached even the most preoccupied of ears. Maybe Cruden bought a copy and pored over it in the solitude of his meagre lodgings. Maybe he even sold copies in his bookshop.

Even if had not been personally and emotionally involved with them, the whole business of the Blackwells must have been very distressing for Cruden. By breaking so many of God's laws at once they were putting their mortal souls in grave danger, and he must have longed to do something to save them. If he had been an ordained minister he would have been better placed to help, if only by encouraging them to pray for forgiveness. But he was not an ordained minister. To the Blackwells, he was nothing. The only consolation was that as far as he knew he was the only person in London who was privy to their dark secret, so there was one small thing he could do for them. If he kept his mouth shut, he could at least make sure that their earthly lives would not be ruined, even if their eternal lives were doomed. So he kept his mouth shut.

In the summer of 1737, soon after the first volume of Elizabeth's *Herbal* had arrived in the bookshops, Cruden took delivery of the first copy of the First Edition of his Concordance. It was a moment of triumph for the little Aberdonian; twelve years of hard work compressed, at last, into one solemn, leather-bound volume. At 1200 pages it could by no stretch of the imagination be called 'handy', but since it contained the ultimate analysis and dissection of that most sacred of books, the Holy Bible, he would surely have considered 'weighty' to be a more appropriate epithet anyway.

In his capacity as *Bookseller by Royal Warrant to Queen Caroline*, Cruden had taken the liberty of dedicating his great work to his royal patroness. His dedication is effusive in the extreme. Dated October 1737, it goes into extravagant detail about 'the fine accomplishments of your mind . . . your inclination and capacity to do good . . . the heroic constancy that determined His Majesty to desire in marriage a Princess more admired for her Christian magnanimity than for the beauty of her person, which had been so universally admired' (he could surely have phrased that particular compliment better), and so on and so on, and finishes with a stylish grovel: 'These are the sincere prayers of him who is, with the most profound respect, May it please your Majesty, Your Majesty's most dutiful and most obedient servant, Alexander Cruden.'

Such obsequiousness may make the modern reader cringe – and has caused his detractors to label Cruden a shameless social climber – but at the time it was the accepted, and expected, style for dedications of books of all kinds. The dedication of the King James Version of the Bible, for example, to which Cruden's great work was the Concordance, rises to even greater heights (or sinks to even deeper depths) of fawnery. It makes frequent references to His Majesty's 'many singular and extraordinary graces', calls him 'a learned and judicious Prince' and 'a most tender and loving nursing Father', and assures him that '. . . whereas it was the expectation of many, who wished not well unto our *Sion*, that upon the setting of that bright *Occidental Star*, Queen *Elizabeth* of most happy memory, some thick and palpable clouds of darkness would so have overshadowed this Land that men should have been in doubt which way they were to walk . . . the appearance of Your Majesty, as of the *Sun* in his strength, instantly dispelled those supposed and surmised mists . . .'. Cruden, in his Concordance, was merely following this most illustrious of examples.

One thousand copies of the First Edition were printed, an impressive number for the time, but before he would allow it to go on sale Cruden was determined to observe the formalities – and allow himself a day to savour. He had the first of these copies specially bound, and then he applied to Sir Hans Sloane for permission to go to St James's Palace and present it in person to his royal patroness. Permission was duly granted. On 3 November 1737, wearing his best coat and the smartest of his three wigs, with the wrinkles smoothed from his clean stockings, and clutching his huge Concordance, Alexander Cruden was ushered into the royal presence.

Caroline of Anspach was fifty-four years old in 1737 and, unbeknown to Cruden, she had been ill for some time. Fittingly, she received her Bookseller in the new library she had commissioned to be built in St James's Palace; Cruden was beckoned forward, and he knelt before Her Majesty and held out his book. The volume was too heavy for her frail hands to grasp, so a Lord-in-Waiting stepped forward to receive it on the Queen's behalf. Caroline then thanked Cruden most graciously for his gift, remarked on the great labour which the Concordance must have necessitated, and told him that she intended to mark her appreciation of the work by making him a grant of £100 from her Privy Purse.

It was a truly wonderful moment; a moment that Cruden would remember – and talk about – for the rest of his life. Too dazzled by the occasion to notice anything amiss, he bowed low and backed out of the royal presence. When he got back to his room he fell down on his knees and gave thanks to Almighty God for His bounteous mercy in allowing a poor sinner to bring his labours to fruition. And he thanked Him, too, for having provided for His servant's earthly needs by guiding the royal hand.

Despite the long list of subscribers to the Concordance, Cruden's purse was empty, his cupboard bare; he was down to his last farthing and Queen Caroline had come to his rescue in the nick of time. A grant of £100 from the Privy Purse would keep him going until his investment in the Concordance started to show some return – and by that time the book would have made his name and his reputation as well. What more could any man want or need or ask for? His efforts were vindicated. He had accomplished his great work for the Lord.

For the first time in his life Alexander Cruden was enjoying a sense of real achievement. It was a very good feeling indeed – and it lasted for exactly seventeen days.

On 20 November 1737, seventeen days after receiving her Royal Bookseller in the library of St James's Palace, and following an unsuccessful operation for an intestinal rupture, Queen Caroline died. Her death dealt Cruden three crushing blows, each more painful than the last. Firstly, his affection and admiration for the Queen had been genuine and deep, and he mourned her passing with real sorrow; secondly, with her death he would no longer be entitled to style himself *Bookseller by Royal Warrant to the Queen*; and thirdly, she had died so suddenly that she had forgotten to give any directions about the grant of £100 to her Royal Bookseller. The money would not now be forthcoming.

Reeling from shock, Cruden surveyed the wreckage of his hopes. He was thirty-eight years old. He had spent twelve years concentrating on his Concordance to the exclusion of almost everything else. But now that he had completed it, instead of finding himself on a comfortable plateau of financial sufficiency and social respectability, his royal patronage had evaporated and he was broke. His savings were gone, he was tired and he was lonely. True, the Concordance might one day provide him with an income of sorts; but there was no telling when or how much. His bookshop was bringing in practically no money since he had never had very many books to sell; and, after a glimpse of a better life as master of his own fate rather than 'a hireling kept in a garret, at hard meat, to write and correct',[9] he found the thought of returning to full-time proof-correcting more depressing than he could bear.

At his wits' end, he made what seemed to him a perfectly logical decision. He would find himself a rich wife.

Not just any rich wife, though; he had someone specific in mind. For many years his fellow-worshippers at Dr Guise's church had included a successful Piccadilly corn-chandler, Bryan Payne, and his wife (to whom Cruden only ever referred as 'Mrs Payne'). The Paynes had befriended him when he had first come to London. He had been in the habit of going to their home for Sunday lunch after the service and had repaid their hospitality by reading to them from the Bible when the meal was over. They jokingly called him their 'private chaplain'. Bryan Payne had died not many months before the Concordance was published, but Cruden had continued to see Mrs Payne at church. Now the happy thought struck him. Here was a wealthy widow who was a good Christian, owned a comfortable house, and presumably served an excellent meal. They were already well acquainted, which would save him the trouble of first finding and then getting to know a stranger. She was, in short, just the sort of person he should marry.

Not surprisingly, since his only previous attempt had landed him in Aberdeen Tolbooth, Cruden was wary of courtship. He took it slowly, spending just a little longer talking to Mrs Payne after church each Sunday, and suggesting shyly that he could resume his custom, discontinued after Mr Payne's death, of taking lunch with her and reading to her from the Holy Scriptures. Because Mrs Payne was fond of the serious little Scotsman and because she knew what it was like to be lonely, she accepted his suggestion. Matters looked promising. But after a month of polite Sunday lunches Cruden began to fret. What now? How did he get the relationship to the next stage? Without the discipline of the Concordance he was having trouble sleeping, his stammer returned, and he contemplated abandoning his scheme altogether. One glance at his finances showed him that he could not afford to do that. He must press the good widow. So the following Sunday he prayed more fervently than usual in church, was as agreeable as he knew how during lunch, and then startled his hostess by blurting out what he himself would later admit was 'an awkward piece of love gallantry'.

Mrs Payne could not have been more surprised had Cruden danced a Highland Fling. It had obviously never occurred to her that the man she thought of as her 'private chaplain' might have a completely different role in mind. She told him in no uncertain terms what she thought of his 'love gallantry' and showed him the door. Back in his lodgings, Cruden agonised over Mrs Payne's reaction to his declaration. Was this how every woman behaved in the early stages of courtship? Maybe she was just being coy. He should have been less diffident, more masterful; he should have stood his ground instead of scuttling away with his tail between his legs like a frightened spaniel; he would have another go. Preparing his ground carefully and summoning all his courage, he wrote Mrs Payne a 'strong letter' telling her he would dine with her on 18 March when, as he later put it, he 'intended to get a plain answer, and to know fully her Resolution from her own Mouth'.

He arrived at the house in Piccadilly on the appointed day with his new plan of action at the ready. To his dismay he found that Mrs Payne had invited two other gentlemen to share what he had hoped would be an intimate dinner *à deux*. One of the guests was John Oswald, who had been Cruden's landlord in Little Britain and who also owned the house in White's Alley where Cruden was now living. The second gentleman, who was introduced to Cruden as Mr William Crookshank, was a stranger. To Cruden's intense frustration, neither gentleman left the room once the whole time he was there. Instead, even before they had dined, it was Mrs Payne who excused herself. On the strange grounds that she had to change her dress, she left the room and she did not reappear. It slowly dawned on Cruden that Mrs Payne had invited Oswald and Crookshank expressly to prevent the intimacy that he had been anticipating. She must have told them that he was coming and why; maybe she had even let them read his 'strong letter'. He was utterly mortified.

Recalling the occasion many months later in circumstances every bit as mortifying, he would say that he had 'tarried some time, being in hopes of her being quickly in a better disposition; but he being afterwards satisfied that he had been misused by Mrs Payne in such a manner that no generous man could bear, he was greatly disobliged, and justly, on the account of the great Encouragement she had given him in his addresses on former occasions'. This version of the events of the fateful day was a face-saving exercise. Mrs Payne had clearly never given his addresses any encouragement at all (although by then he would have good reason to remember things a little differently). In fact he was not so much 'justly disobliged' as burning with humiliation and resentment. When he arrived at church the next morning he was still smarting, and was unable to resist showing Mrs Payne how hurtful 'her haughtiness and bad Behaviour towards him' had been by choosing to 'sit in the Front Seat of the Gallery where Mr and Mrs Payne some years before used to sit, that he might rather triumph over Mrs Payne, than show a mean or servile spirit for the great Disappointment she had given him'. And he spoke the responses in a particularly loud voice so everyone in the congregation would know that his spirit had not been broken by Mrs Payne's 'bad Behaviour'.

By the Monday morning Cruden's normal good nature had reasserted itself, and he was feeling thoroughly ashamed of his unseemly conduct in church. But before he had even started to work out how to make amends, there came a knock at his door; Mrs Grant, his landlady, announced that he had a visitor, and ushered in a man who introduced himself as Robert Wightman.

Wightman looked familiar, and Cruden decided he had met him somewhere before, although he could not recall the occasion. What he did not know was that Wightman was his rival for the hand of Mrs Payne. In fact Wightman, a fellow Scot, considered himself as good as betrothed to the wealthy widow, and had come to take a look at the man who had dared try to worm himself into her affections while he had been out of town on business. But he was all charm and concern, saying that he had heard Cruden was out of sorts, had just been passing and had called in to see if there was anything he could do. Touched by this unexpected kindness on the part of a near-stranger, Cruden found himself agreeing with his visitor's suggestion that the best cure for disordered nerves was bed-rest. A measure of how far he had come since his confinement in Aberdeen Tolbooth was that even Wightman's mention of 'disordered nerves' did not ring any alarm bells. By the time Wightman left, Cruden had the warmest feelings towards his visitor, thinking him 'a sedate man of his own type, serious and courteous, who had treated him with respect and sympathy'.

Cruden could not have been more mistaken. Robert Wightman was totally unscrupulous.

Somehow, Wightman had found out that in his youth Cruden had been incarcerated as a lunatic. Possibly he knew this from his connections in Scotland, or possibly Cruden had confided the story to Mrs Payne in the heat of the moment and she had passed it on to Wightman. Whatever the case, Wightman must have arrived in White's Alley expecting to find a harmless lunatic or a gibbering idiot, either of which would be easily bullied into keeping away from Mrs Payne. He had found, on the contrary, a very plausible suitor for the hand of the rich widow; a perfectly rational man who presented a real threat to his own rosy future. So while Cruden was taking his advice and putting his feet up, Wightman was forced to think up a new strategy. Pausing only to warn Mr and Mrs Grant, Cruden's landlord and landlady, that their apparently mild Scottish lodger was in fact a dangerous madman, he went on his way, deep in thought.

The very next morning, while Cruden was reading quietly in his room, the door burst open. In barged 'a huge man wielding a stick', followed by Mrs Grant, waving her hands about and screeching that Cruden was a lunatic who ought to be sent to a madhouse. These words struck cold terror into Cruden's heart; terror that gave him the strength to leap from his chair, snatch the stick from the intruder and chase him from the room and down the stairs. On the way past he inadvertently knocked the still-screeching Mrs Grant to the floor. Pandemonium ensued. A candle overturned in the confusion and set fire to some of Cruden's papers (a disaster which he had long feared and which would later lead to his being accused of trying to burn the house down). Several passers-by came in through the open front door to see what the commotion was all about. Mrs Grant picked herself up off the floor and ran down the stairs and out into the street, screeching louder than ever and yelling for help, while the intruder (who was apparently a blacksmith) wrestled with Cruden for possession of his stick. The struggle between a large blacksmith and a small proof-corrector was hardly an equal one, so when Cruden lost hold of the stick he dodged the impending blows by diving through a door into the basement. By now Mrs Grant had the support of 'a bloody butcher' (Cruden's words) who had answered her cry for help; between them they managed to force open the door to the basement. The butcher started raining blows on Cruden's head with another stick 'to the great effusion of his blood'. Two new arrivals on the scene, John Duck and John Anderson, took sides with the bleeding Cruden and managed to get rid of the butcher; Mr Grant got Mrs Grant under control; the blacksmith vanished; someone extinguished the fire; someone else called the doctor; and Cruden limped back upstairs to his room to have his wounds tended. Wightman's first, very clumsy, attempt to abduct his rival had failed.

Thoroughly shaken and suffering from a bad headache, Cruden stayed in his room for the next three days. He tried sending for a Constable but was too scared to go out and look for one when none appeared. He refused to speak to the Grants when they brought him food, 'for it was they who had let in upon him the ruffians', and spent most of the time reading his Bible. On the third day a message arrived from Robert Wightman inviting Cruden to visit him at his home in Spring Gardens. Remembering how concerned Wightman had been about his well-being the day before the attack, and without the least suspicion that he had been involved in it, Cruden decided that a sympathetic ear was just what he needed, so he accepted the invitation.

Wightman sent his hackney carriage to collect Cruden from White's Alley. Cruden was handed courteously into the carriage by the coachman's boy, the windows were drawn up and the carriage pulled away down Chancery Lane towards Fleet Street. Spring Gardens was in Whitehall, so Cruden was fully expecting the carriage to turn right into the Strand and head west. Instead it turned left into Ludgate Hill and headed east. Cruden immediately knew something was wrong. He banged on the side of the coach to attract the coachman's attention and tell him he was going the wrong way, but the horses maintained their pace. He managed to lower the window and shout, but the coachman ignored him. Recounting the episode many months later Cruden still found the experience distressing, and, as always when he was under great strain, throughout his account he referred to himself in the third person as 'Mr C'.

*When Mr C saw himself thus imposed upon he expostulated in the following manner: 'Oh, what are you going to do*

*with me? I bless God I am not mad. Are you going to carry
me to Bethlehem? How great is this affliction?' Roberts the
coachman then positively told Mr C that he had orders
from the said Wightman to carry him to country lodgings
near Bow.*

This news was no consolation to the distraught passenger, who
had no choice but to sit tight while the coach carried him ever
eastwards, past St Paul's Cathedral, past the Royal Exchange,
through Aldgate and on towards Whitechapel and the Mile
End Road. Before reaching Bow, the coach turned left towards
Bethnal Green, slowing down through the narrow lanes and
eventually drawing to a halt in front of a large house. Cruden
was bustled out of the coach by the coachman and his boy
and taken in through the front door (which he noticed being
firmly locked behind him), led into a sparsely-furnished room
and handed over to a man who introduced himself as John
Davis. The coachman and his boy then withdrew.

Shaking with fright and indignation, Cruden demanded that
Davis tell him who he was and what kind of place had he
been brought to. Davis replied that he himself was the Under-
Keeper and that the establishment was Matthew Wright's
Private Madhouse.

Alexander Cruden had spent fifteen long years trying to prove
to the world that he was as rational and lucid and sensible as
the next man; that he should never have been locked up in
Aberdeen Tolbooth; that he was not and never had been insane. With his reception at St James's Palace by Queen Caroline,
and the publication of his huge Concordance, he had every
reason to believe that he had finally succeeded. Yet now, within
months of these triumphs and at the whim of a man he barely
knew, he was back where all his troubles had started. Once
again he was being held under lock and key in a madhouse.

# 6

# Receptacles of Misery

In his 1621 *Anatomy of Melancholy*, Robert Burton attributed the sources of insanity to sin and the activities of the Devil. He conceded that there might be other contributory factors – bad air, bad diet, too much or too little exercise, the retention of bodily excretions, emotional disturbance and lack of sleep, 'which causes dizziness of the brain, frenzie, dotage, and makes the body lean, dry, hard, and ugly to behold' – but he had no doubt that 'the original cause of madness was the Fall of Man'. Burton's belief was widely shared. Lunatics were thought to be 'possessed' by some supernatural power whose authority mere mortals had no right to challenge. The insane were accepted as just another strand – if a slightly faulty one – in the chequered fabric of life, and they were seldom locked away.

Even as Burton was propounding his theory, enlightened philosophers were deriding superstition as an evasion of responsibility. Incomprehensible events or situations should not just be attributed to the will of God, the workings of the Devil, or the vagaries of some ill-defined supernatural power. All problems, social, material or spiritual, were susceptible to rational thought. Man could – and should – think for himself. As these new ideas gained ground attitudes started to change; insanity ceased to be regarded as divinely inspired, lunatics were declared sick rather than possessed, and 'by the end of the seventeenth century madness had been reduced to a form of immorality or scandal rigorously to be excluded from the life of moral men'.[1]

As society grew increasingly intolerant of bizarre or disruptive behaviour, provision had to be made for those it was no longer prepared to accommodate. In 1714 an 'Act for reducing the Laws relating to Rogues, Vagabonds, Sturdy Beggars and Vagrants into one Act of Parliament, and for the more effectual punishing such Rogues, Vagabonds, Sturdy Beggars and Vagrants, and sending them whither they ought to be Sent'[2] placed responsibility for the care of the insane on the lunatic's parish. The Act allowed that, on the authority of two or more justices of the peace, lunatics who were 'furiously mad and dangerous' could be confined 'in such secure place as such justices shall direct or appoint', where they could, if it was deemed necessary, be held in chains. The cost of detaining pauper lunatics had to be met from parish funds.

Yet a quarter of a century later, at the time Cruden was carted off to the private madhouse in Bethnal Green, there was still only one publicly-funded lunatic asylum in the whole country – Bethlehem Royal Hospital (also known as 'Bethlem' or, more famously, 'Bedlam') in London's Moorfields, not half a mile from the Royal Exchange. Bethlehem Royal Hospital was a charitable foundation, open to lunatics from the whole kingdom, but it did not admit either the 'moneyed' or those described in the parlance of the day as 'fatuous' (the incurably mad). It limited itself to the poor and the 'furious' (the temporarily deranged who might be expected one day to recover), for whom it had less than three hundred places. In the absence of other dedicated asylums, and given the unsuitability of most jails for such inmates, parish authorities had only two other alternatives: they could place pauper lunatics in their charge in workhouses, or they could place them in private boarding-houses, which establishments gradually became known as 'mad' houses.

Of course not all lunatics were paupers; those whose families could afford to pay for their safekeeping were more likely to be looked after in the closely guarded seclusion of their own homes or, if that was impracticable, in the custody of indi-vidual carers, who were often clergymen. But as confinement of lunatics became socially not just more acceptable but more desirable, so the demand for safe places and good carers rapidly outgrew the supply, and a whole new breed of resourceful entrepreneurs leapt into business 'peddling the promise of discreet silence for families anxious to draw a veil over the existence of insanity in their midst. Considerable fortunes were accumulated by the proprietors of receptacles for the insane, and the private madhouse system grew rapidly in the early part of the eighteenth century.'[3]

The authorities were not slow to take advantage of these private facilities, and used the 1714 Act to coerce madhouse-keepers into accepting a certain number of pauper lunatics alongside their private fee-paying patients. In the case of most authorities, that was the full extent of their involvement in these private establishments. There was no system of licensing, and neither conditions nor treatment were monitored. An inevitable consequence of this official indifference was that the inmates of these unlicensed private madhouses came to be graded – and treated – not according to the extent and severity of their insanity but according to how much the madhouse-keeper was being paid to keep them locked up. While those at the top end of the scale could, if they were lucky, fare reasonably well, the poorest of the paupers were frequently neglected and often half-starved. 'In seventeenth and eighteenth century practice, the madman in confinement was treated no better than a beast; for that was precisely what, according to the prevailing paradigm of insanity, he was.'[4]

The section of the 1714 Act which required 'the authority of two or more justices of the peace' before a lunatic could be confined applied only to pauper lunatics being supported by parish funds. Admission to Bedlam required similar authority. But, crucially for Cruden, no authority of any kind was needed to place a privately funded lunatic into a private madhouse. The system, or lack of it, invited abuse – and not just by the madhouse-keepers. According to an anonymous pamphlet published in 1740, 'Several unfortunates are put into madhouses without being mad. Wives put their husbands in them that they may enjoy their gallants, and live without the observation and interruption of their husbands; and husbands put their wives in them, that they may enjoy their whores without disturbance from their wives; children put their parents in them that they may enjoy their estates before their time; relations put their kindred in them for wicked purposes.' And as long as they were being paid sufficiently well to house the sane alongside the insane, madhouse-keepers colluded in this abomination.

To make matters even worse for those detained in madhouses without just cause, the only legal way by which they could regain their freedom was by a writ of *habeas corpus*. Even then they had to present their case before the Court of King's Bench, which would order an examination of the patient by 'proper persons' before deciding whether they could be released. Daniel Defoe was one of the first serious campaigners for the official supervision of madhouses: 'In my humble opinion all private Madhouses should be suppress'd at once,' he wrote in 1728, 'and it should be no less than felony to confine any person under pretence of madness without due authority. For the care of those who are really lunatic, licensed madhouses should be constituted in various parts of the town, which houses should be subject to proper visitation and inspection, nor should any person be sent to a madhouse without due reason, inquiry and authority.'

Change would come, but only very slowly. In 1754 a proposal that the College of Physicians should undertake the licensing and inspection of madhouses would be dismissed by the College on the grounds that 'its implementation would be too difficult and inconvenient', a decision influenced by the fact that many of the College Fellows had sizeable financial stakes in private madhouses.[5] A 1763 House of Commons Inquiry would be presented with startling evidence of abuses in private madhouses, but since London madhouses confined the relatives of many prominent people, the committee would proceed with extreme caution and no legislation would follow. Even when an Act for Regulating Private Madhouses was at last introduced in 1774, it would recommend only the most timid of reforms which would take many more years to implement.

The private madhouse system therefore continued to flourish well into the nineteenth century and, unsurprisingly, madhouses gained a terrifying reputation. William Pargeter, who gave up his medical career to become an army chaplain but remained closely involved with the care and treatment of the insane, summed up the public perception of what he called these 'receptacles of misery'. 'The idea of a mad-house is apt to excite the strongest emotions of horror and alarm; upon a supposition not altogether ill-founded, that when once a patient is doomed to take up his abode in those places, he will not only be exposed to very great cruelty; but it is a great chance, whether he recovers or not, if he ever sees the outside of the walls.'[6]

There were good madhouse-keepers as well as bad ones, but even the most humane were hampered by the fact that few members of the medical profession had either the inclination or the expertise to treat deranged patients. 'Owing to these circumstances,' says historian William Parry-Jones, 'quack-doctors who specialised in treating the insane flourished, e.g. David Irish, Thomas Fallowes and Thomas Warburton.' The madhouse into which poor Cruden had so ignominiously been dumped was owned by the last named of these three. Thomas Warburton's madhouse in Bethnal Green (also known as Wright's Madhouse after its Keeper, Matthew Wright) was one of the most notorious private madhouses in the country.

Cruden would later publish a minutely detailed 'diary' of his time in Wright's Madhouse. It carried the title *The London Citizen Exceedingly Injured or A British Inquisition Display'd: the unparalleled case of a Citizen of London, Bookseller to the late Queen, who was in a most unjust and arbitrary manner sent on 23rd March 1738 by one Robert Wightman of Edinburgh, a mere stranger, to a Private Madhouse*. Some sixty pages long, this account was designed, as Cruden's entire adult life had been designed, to demonstrate his sanity – only this time to do so for the benefit of a court of law. He was not seeking sympathy, but was trying to present himself in as rational a light as possible. He therefore excluded any hint of any emotion that could have been interpreted by his judges as irrational.

*23rd March 1738*
*Mr C was delivered to John Davis, the Under-Keeper of the said Madhouse. The said Davis locked Mr C up in a room in the madhouse, who was at first much dejected, but after going to prayer was greatly comforted.*

Thank God, as Cruden might have said, for God. For it can only have been his unwavering faith in the Almighty that enabled him to survive the ordeal that lay ahead. His faith in his fellow man, on the other hand, took a hard knock later on that first day when John Davis, the Under-Keeper, unlocked the door and entered accompanied by Robert Wightman. Cruden's immediate thought was that Wightman had come to sort out what had obviously been a dreadful mistake and arrange for his release. But when Davis and Wightman proceeded to carry on a conversation as if he, Cruden, was not even in the room, he realised that it was he himself who had made the mistake.

> *Davis told Wightman that he had not observed any signs of madness about the Prisoner. But Wightman, who pretends to know that a person is mad from the tone of his voice, replied that the madness would show at about 3.00 am in the morning. But he proved a false prophet.*
>
> *When the prisoner went to bed about 8 o'clock Davis came and told him that seeing he was in a madhouse he must allow himself to be used as a madman, and submit to have a chain on the bedstead locked upon his leg, which the Prisoner patiently submitted to.*

Things were getting worse. Now he was not only locked in a madhouse but chained to his bed, and the only person in the world who knew where he was had turned out to be the very person who had put him there. Although he recoiled from the idea of 'telling any body of his being brought to so dismal a place', Cruden was pragmatic enough – and frantic enough – to realise that he had to find some way of getting word of his fate to his friends outside. He therefore told Davis that he had some important instructions for his assistant John Scott regarding the running of his shop, and requested the wherewithal to write him a letter. This request was initially refused. Not until Cruden agreed to let the Under-Keeper read the letter himself did the housekeeper finally bring him pen, ink and paper. The letter was duly written, approved and dispatched, and in the evening of the same day Cruden was rewarded with a visit from John Scott.

The fact that his assistant was allowed to visit him in the madhouse looked encouraging. Scott was able to alert Cruden's friends as to what had happened to him, and they would arrive at the door of the madhouse in considerable numbers during the whole period of his incarceration to visit him. But mostly they were denied admission. And, Cruden suspected, even when they were allowed in to see him, it was only after they had been warned by either the Keeper or the Under-Keeper that, rational as he might seem at that moment, he was subject to bad episodes of insanity at other times. He also discovered that Robert Wightman, in order to justify his drastic treatment of his rival, had spread the word that this was not the first time Cruden had been locked up and labelled insane.

The novelist Tobias Smollett would draw heavily on Cruden's diary when writing his *Adventures of Sir Launcelot Greaves*. Published in 1762, this cock-eyed tale of heroics and derring-do has the eponymous hero ending up locked in a private madhouse. Sir Launcelot's experiences parallel those of Alexander Cruden too exactly to be coincidental. All Smollett had to do was add the drama that Cruden was careful to leave out and he had a perfect, nail-biting climax to his story.

*Our adventurer was no longer in doubt concerning the place to which he had been conveyed; and the more he reflected on his situation, the more he was overwhelmed with the most perplexing chagrin. He could not conceive by whose means he had been immured in a madhouse; but he heartily repented of his knight-errantry, as a frolic which might have very serious consequences with respect to his future life and fortune. After mature deliberation, he resolved to demean himself with the utmost circumspection, well knowing that every violent transport would be interpreted into an undeniable symptom of insanity.*

Just so, Cruden resolved to 'demean himself with the utmost circumspection' as, to the indignity of restraint, was added the doubtful ministration of medicine.

*24th March*
*The Apothecary brought physick with him for the Prisoner by the prescription of Dr Monro, though the doctor did not visit him until 30th March. The Prisoner prudently submitted to take the Physick that evening, for if prisoners in this madhouse refuse to take what is ordered them, there is a terrible iron instrument put into their mouths to hold down their tongues and to force the physick down their throats. That night, to confirm his authority, Davis not only kept the chain on his leg, but added to his misery by chaining his two wrists together with handcuffs.*

Cruden was very wary of the apothecary, a bruiser by the name of Job London, because he knew – perhaps from his experiences in Aberdeen – that the apothecary to a madhouse was not a man to trifle with. 'Mr C didn't think it prudent to fall out with London, being afraid he would poison his medicine.' But more sinister even than the apothecary was the as-yet faceless Dr Monro who so blithely prescribed 'physick' for a patient he had never yet set eyes on, let alone evaluated.

James Monro was Chief Physician to Bedlam. The son of a Principal of Edinburgh University, he was the progenitor of a whole dynasty of Monros who would rule over Bedlam for more than a century. (His son John, grandson Thomas, and great-grandson Edward Thomas would in turn also be Chief Physicians to the infamous asylum, while in 1852 his great-

great-grandson Henry would become Physician to London's second asylum, St Luke's.) 'The prestige and notoriety that accrued to the Monros as physicians to Bethlem,' according to Andrew Scull, 'was sufficient to establish them in the eyes of both their professional peers and patients' families as expert mad-doctors – men whose very name rapidly became synonymous with the trade and to whom the wealthy and aristocratic turned for discreet advice and service.'[7]

Although he was their Chief Physician, James Monro's attendance on the (impoverished) inmates of Bethlehem Royal Hospital took up only a small fraction of his time. Like other physicians in other hospitals, he maintained a highly lucrative private practice outside Bedlam where the wealthy and aristocratic were prepared to pay handsomely for his discreet advice. He was also Visiting Physician to a number of private mad-houses, including Thomas Warburton's in Bethnal Green. In 1738, when Alexander Cruden became one of his 'patients', James Monro was fifty-eight years old, at the height of his professional omnipotence and with a very clear idea of his priorities. His private patients were his first, his second and his third concern. After that, in no particular order, came the inmates of the various madhouses to which he was consultant and the inmates of Bedlam. If there was a queue of (wealthy) private patients demanding his attention, then everyone else just had to wait. And while they were waiting, it was in the best interests of all concerned that they should be in no position to make trouble. Automatically, and without seeing them or knowing anything about them, he prescribed 'physick' to keep them quiet. He would visit them when he had time.

The 'physick' was invariably an opiate.* Its administration

---

* In his *Hypochondriack Melancholy*, written in 1729, Nicholas Robinson extolled 'the virtues of that truly noble drug we call opium' for controlling lunatics.

was a ploy also resorted to by madhouse-keepers themselves when their patients became unruly or when the arrival of potentially inquisitive visitors threatened to uncover their cosy conspiracies. 'The masters of these receptacles of misery,' says William Pargeter, 'on the days that they expect their visitors, get their sane patients out of the way; or, if that cannot be done, give them large doses of stupifying liquour, or narcotic draughts that drown their faculties, and render them incapable of giving a coherent answer.'

However deplorable the collusion between madhouse-keepers and physicians now seems, conditions in these 'receptacles of misery' were not much questioned in the early eighteenth century. It was enough that there were at least a few 'experts' prepared to take on the onerous and un-savoury task of caring for the insane, and at least some places where the insane could be confined. Few outsiders really wanted to know what happened to them once they were confined; if the experts said they needed to be dosed with 'physick' or kept under restraint, well the experts probably knew best.

Certainly no one knew better than the 'experts'; the trouble was that the experts did not know much themselves. When it came to treating the insane, even the most compassionate of mad-doctors was working alone and in the dark. There were no guidelines, no textbooks and no consensus either on the causes of insanity or its treatment. By now, more than a century after Burton's *Anatomy of Melancholy* had declared the sources of insanity to be sin and the activities of the Devil, it was generally accepted that the roots of insanity were physical, with credence being given to the ancient Greek theory that madness resulted from an imbalance of the 'four bodily humours' (blood, phlegm, choler and bile). But for every phy-sician convinced that the best treatment was some form of 'evacuation' of these humours (by bleeding, purging, vomiting, blistering or cupping), there was another who swore by the efficacy of physical restraint.

Sir Richard Blackmore, author of *A Treatise of the Spleen and Vapours*, published in 1725, argued for 'evacuation'. 'If the Juices contained in any of the Bowels degenerate, and become immoderately acid, sharp, pungent and austere, then they urge and vellicate [twitch] the Nerves so much and irritate and scatter the Spirits in such a violent manner, that the whole intellectual and animal Administration is violated and disturbed, while the Mind is deprived of proper Instruments for its Operations.' (The plethora of romantic heroines who suffered from that elegant-sounding condition 'the vapours' would surely have been instantly cured by hearing it attributed to 'fumes wafting up from the guts and smoking out the brain'.)

William Cullen on the other hand, currently practising as a doctor in Glasgow but eventually to become President of the Edinburgh College of Physicians, was a firm proponent of the straitjacket. 'Restraining the anger and violence of madmen is always necessary for preventing their hurting themselves or others; but this restraint is also to be considered as a remedy. Angry passions are always rendered more violent by the indulgence of the impetuous motions they produce; and even in madmen, the feeling of restraint will sometimes prevent the efforts which their passion would otherwise occasion. Restraint, therefore, is useful and ought to be complete.'[8]

As Cruden was soon to discover, the use of one method of 'treatment' did not preclude the use of the other. On the morning of his second day in the madhouse, Job London announced that he was going to administer another dose of 'physick', and that this time he expected Cruden to pay for it.

25*th* *March*
*The prisoner having told the Apothecary that he would not pay him a farthing for his medicines, in the afternoon the*

*Apothecary came and took upon him to order Davis to put a Strait-Waistcoat upon the prisoner's body, made of strong tick [canvas] with long sleeves which came a great way below the end of his fingers, and so the Keeper clasped the arms of the Prisoner upon his breast and his hands round his sides towards his back where his hands were tied very firmly by large strong strings of tape.*

Each madhouse-keeper had his own preferred method of restraint. The most frequently used was the straitjacket (or 'Strait-Waistcoat' as it was then called), but numerous other mechanical devices – hobbles, handcuffs, manacles, leg-locks, muzzles, leather straps and chains – were standard equipment in all madhouses. The keepers of the madhouse in Smollett's *Sir Launcelot Greaves*, like those charged with the care of Alexander Cruden, favoured the strait-waistcoat; when a shouting match between two inmates 'brought the whole house into an uproar, every individual was effectually silenced by the sound of one cabalistic word, which was no other than *"Waistcoat"'*.

Fastening Cruden into his strait-waistcoat, the Under-Keeper of the Bethnal Green madhouse underestimated his newest patient's determination – and overestimated his size. Because Cruden was so slightly built he contrived, after a determined struggle that lasted some hours and involved using the footpost of his bed as a lever, to wriggle his way out of the hateful contraption.

*But he was catched at it by Davis who replaced the Strait-Waistcoat and strongly fettered his arms with chains outside the Strait-Waistcoat. So he was obliged to eat his supper with his mouth like a Dog, as he did his breakfast and dinner the next day. Oh what difficulties he had to perform the Necessities of Nature in a becoming manner. The Strait-*

> *Waistcoat also hindered him from sleep and it was a great*
> *mercy that this barbarous usage did not throw him into a*
> *real disorder.*

Although Cruden would probably not have seen it that way, he did have one reason to thank Robert Wightman. The conditions in which the inmates of the madhouse were kept depended on how much was being paid for their keep. Whether moved by an unlikely compassion, prompted by a guilty conscience, or anticipating his imminent share in Mrs Payne's wealth, Wightman was paying enough money for his rival's keep to secure him a private room rather than a bed in a communal ward. When later in his stay Cruden complained to Matthew Wright, the Head Keeper, that not only was it an outrage that he was there at all but that his accommodation and his food were each as disgusting as the other, Wright informed him that it was costing Wightman the princely sum of one guinea a week to keep Cruden there, and that if he thought his room and his food were intolerable he should see what some of the other inmates had to put up with. According to Cruden's calculations there were some forty or fifty 'public' patients in the madhouse (in addition to an unspecified number of 'private' patients), and according to the Keeper they were living in accommodation worth a mere four or five shillings a week.* Cruden was so upset by the thought of anyone being forced to endure conditions and a diet that were not even half as good as his own that he never complained about either again – although he continued to inveigh against the fact of his incarceration with every ounce of his strength and at every available opportunity.

---

* By 1815 there would be 360 patients, including about 230 paupers, in Warburton's 'White House' at Bethnal Green and 275 patients, including about 215 paupers, in his 'Red House'. Cruden was held in the former.

The third day of Cruden's captivity, 26 March, was a Sunday. He was understandably distressed that since he was still strapped into the straitjacket and tied down with chains he could not mark the Lord's Day by reading the Bible, let alone by going to church as was his invariable custom. So having 'eaten his breakfast with his mouth like a dog', he 'devoted himself to Prayer'. There was still no sign of Dr Monro, but as the Under-Keeper John Davis later informed him, there had been some visitors to see him.

> *The Lord's Day. This day Serjeant-Major Cruden of Dutchy Lane and his wife came and most earnestly desired to see the Prisoner. But to no purpose, for Davis told them he had orders to allow none to see him without the written permission of Wightman, Oswald or Monro.*

This is the first mention of 'Serjeant-Major Cruden of Dutchy Lane'. Presumably he was a relation, but Cruden would always refer to him as 'my friend', and the Sergeant-Major (whose name, inevitably, was also Alexander) would later testify that they had been acquainted 'for seven or eight years'. Whatever their relationship, the Sergeant-Major's first visit to Bethnal Green was in vain; he was not allowed to see his kinsman. He who paid the piper clearly called the tunes. This further proof of his helplessness was enough, even in retrospect, to disturb Cruden's determined equanimity.

'Davis', he wrote in his diary, 'was deaf to all the Prisoner's entreaties to take off the Strait-Waistcoat, and the Prisoner was much disturbed by the blasphemous cursing and swearing of a Patient in the publick parlour which made the place a resemblance of Hell.' Violent language indeed for the least violent of men. The strain was beginning to show. Davis knew it – and decided to turn the screw a little tighter.

*28th March*
*The Prisoner was for the first time taken out of his room*
*into the publick parlour among some of the patients, when*
*the Strait-Waistcoat was taken off but the handcuffs*
*remained and also his leg chained to the chimney-corner.*
*But the Prisoner hated to be chained in the publick parlour*
*with such disagreeable company and earnestly desired*
*rather to be returned to his room, which was granted.*

The patients in the 'publick parlour' were not just in the
madhouse because someone was after their money or because
they were in somebody's way; they were there because they
were truly insane. Those who were not 'chained by the leg to
the chimney-corner' like Cruden but were free to move around
picked at him with twitching fingers and leered at him with
wide unfocused eyes, their ghoulish laughter sent shivers down
his spine, their blasphemous obscenities were as painful to his
ears as to his heart. Had he been less vulnerable himself he would
surely have been moved to great compassion for their plight.
But as it was, their misery was too distressing, too reminiscent
of the Tolbooth, too unbearably painful for him to endure.
So he asked to be returned to his room, 'which was granted'.

*He sat in his room, waistcoated, handcuffed and chained*
*to his bedstead till night, when Davis came and tied the*
*sleeves of the Strait-Waistcoat as before, with his hands*
*behind his back; so that he could go to bed only by entering*
*at the bed's foot, the chain on his leg which was fixed to*
*the foot of the bedstead not being long enough to let him*
*go to bed otherwise. The Prisoner wore the Strait-Waistcoat*
*for four days.*

Davis's ploy had worked. As Cruden ceased to complain about
his room and his food when Matthew Wright told him of the

conditions in which the pauper lunatics were forced to live, so he ceased to complain about the noise from the 'publick parlour' when John Davis showed him who was making it, and why. It was a salutary lesson for the wee man, and he acknowledged it. That night he prayed less for freedom than for forgiveness. He had thought himself a good Christian, but when confronted with the sufferings of his fellow men his first thought had been not to try to help them, but to get away from them as quickly as possible. He was reminded forcibly of the famous Biblical parable – and knew that rather than emulating the Good Samaritan, he had, like the Levite, passed by on the other side. It was not a comfortable thought.

He was still reproaching himself two days later when, a full week after he had been 'admitted' to the madhouse, his lofty physician at last found time to pay him a call.

*30<sup>th</sup> March*
*Dr Monro came in his chariot with Wightman to visit the Prisoner for the first time. The Prisoner not thinking it best to speak much to either of them only expostulated about his unjust confinement and barbarous usage enough to convince them he thought himself greatly injured. Monro ordered him to be bled in the left foot, which was performed by London the Apothecary that evening which took away so much blood that the foot was for some months benumm'd. Wightman told the Prisoner that he had made up an acquaintance* [formed a close relationship] *with Dr Monro, who became entirely Wightman's creature and was devoted to his Service.*

Few would quibble with Cruden's description of his treatment – the purging, bleeding, straitjacketing and so on – as 'barbarous', but far worse barbarities were being inflicted on other inmates of this and other madhouses at the time. 'Lunatics' were being locked up in pitch darkness, having their clothing removed and being left permanently naked, being whipped, being subjected to hot and cold baths or showers applied to different parts of the body – the head immersed in cold water and the body in hot, the feet in cold water and the body in hot and vice versa – or worse; all in the name of 'treatment'. A later apothecary to this same madhouse, Warburton's White House in Bethnal Green, would also allege that the White House was infested with bugs and rats, and that during the winter of 1810–11 over a hundred patients had died of typhus in the two Bethnal Green Houses. Cruden, it seems, was getting off quite lightly.

At this stage of their acquaintance James Monro had no cause to be particularly interested in Cruden – he was just another patient, not mad enough to hold his attention for longer than it took to order him to be bled. And Wightman was not wrong when he boasted to Cruden that Monro was 'his creature'. As with madhouse-keepers, so with physicians – who paid the piper . . .

Two generations of Monros, father James and son John, would reign unchallenged over London's insane for nearly fifty years; the third, James's grandson Thomas, would be called to account for the family's methods. In 1815, by which time the authorities were waking up to the abuses being perpetrated in madhouses all over the country, Thomas Monro was summoned before the House of Commons Select Committee on Madhouses and asked to give details of the way his patients were treated. '. . . [A]ll the patients who require bleeding are generally bled on a particular day,' he testified, 'and after they have been bled they take vomits once a week for a certain number of weeks, after that we purge the patients. That has been the practice invariably for years, long before my time, it was handed down to me by my father and I do not know any better practice.' His hearers must have wondered, as Cruden himself had wondered some seventy years earlier, 'Is there so great Merit and Dexterity in being a Mad Doctor? The common Prescriptions of a Bethlemetical Doctor are a Purge and a Vomit, and a Vomit and a Purge over again, and sometimes a Bleeding, which is no great Mystery.' The members of the Select Committee listened as Thomas Monro went on to state, with true Monrovian *hauteur*, that 'I really do not depend a vast deal upon medicine; I do not think medicine is the sheet anchor; it is more by management that those patients are cured than by medicine; ... if I am obliged to make that public I must do so.' Following these (and other) revelations, Thomas Monro was sacked from his post as Chief Physician to Bedlam. Apparently unabashed by his dismissal, he went back to supervising his own highly profitable private madhouse and indulging his lifelong passion for watercolour painting. Less than a month later the Governors of Bedlam elected his son Edward Thomas as his replacement.[9]

Modern historians of psychiatry like Jonathan Andrews and Andrew Scull insist that it is wrong, at this remove, to be too harsh on the Monros and other early mad-doctors – their methods of treating the insane were 'relatively universally employed'. Besides, these lordly physicians had their reputations to consider. 'In eighteenth century England physicians of all sorts clung tightly to ... their status as gentlemen engaged in the practice of a noble art.' Anxious to avoid 'the socially contaminating effects of anything that smacked of manual labour', they preferred to diagnose their patients from a distance, and to leave 'such menial tasks as inspection and interference with their patients' orifices, the bleeding, purging, and scarifying of their patients' bodies, along with the prescriptions they wrote, to those working with hand rather than head'.[10] While this arrogance might have served to enhance the already considerable self-esteem of the mad-doctors, it did little or nothing to endear them to their patients.

> *Monday April 3rd*
> *This morning the Prisoner took a Vomit, as ordered by Monro and prepared by Job London; but tho' he was unchained, he was again handcuff'd. At night he was chained to his bedstead as usual.*

Although he complained loudly at the time, for the most part Cruden would spare his readers the gruesome details of his 'treatments', which included regular 'purgings' and 'bleedings' as well as 'vomits'. But the ordeal mentioned so casually by the sufferer was on one occasion witnessed by one of his friends, John Robinson, who had no such reticence.

> *I came to visit Mr Cruden and found him in great distress of body, he having taken a Vomit. In the intervals of his excessive straining and reaching he discoursed faintly, but most rationally, telling me he was sure God would make all tend to his good. He never dropt a word tinctured with fretfulness, passion or private or personal revenge. I came four or five times more but was denied access, the under-keeper telling me he was strictly forbid to let any person have access to Mr C without a written order from Wightman.*

There was method in the apparently arbitrary rules laid down by Wightman about who could visit Cruden and when. To have banned visitors altogether would have been to invite an outcry and, for all Wightman knew, the arrival on the mad-house doorstep of a whole posse of Constables called in to investigate Cruden's disappearance. To have allowed in anyone who called whenever they chose, on the other hand, would have left no one in any doubt about Cruden's sanity. Far better to let them in occasionally (and if possible when he was in some distress – like just after he had 'taken a vomit') and hint that they were fortunate to coincide with a brief moment when the poor man was lucid. Cruden was wise to this scheme:

> *The Prisoner's pretended Disorder ebbed or flowed as it served the Interest and Ends of Wightman and his creature Monro. Sometimes his friends had access to him at Bethnal Green and at other times were refused when it was said that he was not fit to be seen. But this is abominably false, for his adversaries would have been glad to let any body see him if he had not been fit to be seen.*

Knowing from long experience how impossible it was to refute allegations of intermittent insanity, and knowing also how distressing he himself had found the behaviour of his fellow inmates, Cruden did not blame his friends for turning away. 'People are naturally shy of concerning themselves with a person in the prisoner's afflicted situation,' he commented sadly. Luckily Sergeant-Major Cruden was not so shy.

> *My wife and I* [he would later testify] *had great difficulty in getting to see Mr C in Bethnal Green, for we were told by John Davis that he had strict orders to let no one see him without permission from Wightman or Monro. My wife and I went to Wightman for a Ticket to visit, but Wightman told us that* [Mr Cruden] *was very ill and not fit to be seen. My wife and I eventually prevailed with Dr Monro to give them a Permit for visiting* [Mr C], *and upon seeing him, my wife and I found him very composed and perfectly in his senses, and as well as we had ever seen him.*

When the Sergeant-Major (and his wife) did finally gain admission to the madhouse, Cruden was doubly pleased to see him. Not only was he confident that the more people who could see that he was 'perfectly in his senses', the greater chance there would be of his regaining his freedom, he also needed his military relative to lend him some money. As Tobias Smollett knew (or learned from Cruden), one of the perks of the otherwise grim job of working as a servant in a private madhouse was being able to raid the pockets of new arrivals. Smollett's fictional hero Sir Launcelot Greaves was 'not without hope of being able to move his jailor by a due administration of that which is generally more efficacious than all the flowers of elocution; but when he rose in the morning, he found his pockets had been carefully examined, and emptied of all his papers and cash'. Exactly the same thing happened to Cruden – but he was less handy with the 'flowers of elocution'. 'The Prisoner's pockets having been rifled,' he grumbled, 'he had no money and therefore when he called on the servants in the Madhouse they did not answer him.'

As soon as Cruden had 'got a few shillings' from the Sergeant-Major, he was 'able a little to gratify the servants', and his conditions started to improve. The straitjacket was removed, as (for a few hours each day) were the chains, and a couple of times he was even allowed to 'walk a little in the garden' restrained only by handcuffs. He railed against the injustice of having to pay for such privileges; he castigated Matthew Wright and his wife for having 'such an insatiable thirst after Money that if the most judicious and prudent persons upon earth were sent thither with a good weekly allowance they must be their Prisoners'; but he was not so pig-headed as to refuse to play the game. 'The Prisoner,' he admitted, 'found it convenient to Study to Please the Servants.'

*6th April*
*The Keeper knowing that Dr Monro was coming to visit the Prisoner, thought fit to take off his handcuffs and chains,*

*and the Doctor came between eight and nine in the morn-*
*ing, and Wightman with him. The Prisoner expostulated*
*with Monro about his unjust Confinement, but Monro, like*
*a bird upon the Wing, made only a standing visit.*

Although several of his friends were allowed in to see Cruden
over the next few days, the madhouse-keeper made certain
that these visits were kept short, insisting that more than a
few minutes of anyone's company at a time would be too
much for Cruden's nerves to stand. One friend brought him
a Bible, another 'half a pound of Green-Tea', a third more
writing materials, and they all reassured him that they could
see that he was 'as sensible and rational as they had ever known
him', and that of course they would do everything they could
to get him out. As they left they were taken aside by the Keeper
and congratulated, in tactful whispers, on their good fortune
in having happened to arrive when the prisoner was enjoying
one of his all-too-brief moments of sanity.

*10<sup>th</sup> April*
*The Prisoner being unchained by Davis was not handcuffed*
*till noon and having received Pen Ink and Paper the day*
*before wrote some letters which he delivered to the servant*
*of the barber with money to put them in the Penny-Post.*
*But [one of the guards] soon after pursued the barber's*
*assistant and took from him the letters and the money,*
*which the Prisoner didn't know of till some months later.*

His letters were pleas for help, written to everyone he could
think of who might be able to assist him – including (surely
an act of desperation at a distance of five hundred miles) his
by now aged father in Aberdeen. Not one of these letters
reached its destination. They were all intercepted and confiscated by Wightman. And as the days passed and Cruden

received no response to any of them, his spirits, which had been considerably raised by the improvements in his living conditions, started to sink again. The vomits and the bleedings and the doses of 'purging physick' continued. Every night he was handcuffed and chained securely to his bed.

He had now been in the madhouse for three weeks. Fighting for his dignity, battling to maintain his composure, he was hard-pressed to keep a grip on that very sanity of which the world seemed determined to deprive him. A later inmate of the same madhouse, John Mitford, would swear that Warburton's House had an unwritten rule to the effect that 'if a man comes in here mad, we'll keep him so; if he is in his senses, we'll soon drive him out of them'.[11] As Daniel Defoe so indignantly demanded, 'Is it not enough to make anyone mad, to be suddenly clapped up, stripped, whipped, ill fed and worse used? If this tyrannical inquisition . . . be not sufficient to drive any soul stark staring mad . . . I have no more to say.'

# 7

# A Hundred Hairs to Hang by

When asked, some years later, how he had found the strength to persist in the face of so much frustration, Cruden would rather apologetically explain that it was just in his nature. 'I am somewhat of a disposition,' he would write, 'that if I had a hundred hairs to hang by and ninety nine should fail, I would endeavour to hang on by the hundredth, and if that should fail I then submit to the will of God.'

Such self-analysis would surely have been beyond the powers of a conventional 'madman'. Nothing if not dogged, Cruden clove to his sanity much as he had devoted himself to his Concordance. When it became clear that the ninety-nine hairs had well and truly failed him, he tightened his grip on the hundredth and hung on for all he was worth, grimly determined not to go 'stark staring mad' under the 'tyrannical inquisition'.

He might have found his lot a little easier had he known that his tormentor was not having everything his own way either. In fact Robert Wightman had suffered a serious reverse. Mrs Payne had given him his marching orders. If it had indeed been she who let slip that Cruden had been locked up as insane in his youth, the discovery that Wightman had used her indiscretion so ruthlessly to his own advantage must have been deeply embarrassing to her. But instead of trying to put matters right, the widow had taken the easier option of deciding that she would have nothing more to do with either of her suitors. This left Wightman not only sorely disappointed but in something of a quandary. It was costing him a guinea a week to keep Cruden in Bethnal Green;* money that he could not, and now presumably would never be able to, afford. Yet he knew that as soon as he stopped paying the money, Cruden would be turned out of the madhouse. And once he was released, he might not be willing just to disappear quietly into the undergrowth. On the contrary; the contents of Cruden's confiscated letters gave Wightman reason to believe that the prisoner was planning to pursue his captors 'in a legal manner' for having incarcerated him in the first place.

Wightman wrestled with this problem for a few days and then decided to pay his victim another visit. Although still chained to his bed, Cruden was far from cowed, receiving his visitor 'very coldly' and demanding with some vigour to know by what right 'a stranger very slenderly acquainted with his affairs' had so summarily deprived him of his liberty. Cruden's demeanour left Wightman in no doubt about the chances of him quietly disappearing. They were non-existent; and Wightman 'went away very abruptly' to think again.

Cruden would later discover that Robert Wightman, the man he called 'the great actor in this barbarous affair', was already 'notorious in Scotland for his wild projects'. These had included a scheme for developing Leith pier 'which hath run the city of Edinburgh into debt many thousands of pounds

---

* The equivalent of about £100 a week today.

sterling' and had ended in a court case involving the Earl of Hopetoun. And as Wightman was now about to demonstrate, he had no scruples about embroiling others in his schemes as soon as they started to go awry. Faced with the problem of what to do with Cruden, he now invited Dr Monro, Matthew Wright, John Davis, John Oswald and Cruden's clerical friend Dr Guise to a meeting at his lodgings. Here, in an attempt 'to flip the collar off his own neck' (as Cruden nicely put it), Wightman told them that although he thought Cruden was probably well enough to be allowed to leave the madhouse, he knew him for a disputatious man who might thereafter make trouble for them all. That being the case, Wightman suggested, they would be well advised to write him a collective letter explaining that they had acted in what they had believed to be his best interests, and get him to sign an agreement promising that he would behave in a peaceable manner once he was released. The plan sounded quite reasonable to the assembled company, was duly agreed, and a draft letter was signed. But 'like thoughtless men, the members of this "Blind Bench" did not demand to see the Letter that was to be sent under their names [thus 'blind'], but acted by implicit faith in Wightman, leaving the forming of it wholly to him'. By the next afternoon, when Wightman showed the letter to Cruden, it had evidently undergone some subtle changes.

*15th April*
*Davis having unchained the Prisoner in the morning gave him some purging physick; and in the afternoon Wightman came with a letter which he instructed Mr Cruden to read. The letter, which Wightman had drawn up and which the Prisoner was expected to sign, absolved Wightman of all wrongdoing: 'I shall not blame you or your friends for anything that has happened or may happen.' Mr C was given to understand that if he signed this letter, Wightman*

*would permit him to be released. In the circumstances it
can hardly be thought surprising that Mr C refused to sign.*

The fact that the letter purported to come not just from
Wightman, Monro, Davis and Oswald but also from his 'faithful and beloved pastor' Dr Guise was deeply upsetting to
Cruden. He suspected that Wightman had involved Dr Guise
because he thought the word of his spiritual adviser would
carry extra weight with the prisoner. Later he would put his
old friend's involvement down to the cleric's naïve inability
to believe ill of anyone – including Wightman; but at the time
he was left feeling more lonely and abandoned than ever.
Wightman, for his part, was not used to being thwarted.
Cruden's recalcitrance made him angry as well as anxious.
He issued his prisoner with an ultimatum; and wittingly or
unwittingly, he hit upon the one threat above all others that
would bring Cruden near to breaking point.

*He told Mr C that if he did not sign the letter he would
be sent to Bedlam. To be sent to Bethlehem was the sorest
evil that could befall him and which he dreaded more than
death.*

Wightman was bluffing. As previously noted, it required not
just the 'authority of two or more justices of the peace', but
also a signed medical certificate before any patient could be
admitted to Bedlam. But Cruden was apparently unaware of
these safeguards. To him it seemed perfectly logical that if he
could be detained in Wright's Private Madhouse for nearly a
month without any authority, he could also, and quite as
easily, be sent to Bedlam; and once he had disappeared into
that dark and dreadful place he doubted if he would ever see
the light of day again. The very idea made him feel sick. But
he still refused to sign the letter.

Wightman's next ploy was to decree a change in his prisoner's regime. If the threat of Bedlam was not enough to make him sign the letter absolving him and the 'Blind Bench' from all blame, maybe some strict solitary confinement would change his mind. On 20 April Dr Monro paid his fourth (and last) visit to Cruden. The prisoner, as usual, 'expostulated about his unjust imprisonment, having never been disordered or mad'; Dr Monro, as usual, declined to respond. As soon as the doctor had departed the dreaded strait-waistcoat was once again produced, Cruden was once again trussed like a chicken, and he received no more visitors for five days.

His resolve not to sign Wightman's letter was unshaken by his solitude and, as ever, he found great consolation in prayer. But he admitted to being hugely relieved when, on the sixth day, he heard a familiar voice outside his door. Sergeant-Major Cruden was not about to let Wightman or anyone else keep him away from the madhouse, no matter how many decrees the 'Blind Bench' might pass. He (and his wife) had camped on James Monro's doorstep and, with a stubbornness that would have done credit to Cruden himself, refused to budge until they had been given written permission to visit the prisoner.

When they finally gained access to Cruden's room the loyal pair were agreeably surprised to find that, contrary to what they had been led to believe, 'the prisoner' was 'entirely in his right mind'. He was nevertheless in a high state of indignation: 'The Prisoner told his friends that he could easily get out would he sign a Pardon for Wightman, but that he would never do it, thinking it a dishonourable thing.' The Sergeant-Major sympathised, but begged him to reconsider. This was a moment when pragmatism might be more profitable than pride. 'Cunning and powerful enemies' were ready to move against him if he continued to refuse. That very morning he had heard rumours that Cruden was to be sent to Bedlam 'on

Saturday se'ennight' (i.e. a week on Saturday). He strongly advised him to disregard his honour and do whatever was necessary to get out of that dismal place – even if it meant signing the pardon.

But Cruden was adamant. He would not sign. Like the Christian martyrs, he refused to recant. Like them he paid a price.

*27<sup>th</sup> April*
*Davis did not even open the sleeves of the Strait-Waistcoat and the Prisoner was forced to stay in bed till the afternoon. After dinner it was Davis's sovereign will and pleasure to chain him again to his bedstead, but before he did it he gave the Prisoner a blow in the face which almost beat out his eye and much disfigured his face, of which he was not recovered for some weeks.*

Cruden's was by no means an isolated case. In 1763 an anonymous writer sent an account of his experiences to the *Gentleman's Magazine* under the title 'A Case Humbly Offered to the Consideration of Parliament'. It could have been written by Alexander Cruden himself, except that, if it had been, he would have said so.

*When a person is forcibly taken or artfully decoyed into a private madhouse, he is, without any authority or any further charge than that of an impatient heir, a mercenary relation, or a pretended friend, instantly seized upon by a set of inhuman ruffians trained up to this barbarous profession, stripped naked, and conveyed to a dark room. If the patient complains, the attendant brutishly orders him not to rave, calls for assistants, and ties him down to a bed, from which he is not released until he submits to their pleasure. Next morning, a doctor is gravely introduced who, taking the report of the keeper, pronounces the unfortunate person a lunatic, and declares that he must be reduced by physic. If the revolted victim offers to argue against it by alleging any proofs of sanity, a motion is made by the attendant for the doctor to withdraw, and if the patient, or rather the prisoner, persists in vindicating his reason, or refuses to take the dose, he is then deemed raving mad; the banditti of the whole house are called in, the forcing instruments brought, upon which the sensible patient must submit to take whatever is administered. When the poor patient thus finds himself deprived of all communication with the world, and denied the use of pen and paper, all he can do is to compose himself under the unhappy situation in the hope of a more favourable report. But any composure under such affliction is immediately deemed a melancholy or sulky fit by the attendant, who reports it as such to the doctor in the hearing of the despairing prisoner, whose misery is thus redoubled in finding that the doctor prescribes a repetition of the dose, and that from day to day, until the patient is so debilitated in body that in time it impairs his mind. Weakened by physic, emaciated by torture, diseased by confinement, terrified by the sight of every instrument of cruelty and the dreadful menaces of an attending ruffian, and hardened against all the tenderness of human nature, what must a rational mind suffer that is treated in this irrational manner?*[1]

Cruden would be careful to make no mention of his mental suffering; it would almost certainly have been held against him as proof of mental frailty. But he was very willing to complain about his physical suffering. When, the day after his beating, Davis untied the sleeves of the straitjacket so that he could eat his meal, he took advantage of his relative liberty to scribble some more letters. Having despaired of his friends who, despite his pleas, had seemed unable to help him, he wrote a second frantic letter to his father in Aberdeen, plus what he called 'an Advertisement, giving an account of his unjust and barbarous Treatment' to be printed in the newspapers. When his assistant John Scott arrived to visit him that afternoon, Cruden pressed the papers into his hand and told him to put the letter in the post and hand the Advertisement to the printers of the newspapers carefully and without delay.

What Cruden had not realised was that by this time Scott, too, had been bribed or bullied into betraying his afflicted employer. Instead of delivering the precious papers to the post or to the printers, the treacherous apprentice handed them directly to Wightman. Within hours of Scott's departure Cruden found his room and his bed being searched by 'the Tyrant Wright', the store of pens and paper which he had 'artfully concealed' under his bed being violently seized, his shoes being pulled from his feet and his leg once more being chained to the bedstead. From that moment on he was kept in chains, 'so that every night he was forced to go in by the foot of the bed and his breeches were never off for the space of five weeks'.

If the solitude, the withdrawal of such privileges as having access to pen and paper, the constant and debilitating terror of being dragged off to Bedlam, and now the almost unbearable indignity of never being allowed to change his clothes or wash himself, were not quite driving Cruden mad, they were certainly beginning to wear him down. He sought his customary consolation in prayer, but the power of even that normally infallible remedy seemed to be waning.

*2nd May*
*The Prisoner being still chained night and day had no visitors, and could only converse with himself and his God.*

*6ᵗʰ May*
*The Prisoner still being chained day and night devoted the*
*day to Prayer. He was uneasy and cast down in spirits,*
*fearing the Porters of Bethlehem should come to fetch him*
*thither.*

When, a few days later, the strait-waistcoat was removed and
did not reappear, he thought it must be because the madhouse-
keepers believed they had finally managed to break his spirit.
In fact it was because they had seen an angry letter from
Sergeant-Major Cruden to Robert Wightman.

*Last Saturday* [the Sergeant-Major wrote] *I received a*
*very threatening letter from one John Scott that looks after*
*Mr Cruden's shop, setting forth that my conduct in writing*
*to Mr Cruden's friends that Mr Cruden is not disordered*
*and is ill-used in being placed at Bethnal Green, is very*
*much resented by Dr Monro and you. As I found him*
*restrained from the use of pen ink and paper I writ, at my*
*friend's desire, not only to them but to a great many more*
*of his acquaintance, intimating to all of them that he was*
*very well in his senses.*

The cat, as Wright and Davis realised, was now well and truly
out of the bag. Cruden's letters had all been safely intercepted,
but those written by his loyal kinsman the Sergeant-Major had
not; and the madhouse-keepers were suddenly having second
thoughts about the wisdom of their continued severity towards
their prisoner. Hence the disappearance of the strait-waistcoat
(they did not go so far as to remove the chains), and hence
the unexpected change of attitude, first of Under-Keeper John
Davis, who visited Cruden's room on 15 May and 'declared
his sorrow for the Blow he had given him', and then, on 16
May, of Matthew Wright. According to Cruden, the 'tyrannical

Keeper' came into his room, took him kindly by the hand, told him that he had been ordered by Robert Wightman to act as he had, and asked Cruden why he did not 'make matters up with Wightman, and get from here, and be thankful for being well?'

When Dr Monro made his customary tour of the madhouse later that same week, Cruden was interested to know if he, too, had undergone a change of heart and was suddenly going to be more friendly. Hearing the mad-doctor's voice in the next room, Cruden called for him to come through; Monro declined the summons, saying – loudly enough for Cruden to hear – that he had no wish to speak to that particular prisoner and indeed wanted nothing more to do with him. Dr Monro was evidently off the case but felt under no obligation to apologise.

Despite the removal of the strait-waistcoat and the apologies from Wright and Davis, it quickly became clear to 'the Prisoner' that nothing had really changed. Wightman was still issuing the orders, and unless and until Cruden signed his letter he was obviously doomed to stay in the madhouse. On 19 May, however, came a glimmer of hope. After a gap of more than two weeks the Sergeant-Major returned, bringing with him brothers Kelsey and Frederick Bull, a linen-draper and tea-broker respectively, who were described by Cruden as his 'particular friends' (the latter had been responsible for providing Cruden with 'half a pound of Green-Tea' some five weeks before). Alarmed to find Cruden in such low spirits, the three men did their best to convince him that it was not in Wightman's power to have him sent to Bedlam.

*But Mr Cruden was still under disquieting fears of being carried thither, and wrote as moving and affecting a letter as could be penned, that could not fail to make an impression upon Men of Humanity and Compassion, to the Governors of Bedlam, which Mr Frederick Bull took care to get presented to them the next day by his uncle* [who worked at the asylum]. *One of the Governors asked if it related to the Queen's Bookseller. Mr Bull said it did. The Governor replied 'I know him, and tell him to be easy, for he shall not be brought to this house.' But the Prisoner, knowing nothing of this kind message, continued under his racking fears.*

Cruden's friends were not powerful men. A sergeant-major, a linen-draper and a tea-broker, however loyal and concerned they might be and however many impassioned letters they might write on his behalf, could bring no useful pressure to bear on anyone in authority to secure his release. He was the victim not simply of individual malice but of a pernicious system. Even the most frequent of his other visitors, 'Dr Rogers of Stanmore', who was not just a medical man but the inventor of a 'famous' brand of gout-oil, seemed at a loss to know how to help him (apart, presumably, from treating his gout). And to Cruden's deep disappointment none of these friends visited him again. He suspected that Wightman had told Matthew Wright that from now on he was to be allowed absolutely no visitors of any description. The hundredth hair was coming under severe strain.

Somehow his willingness 'to submit to the will of God' saw him through another week, his ninth in the madhouse. He prayed almost continuously, as he had prayed every day for the last sixty-three days; he recited the Psalms – every one of which he had committed to his prodigious memory: the 22nd Psalm: '*Be thou not far from me, O Lord: O my strength, haste thee to help me*'; the 69th Psalm: '*Deliver me out of the mire, and let me not sink: let me be delivered from them that hate me*'; the 71st Psalm: '*Deliver me in thy righteousness, and cause me to escape . . .*'; 'cause me to escape . . . cause me to escape . . . cause me to escape . . .'

*27th May*

*The Prisoner still being chained day and night in this hot season, and being alarmed with being sent to Bethlehem, happily projected to cut the bedstead through with the knife with which he ate his victuals. He made some progress in it this day.*

For the first time since he had made the decision to woo Mrs Payne, Cruden was happily engaged. His spirits soared as each whittled flake was secreted in his bedding.

The madhouse beds were made of wood, and the wood of his had seen better days. Even so it was extremely hard work, and not only did he have to be very careful not to be 'catched at it', he also had to make certain that no one noticed the effects of his labours on either the bed or his person. A few minutes' sawing was enough to have him in a muck sweat from the unaccustomed exertion and to raise blisters on both hands from grasping the knife-handle. But, as ever, he persevered.

*28th May*

*The Prisoner being again chained to his bedstead, made up his bed very early to conceal his design. He wrote a letter to Sergeant Cruden to send him a handsaw, doubting the strength of his knife, but providentially did not send it or his escape would have been prevented.*

For three days he chipped and sawed and chiselled with the knife, cushioning the blisters on his hands with the sheet. On the fourth day he was so encouraged by his progress that he worked for most of the day and far into the night.

*29th May*

*The Prisoner was again chained to his bedstead. He went to work again, prayed hard and wrought hard till his shirt*

*was as wet as if dipt in water. And as if he had received
more than common vigour and strength he finished the
great operation about 4.00 in the morning.*

He jammed the now three-legged bed against the wall to steady
it, draped the sheet over his handiwork, fell back exhausted
among his chains and slept until midday. The next day, his
sixty-eighth in detention, would also be his thirty-ninth birthday. How better to celebrate than by escape?

*31ˢᵗ May*
*The Prisoner's birthday. He awoke early, performed his
Devotions, held his chain in his hands still fastened to his
leg, and deliberately got out at the window to the garden,
mounted the garden wall with much difficulty, lost one of
his slippers and jumped down into the back way just before
the clock struck 2* [a.m.].

Bethnal Green, like Southgate, is now part of London (one
stop east of Liverpool Street on the Central Line); in 1738,
again like Southgate, it was a separate community. But where
the residents of Southgate belonged in the main to the prosperous bourgeoisie, Bethnal Green was an area of 'such poverty
as few can conceive without seeing it'.[2] Although still described
as a hamlet, it was estimated in 1743 to have 'a population of
more than fifteen thousand, mostly weavers and dyers and
their dependants . . . crowded into narrow streets and courts
. . . three or four families to a house'.[3] Ironically, considering
he had been a 'resident' of Bethnal Green for more than two
months, it was an area that Cruden knew not at all. Once over
the garden wall of Wright's Private Madhouse and into 'the
back way', he had no idea which way to go. It was pitch dark,
'his left foot that wanted the slipper was sorely hurt by the
gravel-stones which greatly afflicted him', and he was still

clutching the chain that was shackled to his ankle. Eager to put the greatest possible distance between himself and the madhouse before the alarm was raised, he transferred his right slipper to his slipperless left foot to protect it from further injury and set off through the maze of narrow alleys, his ears pricked for the sounds of pursuit. Wrong turnings led him into dead ends, he slipped in the filth of open drains, tripped over noisome piles of refuse and stumbled on uneven cobblestones until his cut foot was so painful that 'he hardly knew how to go on'; but eventually he found himself in Mile End. He paused to rest and get his bearings, found a signpost which showed him that he had not strayed too far in the wrong direction, and set off westwards back along the Mile End Road towards Whitechapel.

As he hobbled through the darkness he became aware of footsteps behind him. They were coming closer. He knew he was being followed. Since he was quite unable to run he had no chance of outstripping his pursuer, so he resigned himself to imminent recapture.

By a stroke of good fortune his imagined pursuer turned out to be 'a kind soldier' somewhat the worse for drink. To anyone else a man only half-dressed, his unwashed clothes and unkempt hair further disordered by his scrambling 'with much difficulty' over the wall, barefoot from having lost his remaining slipper so with both feet now bleeding, and his shackle and chain leaving no doubt that he had recently escaped from some kind of imprisonment, must have appeared suspicious if not downright dangerous. But the soldier listened to Cruden's story, apparently had no difficulty in believing it, and suggested they should try and find a coach to carry them the rest of the way into London. That a sympathetic coachman might have been tooling down the Mile End Road in the middle of the day with room to spare in his vehicle for two ill-favoured individuals needing a lift would have been unlikely enough; for such a convenient personage and such a handy equipage to have appeared at their side out of the darkness at three o'clock in the morning would have been nothing short of miraculous. But Cruden appreciated the thought.

> *The kind soldier endeavoured to get him a coach, but in vain. Therefore he and the soldier walked undiscovered until they came to Aldgate where the watchman, perceiving a chain and suspecting him to be a person broke out of jail, called the Constable and brought him back to Aldgate Watchhouse.*

Aldgate – the 'old gate' – was one of the six original gates into London and still barred the way into the City (although it would be demolished in 1761 and, briefly and coincidentally, re-erected in Bethnal Green). On the orders of the Lord Mayor, the gate was guarded by relays of watchmen whose duty was to detain any passing undesirables in their adjacent Watchhouse and then to call the constables to deal with them. Before the creation of a police force, watchmen were 'the lowest ranks of the law-keeping establishment, often old and decrepit, armed only with a staff, and paid a pittance to patrol far more than they could manage'.[4] Parish constables, one step up from watchmen but often only marginally more impressive, were 'responsible for apprehending malefactors'.

Half dismayed at having been detained and half relieved that he would now at least be able to sit down, Cruden bade farewell to his companion and followed the watchman into the Watchhouse. Minutes later, not one but two constables, who rejoiced in the names 'Mr Ward and Mr Wardly', arrived in answer to the watchman's summons and invited Cruden to explain his most suspicious appearance.

*Mr C acquainted the two Constables with his Case, which did much affect them. They allowed him some refreshment, but sent the Watchman privately to Bethnal Green to know the certainty of the Account; upon which Davis and two more of Wright's bull-dogs came to the Watch-house with handcuffs to carry the Prisoner back to the madhouse.*

# 8

## *Coup de Grâce*

Few incidents in Cruden's story offer more persuasive evidence of his sanity than this encounter in the early hours of the morning of his thirty-ninth birthday. Dishevelled, distraught, shackled to a chain, and freely admitting to having just escaped from a madhouse, he must have looked every inch a lunatic and his custodians would certainly have been forgiven for thinking him one. Yet by the time the watchman reappeared in the Aldgate Watchhouse with John Davis and his 'bull-dogs' in tow, Cruden had managed to satisfy both constables by his 'meek and sedate conversation' that he was no such thing. Had they had the slightest doubt, it would have been the easiest thing in the world for them to hand him straight over to Davis and rid themselves of a potentially troublesome charge. Instead they agreed not to send him back to the madhouse before he had had a chance to present his case to a higher authority. They also dismissed Davis and the 'bull-dogs' with a message for Matthew Wright to present himself at Grocers' Hall at eleven o'clock in the morning. And since it was by now five o'clock and Cruden was clearly exhausted, they took him to a nearby coffee-house where he could get some rest. Concerned for his charge's well-being, Constable Ward offered to remove the shackle from Cruden's leg so he could sleep; Cruden politely but firmly declined. The chain, he said, was his only witness; physical proof of his ordeal, he wanted the Lord Mayor to see it *in situ*, still attached to his leg.

Five hours later, feeling 'much refreshed and heartened', Cruden prepared to accompany Constable Ward to Grocers' Hall. As well as being the headquarters of the Worshipful Company of Grocers, Grocers' Hall was at that time the official residence of Cruden's chosen higher authority, the Lord Mayor of London.* The current Lord Mayor, like his predecessors and his successors to this day, owed his tenure of the office to his sole electors, the liverymen of the City Livery Companies. Himself a liveryman of the Stationers' Company and therefore one of those electors, Cruden was confident that the Lord Mayor was the one higher authority upon whose impartiality – possibly even upon whose favour – he could rely. But when they entered the imposing Hall he found that although there was no sign of Matthew Wright, Robert Wightman had arrived ahead of him and had already had an audience with the Lord Mayor, Sir John Barnard.

*The Prisoner had been several hours in bed at North's Coffee-House and had not had time to send for his friends; but Wightman was surrounded both with friends and Wretched Tools; for* [Job] *London the Apothecary and Grant of White's Alley* [husband of Cruden's screeching landlady] *both took their oath before His Lordship that the Prisoner was a Lunatick, tho' Grant knows no more what*

---

* The foundation stone of today's Mansion House would be laid the following year, 1739.

*is meant by 'Lunatick' than a Child of a year old, and had not seen the Prisoner for nine weeks and six days.*

As Cruden had hoped, however, the Lord Mayor wanted to hear both sides of the story.

*The Constable told his Lordship the situation of the Prisoner when he seized him, and the Prisoner gave his Lordship a just and full account of his illegal Imprisonment. His Lordship for a while made no reply, and then he asked why he appeared before him with his Chain. To which the Prisoner replied that this chain being put upon him by an illegal power, he was resolved to have it taken off by legal authority; and accordingly the Constable unlocked the chain in the presence of his Lordship.*

The arguments swung to and fro. Wightman cited Dr Monro's attendance on Cruden as proof that he must be mad. Cruden responded with a letter from his friend Dr Rogers ('of gout-oil fame') testifying to his sanity. Wightman insisted that Cruden was so demented that no lodging-house keeper would be prepared to rent him a room; therefore the only safe place to put him was back in the madhouse. Cruden countered that this was 'abominably false' and named an 'honest family that would heartily receive him'. When it was clear they were getting nowhere, Sir John Barnard suggested they submit the case to the judgement of that most reputable of mad-doctors, James Monro. Cruden's heart sank, and the smirk on Wightman's face told him that he too interpreted this as a sign that matters were going in his favour.

*When the Prisoner saw Wightman endeavouring still to have him under his care, he fell on his knees before Sir John Barnard and begged most earnestly not to be delivered*

*into the hands of cruel Wightman or his Creature Monro
who had uttered such gross lies and calumnies against him,
but rather into the hands of an honest Constable, or any
body his Lordship pleased.*

This heartfelt plea was sufficiently eloquent for Sir John Barnard to arrive at least at an interim decision. Whatever had been the case previously, at this moment the man before him was clearly not out of his mind, and there was nothing in his demeanour or language to suggest that he was either a danger to the public or unable to take care of himself. Barnard therefore ruled that Cruden should be set at liberty, gave him the address of a lodging house where he must agree to stay for seven days, and instructed both parties to come before him again at the end of that time to hear his final decision.

*So Mr C, glad to be delivered out of Wightman's power,
went in a Coach from Grocers' Hall to Mr Morgan's lodging
house in Downing-street near Hide-park-corner this 31<sup>st</sup>
May 1738. Wightman was much chagrined at the Prisoner's
escape.*

Cruden's 'Downing-street near Hide-park-corner' was not the Whitehall Downing Street of 'No. 10' fame, but a small street of modest houses running north from Piccadilly (and soon to be renamed Down Street to avoid confusion with its more distinguished namesake). Here Jacob Morgan, a joiner, and his wife Sarah took such good care of their new lodger that after a bath, a meal, another sleep and Mrs Morgan's solicitous attentions to his 'much swelled' feet, Cruden declared himself fit for anything.

Word of his escape had spread quickly round his friends, and a succession of visitors arrived to congratulate him on his 'miraculous deliverance': Sergeant-Major Cruden and his wife were the first, followed by the brothers Kelsey and Frederick Bull, then an old Aberdonian friend William Simpson, Dr 'Gout-Oil' Rogers, and several members of Cruden's church congregation. All were agog to know how he had contrived so dramatically to break out of the madhouse. One of his more fervent fellow-worshippers exclaimed that his story put her in mind of her favourite Biblical character, Joseph, who had also been imprisoned on trumped-up charges, had also been miraculously delivered and who had gone on to become a prosperous and powerful man. Cruden, she said, was like 'a second Joseph' – an idea which greatly tickled his fancy. The Sergeant-Major then pressed his kinsman to a celebratory tankard of beer, but Cruden declined – he knew he was on probation and dared not risk doing anything that might prejudice his continued freedom. For twenty-four hours he held court in his Downing Street lodging and then he sallied forth to savour that freedom. His diary entries for the next few days are almost jaunty.

*Friday June 2nd.*
*Mr C went up the River with an acquaintance for his amusement, and came home at night.*
*Saturday June 3rd.*
*Mr C visited several friends, and in the afternoon walked in Hide Park and in St James Park.*
*Sunday June 4th.*
*The Lord's Day. Mr C attended publick worship in Swallow-Street all day.*

To be free to attend 'publick worship' was undoubtedly his most precious freedom of all. In the ten weeks since he had last been able to go to church he had missed the prayers and the sermons and the fellowship of like-minded worshippers in the House of the Lord much as a married man might have missed his wife and family, and he could hardly bear to tear himself away.

Monday brought another boost to his spirits when 'a gentleman of Richmond' complimented him on his Concordance, and he realised to his amazement that he had not given his Great Work more than a passing thought for months. But he had no time to dwell on the satisfaction; he had to prepare for his second hearing before the Lord Mayor.

*Tuesday June 6th*
*In order to convince the Lord Mayor of his sound mind, and of Wightman's unaccountable management, Mr C desired his landlord and landlady to give him a written Certificate, which they wrote as follows:*
*'We hereby testify that Mr Alexander Cruden, our Lodger, is of a peaceable and agreeable Temper, and behaves every Way to so great Satisfaction that we cannot desire a better Lodger. We discover nothing of Disorder about him and think that there is not the least Occasion for any Person to look after Mr Cruden for he is very capable to take care of himself.'*
*Given at Downing Street nr Hide-park-corner, Piccadilly, June 6 1738.*

*Jacob Morgan*
*Sarah Morgan*

On the Wednesday morning, accompanied by his tea-broking friend Frederick Bull, armed with the Morgans' commendation and confident of vindication, Cruden presented himself at Grocers' Hall. His confidence turned out to be fully justified; Sir John Barnard declared that he could see no reason why Cruden should be returned to the madhouse.

Had he been blessed with the gift of prescience, Cruden might well have settled for having successfully convinced the

Lord Mayor that he was not mad. But he had come to Grocers' Hall with two objectives, and that was only one of them. Not a man to leave things half done, he thanked Sir John profusely for his ruling and immediately launched into a 'full account of the Injuries done him by Robert Wightman'. The Lord Mayor stopped him in his tracks. Since Cruden was at that moment at liberty in the City of London, Barnard explained, the Lord Mayor of London had the authority to rule that he be allowed to remain at liberty. Allegations of wrongful imprisonment in a madhouse in Bethnal Green, on the other hand, were beyond his jurisdiction. 'His Lordship said that the Action did not properly come before him, but was an Action at Law'.

As he had already determined on an 'Action at Law' against his persecutors, Cruden scarcely needed encouragement. But he took Sir John's words as an endorsement of his plan and straight away started to assemble his case. He wrote a succession of letters to Wightman demanding the return of the money and possessions that he had been forced to abandon at Bethnal Green and which his 'chief adversary' was intent on using to offset the cost of keeping him there. The only response was a message 'that Mr Wightman regarded none of his letters, and that he would trounce all Persons that came to trouble him about the affairs of Mr C'. This was not unexpected; in fact Cruden welcomed this proof (since proof would presumably be needed) that Wightman was a thief as well as a bully. The next, and even more important, proof he needed was that of his own sanity. With the assistance of his friend Dr 'Gout-Oil' Rogers, he arranged for a consultation with no fewer than three London physicians and asked them to testify to his state of mind.

*We whose names are underwritten have seen and conversed
with Mr Alexander Cruden, Bookseller to her late most*

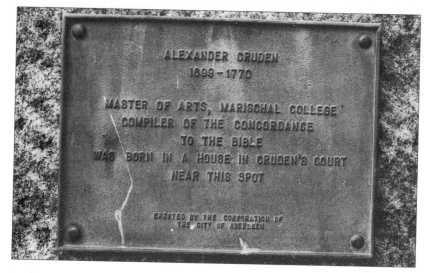

In the very heart of Aberdeen, in a passage which leads to a staircase which leads to a car park, the plaque commemorating the birth of Alexander Cruden is as modest as it is hard to find.

A view of Netherkirkgate, c.1750. In the foreground the townhouse of the Keiths of Benholm, in the background St Nicholas Kirk where Alexander Cruden was baptised in June 1699.

The Old Grammar School, Aberdeen. Only particularly gifted boys were admitted before the age of nine; Alexander Cruden started at the Grammar School when he was eight.

Marischal College, c.1780. Aberdeen's second university, Marischal College was established in 1593 in the redundant Greyfriars Monastery as a Protestant rival to Catholic King's College. The two colleges combined in 1860 to become the University of Aberdeen.

The crenellated stone tower in the corner beneath the clock spire is all that remains of the infamous Aberdeen Tolbooth, scene of Cruden's first incarceration.

Reverend Thomas Blackwell, Professor of Divinity and Principal of Marischal College. His influence would not just govern Cruden's university career; it would dictate the course of his entire life.

Thomas Blackwell Junior. Highly qualified and professionally successful, he was variously described as pedantic, pompous, dignified and self-important, and in later life 'he brought on a consumptive habit by great abstemiousness'.

Jameson's House in Schoolhill. As Daniel Defoe remarked in 1706, 'the Streets [of Aberdeen] are very handsome and well-built, the Houses lofty and high ... built of Stone, with handsome Sash-windows and very well furnished within'.

John Strype's *Plan of the City of London*, c.1720. The city's population of half a million lived at close and crowded quarters in an area barely three miles by two.

James Stanley, 10th Earl of Derby. By 1729, when he employed Cruden as his French reader, Lord Derby had retired from public life to spend his time indulging his love of books and works of art and improving his estates at Halnaker and Knowsley.

Caroline of Anspach, wife of George II. Cruden dedicated the first edition of his Concordance to the Queen he described as 'possessed of all those talents which make conversation either delightful or improving'.

### ABASE.

JOB 40. 11. behold every one that is proud, and *a*. him
*Isa*. 31. 4. as the lion will not *a*. himself
*Ezek*. 21. 26. and *a*. him that is high
*Dan*. 4. 37. that walk in pride, he is able to *a*.

### ABASED.

*Isa*. 32. † 19. the city shall be utterly *a*.
*Mat*. 23. 12. whosoever shall exalt himself shall be *a*. | *Luke* 14. 11. | 18. 14.
*Phil*. 4. 12. I know how to be *a*. and abound

### ABASING.

2 *Cor*. 11. 7. have I committed an offence in *a*.

### ABATED.

*Gen*. 8. 3. after 150 days the waters were *a*.8,11.
*Lev*. 27. 18. it shall be *a*. from thy estimation
*Deut*. 34. 7. nor was Moses natural force *a*.
*Judg*. 8. 3. then their anger was *a*.

### ABBA.

*Mark* 14. 36. *a*. father, all things are possible
*Rom*. 8. 15. the Spirit whereby we cry *a*. father
*Gal*. 4. 6. sent Spirit into your hearts crying *a*.

### ABHOR

Signifies, [1.] *To loathe or detest*, Deut. 32.19. Job 42. 6. [2.] *To despise or neglect*, Psal. 22. 24. Amos 6. 8. [3.] *To reject or cast off*, Psal. 89.38.
*Lev*. 26. 11. and my soul shall not *a*. you
15. or if your soul *a*. my judgments
30. and my soul shall *a*. you
44. nor will I *a*. to destroy them utterly
*Deut*. 7. 26. but thou shalt utterly *a*. it
23. 7. not *a*. an Edomite, not *a*. an Egyptian
1 *Sam*. 27. 12. hath made his people to *a*. him
*Job* 9. 31. my own clothes shall *a*. me
30. 10. they *a*. me, they flee far from me
42. 6. I *a*. my self and repent in dust and ashes
*Psal*. 5. 6. the Lord will *a*. the bloody man
119. 163. I hate and *a*. lying.
*Prov*. 24. 24. nations shall abhor him
*Jer*. 14. 21. do not *a*. us for thy names sake
*Amos* 5. 10. they *a*. him that speaketh uprightly
6. 8. I *a*. the excellency of Jacob
*Mic*. 3. 9. hear, ye that *a*. judgment
*Rom*. 12. 9. *a*. that which is evil

### ABHORRED.

*Exod*. 5. 21. you have made our favour to be *a*.
*Lev*. 20. 23. and therefore I *a*. them
26. 43. their soul *a*. my statutes
*Deut*. 32. 19. when the Lord saw it, he *a*. them
1 *Sam*. 2. 17. men *a*. the offering of the Lord
2 *Sam*. 16. 21. hear, thou art *a*. of thy father
1 *Kin*. 11. 25. Hadad *a*. Israel and reigned
*Job* 19. 19. all my inward friends *a*. me
*Psal*. 22. 24. nor *a*. the affliction of the afflicted

*Psal*. 78. 59. he was wroth, and greatly *a*. Israel
89. 38. but thou hast cast off and *a*.
106. 40. he *a*. his own inheritance
*Prov*. 22. 14. *a*. of the Lord shall fall therein
*Lam*. 2. 7. he hath *a*. his sanctuary
*Ezek*. 16. 25. thou hast made thy beauty to be *a*.
*Zech*. 11. 8. and their soul also *a*. me

### ABHORREST.

*Isa*. 7. 16. the land thou *a*. shall be forsaken
*Rom*. 2. 22. thou that *a*. idols

### ABHORRETH.

*Job* 33. 20. so that his life *a*. bread
*Psal*. 10. 3. blesseth the covetous, whom Lord *a*.
36. 4. he deviseth mischief, he *a*. not evil
107. 18. their soul *a*. all manner of meat
*Isa*. 49. 7. to him whom the nation *a*.

### ABHORRING.

*Isa*. 66. 24. they shall be an *a*. to all flesh

### ABIDE

Signifies, [1.] *To stay or tarry*, Gen. 22. 5. [2.] *To dwell or live in a place*, Gen. 29. 19. Psal. 15. 1. [3.] *To bear or endure*, Jer. 10. 10. Joel 2. 11. [4.] *To be*, Gen. 44. 33. [5.] *To continue*, Eccl. 8. 15. Joh. 14. 16. [6.] *To wait for*, Acts 20. 23. [7.] *To rest*, Prov. 19. 23. [8.] *To live*, Phil. 1. 24. [9.] *To stand firm*, Psal. 119. 90. 125. 1. [10.] *To rule or govern*, Psa. 61. 7.
*Gen*. 19. 2. we will *a*. in the street all night
22. 5. *a*. you here with the ass
24. 55. let the damsel *a*. with us a few days
29. 19. better I give her to thee, *a*. with me
44. 33. let thy servant *a*. instead of the lad
*Exod*. 16. 29. *a*. ye every man in his place
*Lev*. 8. 35. therefore *a*. at the door of tabernacle
19. 13. wages of hired shall not *a*. with thee
*Num*. 35. 25. *a*. to death of the high priest
*Ruth* 2. 8. *a*. here fast by my maidens
1 *Sam*. 1. 22. before the Lord, and *a*. for ever
5. 7. the ark of God shall not *a*. with us
22. 23. *a*. thou with me, fear not
30. 21. whom they made *a*. at brook Besor
2 *Sam*. 16. 18. his will I be, and with him *a*.
*Job* 24. 13. *a*. not in the paths of the light
38. 40. and *a*. in the covert to lie in wait
39. 9. will the unicorn *a*. by thy crib
*Psal*. 15. 1. who shall *a*. in thy tabernacle
61. 4. I will *a*. in thy tabernacle for ever
7. he shall *a*. before God for ever
91. 1. shall *a*. under the shadow of the Almighty
*Prov*. 7. 11. her feet *a*. not in her house
19. 23. and he that hath it shall *a*. satisfied
*Eccl*. 8. 15. that shall *a*. with him of his labour
*Jer*. 10. 10. nations not able to *a*. his indignation

*Jer*. 42. 10. if ye *a*. in this land I will build you
49. 18. no man shall *a*. there, 33. | 50. 46.
*Hos*. 3. 3. thou shalt *a*. for me many days
11. 6. the sword shall *a*. in his cities
*Joel* 2. 11. the day is terrible, who can *a*. it
*Mic*. 5. 4. they shall *a*. for he shall be great
*Nab*. 1. 6. who can *a*. in fierceness of his anger
*Mal*. 3. 2. who may *a*. the day of his coming
*Mat*. 10. 11. there *a*. Mar. 6. 10. Luk. 9. 4.
*Luk*. 19. 5. to day I must *a*. at thy house
24. 29. *a*. with us. || *Joh*. 15. 4. *a*. in me, 7.
*Joh*. 12. 46. believes, should not *a*. in darkness
14. 16. another Comforter that he may *a*.
15. 6. if a man abide not in me, he is cast
10. ye shall *a*. in my love, *a*. in his love
*Acts* 15. 34. it pleased Silas to *a*. there
16. 15. come into my house and *a*. there
20. 23. that bonds and afflictions *a*. me
27. 31. except these *a*. in the ship
1 *Cor*. 3. 14. if any man's work *a*.
7. 8. it is good if they *a*. even as I do
20. every man *a*. in the same calling
40. happier if she so *a*. in my judgment
*Phil*. 1. 24. to *a*. in the flesh is more needful
25. I know that I shall *a*. with you all
1 *Tim*. 1. 3. I besought thee to *a*. at Ephesus
27. ye shall *a*. in him || 28. children *a*. in him

### ABIDETH

2 *Sam*. 16. 3. behold he *a*. at Jerusalem
*Psal*. 49. 12. man being in honour *a*. no
55. 19. even he that *a*. of old
119. 90. thou hast established the earth, and it *a*.
125. 1. like mount Zion which *a*. for ever
119. 90. heareth reproof, *a*. among the wise
*Eccl*. 1. 4. but the earth *a*. for ever
*Jer*. 21. 9. that *a*. in this city shall die
*John* 3. 36. but the wrath of God *a*. on him
8. 35. the servant *a*. not, but the son *a*.
12. 24. except a corn of wheat die, it *a*. alone
34. we have heard that Christ *a*. for ever
15. 5. he that *a*. in me bringeth forth fruit
1 *Cor*. 13. 13. now *a*. faith, hope, charity
2 *Tim*. 2. 13. if we believe not, yet he *a*. faithful
*Heb*. 7. 3. Melchisedec *a*. a priest continually
1 *Pet*. 1. 23. word of God which *a*. for ever
1 *John* 2. 6. he that saith he *a*. in him
10. that loveth his brother *a*. in light
14. ye are strong, and word of God *a*. in you
17. that doth the will of God *a*. for ever
27. anointing oil *a*. in you and teacheth
3. 6. whosoever *a*. in him sinneth not
14. loveth not his brother, *a*. in death
24. and hereby we know that he *a*. in us

B     2 *John*

St James's Palace (c. 1750). On 3 November 1737 Alexander Cruden presented a copy of his Concordance to Queen Caroline at an audience in the library of the palace.

Elizabeth Blackwell. 'She had in her girlish days practised the drawing and colouring of flowers – a suitable and amiable accomplishment for her sex.'

The illustrations in Elizabeth Blackwell's *Curious Herbal* have been dismissed by one critic as 'the work of an industrious amateur, showing no touch of genius'. Others disagree, judging that she depicted the plants 'with extreme skill and delicacy'.

Alexander Cruden MA. Engraved by W.C. Edwards c.1762, from an original drawing by T. Fry.

*The Demonisation of Alexander Cruden – how a distinguished, even good-looking middle-aged man was transformed into a dangerous, importunate lunatic.*

Alexander Cruden MA. Engraved by T. Cook (unknown date), from an original drawing by T. Fry.

Alexander Cruden. Derived by Rex Whistler c.1934 from T. Cook's engraving after R. [sic] Fry.

Dr James Monro (1680–1752). The son of a Principal of Edinburgh University, James Monro was the progenitor of a whole dynasty of Monros who would rule over Bedlam for more than a century.

Dr John Monro (1715–1791). Maybe because John Monro was a little less pleased with himself and a little more inclined to listen to his patients than was his father, doctor and patient found, probably to the surprise of each, that they got on very well.

'Scene in a Madhouse' (i.e. Bedlam), Plate 8 from Hogarth's *Rake's Progress*. The very idea of Bedlam made Cruden feel sick. 'To be sent to Bethlehem was the sorest evil that could befall him and which he dreaded more than death.'

Lord Chief Justice Sir William Lee, KC. As Chief Justice of the Court of King's Bench, Lee was breaking with tradition by presiding over the Court of Common Pleas.

*Below:* Interior view of Westminster Hall showing the Court of Common Pleas in Session, by Pugin et al.

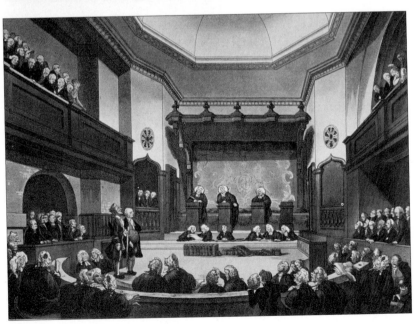

|  | Book | Line |  | Book | Line |
|---|---|---|---|---|---|
|  |  |  | Vide Satan |  |  |
| Return from thence, after-diffen- ) fions, &c. to the birth of the ) Meffiah, &c, | xii. | from 345 to 359 | Luft, Carnal, the firft Effect of ) Adam's, &c. fall | ix. | 1011 |
| Ifis, (a fall'n Angel) | i. | 478 | The Solace of it | ix. | 1042 |
| Ithuriel (a guardian Angel of Paradife) | iv. | 788 |  |  |  |
| Detects Satan's firft attempt on ) Eve there | iv. | 810 | **M** |  |  |
|  |  |  | Mammon (a fall'n Angel) | i. | 678 |
| **K** |  |  | His Speech in the council call'd ) by Satan after their fall | ii. | 229 |
| Knowledge of good and evil, the ) tree of it, how fituated | iv. | 220 | Man fall'n the Object of grace, why | iii. | 130 |
|  | ix. | 626 | His long Refiftance of it alone ) exclufive | iii. | 198 |
| Defcrib'd | ix. | 575 | Redemption propos'd by God the ) Father | iii. | 203 |
| Forbidden to Adam ) | vii. | 542 | Undertaken by God the Son | iii. | 227 |
|  | viii. | 323 | The Son's Merits alone imputa- ) tive to him, towards it, how | iii. | 290 |
| Satan's Encomium of it | ix. | 679 | Man created to repair the lofs of the ) fall'n Angels | iii. | 667 |
| Eve's ) | ix. | 795 |  | ix. | 143 |
|  | ix. | 863 | His Creation (part of the fixth ) day's) defcrib'd | vii. | 524 |
| Knowledge (or Opinion) the re- ) fult of reafon and fancy | v. | 100 | Dominion over the reft | vii. | 520 |
| Without reftraint, folly ) | vii. | 126 | Love to Woman, how confiftent ) with his fuperiority | viii. | 567 |
|  | viii. | 188 | The whole creation in little | ix. | 109 |
|  | xii. | 561 | Angels, his guardians | ix. | 154 |
| Of things neceffary, wifdom | viii. | 192 | His Superiority over the Woman ) given him by God | x. | 145 |
| Knowledge of future events, the ) defire of it reprehended | xi. | 770 |  |  | 195 |
| Its fum, the love, fear, &c. of God | xii. | 557 |  |  |  |
| In animal creatures afferted | viii. | 369 |  |  |  |
| Vide Similies. |  |  |  |  |  |

It was at Auditor Benson's specific request that Cruden was asked to compile an Index of Matters to Newton's edition of *Paradise Lost* (published in 1749), a task which Alexander Chalmers described as 'second only in magnitude to the compilation of his Concordance'.

### XXVIII.

And ever and anon, when none was ware,
With fpeaking looks, that clofe embaffage bore,
He rov'd at her, and told his fecret care:
For all that art he learned had of yore.
Ne was fhe ignorant of that lewd lore,
But in his eye his meaning wifely read,
And with the like him anfwer'd evermore:
She fent at him one firy dart, whofe head
Empoifned was with privy luft, and jealous dread.

### XXIX.

H efrom that deadly throw made no defence,
But to the wound his weak heart open'd wide;
The wicked engine through falfe influence
Paft through his eyes, and fecretly did glide
Into his heart, which it did forely gride.
But nothing new to him was that fame pain,
Ne pain at all; for he fo oft had tride
The powre thereof, and lov'd fo oft in vain,
That thing of courfe he counted, love to entertain.

Verses from Spenser's *Faerie Queene* in the 1753 edition corrected by Alexander Cruden. The first line of Verse XXIX proves that typesetting errors could creep past even the most vigilant of proof-correctors.

Profile of Alexander Cruden set into the wall above No.45 Camden Passage, Islington.

Cruden's profile and memorial plaque in Camden Passage were unveiled by the future Poet Laureate John Betjeman in 1965. The plaque was blessed by Revd D.E. Nineham, Professor of Divinity at the University of London, and the unveiling ceremony was accompanied by madrigal singers from the Royal College of Music.

*Excellent Majesty, and do think him in good Health and Order, and that it is a most injurious and unaccountable thing to propose to send him to Bethlehem. Given at London, the seventh day of July in the Year of our Lord 1738.*

> *Alexr. Stuart M.D.*
> *William Stukeley M.D.*
> *Robert Innes M.D.*

Of this impressive trio of witnesses, William Stukeley was the best known. An ordained clergyman as well as a Fellow of the Royal College of Physicians, Stukeley had written numerous antiquarian and medical books. These included *Of the Spleen, its Description and History* and *A Treatise on the Cause and Cure of the Gout*, which Cruden himself had published in 1736.* Alexander Stuart, unusually, was a Fellow of both the College of Surgeons and the College of Physicians. Robert Innes' fame – if he had any – was less enduring; Cruden described him merely as 'a Physician in London of long Practice'. Confident that the word of these experts would carry enormous weight, Cruden tucked this precious 'certificate of sanity' into his pocket and moved on to the next step in his campaign. Hiring an attorney to initiate an 'Action at Law' against Wightman, he swore an affidavit before a judge in an attempt to get Wightman 'held to bail'. Here he hit a snag. The judge, Lord Comyns, ruled that bail in such a 'very uncommon and unprecedented case' could not be imposed by one judge sitting alone, and since his fellow judges had all left town for the summer, he 'suspended the consideration of the affair'.

---

* It would seem from his connections with both Stukeley and Dr 'Gout-Oil' Rogers that Cruden must have suffered from gout, but he never mentioned it. Presumably that was because this painful condition was among the least of his worries.

The Sergeant-Major, for one, welcomed this ruling. He had been watching Cruden closely, had seen his strength and his spirits flagging as the entirely predictable reaction to his long ordeal set in, and had been trying for some time to make him ease up. Now there was no alternative. On 22 August Cruden left London for Southgate. In the home of his former employers the Coltmans, 'Madam Coltman kindly entertained him for two months'.

It is curious how the fortunes of Alexander Cruden and Elizabeth Blackwell moved to such similar rhythms. Both would suffer deep adversity; both would enjoy remarkable success. Yet their respective travails and triumphs never seemed to coincide. When one was down, the other was up. It is hard to believe that in such a small world, and with so many things in common, they never met each other on the way.

In the summer of 1738, while Cruden's attempts to bring Robert Wightman to justice were stalled, Elizabeth Blackwell was persevering with the second volume of her *Curious Herbal.* The first volume of 252 plates had sold well and the appeals for more had been loud enough to prompt the publication of an interim edition, a kind of 'volume one-and-a-half'. Containing a further 132 plates, this appeared in May 1738 while Alexander Cruden was being held in Bethnal Green (and Alexander Blackwell was being held in Highgate). But Elizabeth still had more than a hundred plates to complete before reaching her proposed five hundred.

There were formidable obstacles in the path of any 'respectable' female who was obliged to make her own living. Eighteenth century notions of what constituted an appropriate feminine activity were woefully limited; 'hand-painted engravings of garden flowers intended as models for embroidery and silk-painting' were unexceptionable, and the study of natural history was allowed to be a suitable occupation for a lady so long as such study was undertaken in the interests of refining these pretty skills. But if a lady – and particularly a lady on her own – wanted to safeguard her reputation she had to steer clear of anything too scientific. 'Botany has lately become a fashionable amusement with ladies,' wrote the Reverend Richard Polwhele in 1798, 'but how the study of the sexual system of plants can accord with female modesty I am not able to comprehend.' 'Several times,' he added darkly, 'I have seen boys and girls botanizing together.'[1] Even the best part of a century later the idea of a lady writing a book still had the power to raise the more reactionary of male eyebrows. This was one of the many things that had poor James Bruce in such a fluster when he was updating his *Eminent Men of Aberdeen*. Lacking the courage to go into the details of Elizabeth Blackwell's marital state, he vented his disapproval instead on 'literary ladies' in general:

> *There is something offensive in a woman putting out a book except on some such subject as dancing or cookery or anything of that kind. When they go to the lengths of writing sonnets, political economy, theories of morals, essays on population, theological discourses etc it is perfectly unbearable. Literary men are seldom agreeable companions, but literary ladies are generally allowed to be insufferable.*[2]

Fortunately Elizabeth Blackwell had an array of distinguished sponsors to shield her from such puritanical censure and the most compelling of motives to see her project through. Her husband/brother Alexander was still providing her with the scientific nomenclature for her illustrations from his prison cell in Highgate; he was also paying close attention to the income generated by the *Curious Herbal*. Fearing that this might fall short of the sum required to pay off his debts and thereby gain his release, he had arranged to sell a third share in the copyright of the complete work for £150 to a bookseller named John Nourse. Elizabeth raised no objections, and by the beginning of 1739 this money, together with the sum realised from the sales of Volumes One and One-And-A-Half, was sufficient to settle Alexander's outstanding debts in full. He was released from Highgate Prison just in time to help Elizabeth celebrate the publication of Volume Two.

The first volume of *A Curious Herbal, containing Five Hundred Cuts of the most Useful Plants which are now used in the Practice of Physic* had been dedicated to Dr Richard Mead. The chief dedication of Volume Two was now inscribed by Elizabeth Blackwell to Isaac Rand, the Curator of Chelsea Physic Garden, 'in an address breathing a spirit of fervent gratitude, and acknowledging that, in her own ignorance of Botany, she was entirely obliged to him for the completeness of the work'.[3] There were secondary dedications too, to Sir Hans Sloane and again Dr Richard Mead, as well as to Dr Thomas Pellett, President of the Royal College of Physicians and Dr Alexander Stuart, the physician, who 'showed some of the first drawings at a public herbarizing [sic] of the worshipful company of Apothecaries'.[4]

This list of dedicatees is further evidence of how small a world was Enlightenment London. That the list of subscribers to Cruden's Concordance had so many names in common with that to Dr Johnson's *Dictionary* is not surprising; most of them were booksellers. The list of Elizabeth Blackwell's dedicatees produces stranger coincidences. Dr Richard Mead was closely associated with Cruden's mad-doctor James Monro; according to Monro's son, not the least of his father's claims to regard was that 'the illustrious Mead chose you as a companion and loved you as a friend'.[5] Dr Alexander Stuart, in another coincidence, was the self-same 'Alexr. Stuart M.D.' who a few months previously had examined Alexander Cruden and testified to his sanity. The most significant dedication of all, though, was the one Elizabeth Blackwell left to last. It was addressed to Dr John Johnston, Regius Professor of Medicine at the University of Glasgow.

*As this work has met with a more favourable reception from the publick, both at home and abroad, than I could have expected, knowing my own insufficiency for the under-taking, this success must be ascrib'd in great measure to the prevailing influence of these worthy gentlemen who kindly honoured it by their recommendation, amongst them I am in a particular manner indebted to your goodness, in making it acceptable at Glasgow.*

*Your much obliged niece*
*Elizabeth Blackwell.*
*17th January 1739[6]*

John Johnston, as mentioned, was the brother of Christian Blackwell (*née* Johnston), mother to both Elizabeth and Alexander Blackwell. Wittingly or unwittingly, Elizabeth thus provided the final clue to the true nature of her relationship to her 'husband' Alexander Blackwell.

What constituted John Johnston's goodness in making *A Curious Herbal* 'acceptable at Glasgow' is not recorded. Nor do we know why Elizabeth was prepared to risk the exposure of her secret by making such a public dedication. Johnston's career as Regius Professor of Medicine at Glasgow University was not exactly illustrious – indeed 'it is not certain that he ever gave any instruction on the subject'[7] – but Elizabeth was probably pleased to be able to parade a family member who was a medical academic, and perhaps obliged to him not just for support but for discretion. Maybe, after fifteen years of 'marriage' and with the praises of the 'extraordinary merit' of her work as of 'great practical value' and 'a touching and admirable monument of female devotion' ringing in her ears, she was confident that the significance of this one small detail would be overlooked. If so, she was right. Its significance would indeed be overlooked for more than two hundred years.

For historians of botanical illustration the Blackwells offered other mouth-watering material. 'With Mrs Elizabeth Blackwell, artist and engraver of *A Curious Herbal*,' wrote Wilfrid Blunt and William T. Stearn, the authors of *The Art of Botanical Illustration* (1950), 'we become entangled in a little drama of heroism, intrigue and torture which seems strangely out of place in the sober chronicles of botanical illustration.' The heroism in question was Elizabeth's in so gallantly coming to the rescue when Alexander was imprisoned. Although Blunt and Stearn were ultimately dismissive of her artistic talents, they thought it only right that the drawings and engravings which led to her husband's release should have 'made her famous'. As for the 'intrigue and torture', they were still, in 1739, some years off. 'It would be pleasant,' Blunt and Stearn agreed, 'to be able to relate that the re-united pair lived happily ever after. And for a while, indeed, all went well.' Chalmers concurs: 'Blackwell, after his release, lived for some time at Chelsea with his wife and, on her account, was much respected.'

By January 1739, when the second volume of Elizabeth's *Curious Herbal* was published, Alexander Cruden had returned to London and was lodging with the steadfast Sergeant-Major. His sojourn in Southgate with Mrs Coltman had quickly restored him to physical health, but he had needed every moment of the two months he spent there to recover his spirits. (Mrs Coltman had probably not been in the best of spirits herself – her husband, the 'valuable Henry', had died some years previously, and her only son, Cruden's former pupil, had met a premature and 'much lamented' death in 1736.) Now that he was back in town, Cruden was more determined than ever that his persecutors, Robert Wightman, James Monro, Matthew Wright and John Oswald, should be called to account for 'their Unjust and Barbarous Treatment of Mr C at Bethnal Green'. So he started preparing his diary for publication.

His motives for so vigorously pursuing his persecutors may not have been absolutely clear even to Cruden himself. It is tempting to think that he must have been driven at least in part by a desire for revenge, but by all accounts he was the most benign and least vengeful of men. Had it been anything other than his sanity that had been impugned by the actions of Wightman, Monro, Wright and Oswald, he might well have 'turned the other cheek' and let it pass. But his sanity was all he had – indeed, besides life itself, it is all anyone has – and the more it was called into question, the more desperately he needed to establish it. Legal action against his persecutors would give him the perfect chance to prove not just in a court of law but before all the world that *Alexander Cruden was not and never had been mad.*

He had another motive too. 'He made his persecution the basis of an eloquent plea to the legislature ". . . plainly showing the absolute necessity of regulating Private Madhouses in a more effectual manner than at present".'[8]

*It seems necessary* [wrote Cruden] *that Private Madhouses should be licensed, and under proper Regulations, and that the poor Patients should be visited at least once a Month by Persons of Authority, and have the Liberty of offering their Petitions . . . it seems that there is a sort of Defect or Oversight in the Legislature in not making full Provision against the Evils of Private Madhouses.*

Cruden had experienced some of these evils, but he had witnessed more. The memory of his encounter with the miserable creatures in the 'publick parlour' of Wright's Private Madhouse would stay with him for the rest of his life, as would his shame at having so cravenly recoiled from their sufferings. His campaign for the licensing of private madhouses, and his later 'benevolent exertions' in the cause of prison reform, were prompted by a need to make amends for his own personal failure as well as by a sincere desire to right official wrongs. And knowing that no cause, however deserving, would benefit from the support of a man who was thought to be mad, it was as much for the sake of this campaign as for his own sake that he had to prove that he was not.

Cruden already had the precious 'certificate' signed by the doctors, but he wanted more. The prodigious memory that had served him so well ever since his schooldays now helped him recall every detail of his sixty-eight days of imprisonment, and allowed him to fill in the gaps in his diary where the constraints of the chains and the straitjacket had prevented him from writing. By the beginning of March it was ready, and on 21 March 1739 – a year almost to the day since he had been abducted – he published it, with a postscript:

> *If any can disprove any of the horrid Facts in the above mentioned Pamphlet, they ought, in Justice to themselves and the Public, to answer it; else their Silence will be justly construed to be a full Proof of its being Unanswerable, and the Crimes as black as they are here represented.*

The publication of his 'diary' brought Cruden an avalanche of letters expressing support for his cause and sympathy for his sufferings. His friend Dr 'Gout-Oil' Rogers wrote: 'I am surprised how you bore up under so many cruelties. Thousands would have gone mad had they suffered a tenth part of the tyrannies and oppressions that were laid upon your shoulders.' Mr Frewen, a complete stranger, wrote likewise: 'I congratulate you on being out of the power of your merciless persecutors. A hundredth part of the cruel treatment you met with would have been enough to get the better of any man's reasoning. My notion is that you have been most injuriously and most barbarously treated, and I hope the law will give you all possible reparation.' He even received letters from Aberdeen – some of which were more helpful than others: 'The God of your Life will bring his own Glory and your Good out of all those strange Providences that have passed over you,' wrote the Reverend Mr Wilkinson. 'His wise and holy Hand hath order'd this heavy Trial for you, and I know you will adore Him with Humility and Silence.' The Reverend Mr Moffat, on the other hand, expressed his fervent hope that 'your malicious Enemies will be obliged to make just Satisfaction and Reparation for the Injuries done you ... I pray God may cause your Integrity and Innocence to shine as the Light at Noon-day.'

The fact that the publication of his diary produced so many letters of support and not a single letter challenging its contents might suggest that adverse comment had been suppressed. But Alexander Cruden was not given to dissimulation, nor could he afford to ignore criticism. Had he received even a single assertion that his treatment in Bethnal Green had been justified, he would have been unable to resist a loud and public refutation. Besides, had any such assertion come to light without him having refuted it, doubts would have been cast on his honesty as well as his sanity. As he put it, 'Mr C would rather be confin'd again, even at Bethnal Green, than be guilty of the abominable Crime of Fraud and Falsehood, the Weapons of his enemies.' The comforting letters of support joined the doctors' certificate squirreled away in Cruden's capacious pockets and he set about recruiting witnesses who would be prepared to stand up in court and testify on his behalf. So successful was he in this quest that, as the date set for the court hearing approached, he felt increasingly confident that his case was indeed unanswerable.

On Cruden's instructions, his attorney had brought two separate actions, one against Robert Wightman for having illegally taken possession of his effects, and another against James Monro, John Oswald, Matthew Wright and John Davis for 'Trespass, Assault and Wrongful Imprisonment'. Unfamiliar as he was with the complexities of the legal process, Cruden raised no objection when the hearings, initially set for 17 June 1739 in 'the Sheriff's Court at Guildhall', were postponed and the cases then transferred, first to the Lord Mayor's Court and then back to the Sheriff's Court before finally being moved to the Court of Common Pleas. Nor, at that stage, did he appreciate the significance of the court's decision that the action against Monro, Oswald, Wright and Davis for 'Trespass, Assault and Wrongful Imprisonment' should be heard first, with that against Robert Wightman to be heard a week later. On 17 July 1739 the Court of Common Pleas convened in Westminster Hall, with 'Henry Jenkin for Cruden, William Round for Monro, Wright & others, and with Lord Chief Justice Lee presiding.'

Although the building was essentially the same, the interior of Westminster Hall was not the hushed, cathedral-like atrium today reserved for the grandest of ceremonial occasions. For five hundred years it had been the home of the Law Courts, and as such more closely resembled the tumultuous floor of the Stock Exchange. The four corners of the huge hall were occupied by the four Courts of Justice – Court of King's (or Queen's) Bench, Court of Common Pleas, Court of Exchequer and Court of Chancery – each with its attendant swarm of judges, lawyers, clerks, jurymen, witnesses, supplicants, petitioners and all manner of disputatious litigants. Onlookers packed the (long gone) gallery. Bookstalls lined the walls between the courts. Members of the public wandered in and out at will. The volume of noise generated by all this judicial, commercial and social activity in one vast echoing chamber must have made it extremely hard to concentrate on whatever proceedings were in hand.

Too engrossed in the proceedings in the Court of Common Pleas to be distracted by any amount of noise, Cruden watched intently as the judge made his stately entrance. Reluctant to incur the wrath of so puissant an individual and thereby risk ending up in the dock himself, he did not dare mention Lord Chief Justice Lee by name; he would refer to him either as 'the Judge' or, when making anything approaching an allegation of injustice, merely as 'a certain Person'.

> *Dr Monro was sitting on the Bench when 'a certain Person' came into the Court, and this Person en passant shook Dr Monro very familiarly by the hand. This did not escape the Notice of some, tho' it was done with Quickness and Dexterity, and was looked upon by some as a Sign of what followed.*

Sir William Lee KC had been appointed Chief Justice of the Court of King's Bench in 1737 after a long and distinguished career as a lawyer and politician (Latin Secretary to George I and George II, Recorder of Buckingham, MP for Chipping Wycombe, Attorney-General to Frederick Prince of Wales, Privy Councillor etc etc). Given that Lee was as comfortably ensconced in the legal establishment as James Monro was in the medical establishment, and given, again, that anyone who was anyone in Enlightenment London knew everyone else who was anyone, it is not surprising that two such successful men should be well acquainted. Cruden, however, naïve in the ways of the world and deeply suspicious of the doctor, was inclined to see something sinister in the coincidence. It is of course possible that Lee had chosen to preside over a case in which one of the accused was a friend in the hope of guiding it to a satisfactory outcome (and it is interesting to note that, as Chief Justice of the Court of King's Bench, Lee was breaking with tradition by presiding over the Court of Common Pleas – and to learn that the previous day he had apparently been too ill to preside over any court); but it is also possible that there were no judges available to hear the case who were *not* acquainted with Monro. Either way, before the trial began Lord Chief Justice Lee made a statement to the court 'saying honestly that he was prejudiced in favour of Dr Monro, but also adding that he would endeavour to guard against it', a statement that not surprisingly did little to allay Cruden's fears. The jury was then sworn in and the proceedings opened with the charges (couched in what either the plaintiff or his lawyer considered to be suitable legalese) being read aloud to the court.

*That Matthew Wright, John Davis, James Monro and John Oswald, together with Robert Wightman, did make an Assault upon Alexander Cruden, the Plaintiff, and him did beat, wound, evilly treat and imprison; and him, there in Prison, contrary to the Laws and Customs of England, against his will did detain; his Letters and Messages stop and intercept, and him from the Assistance, Comfort and Conversation of his Friends did keep, obstruct and hinder; and Iron Fetters, Chains, Cords and other Instruments of Cruelty and Oppression on him did put, and for a long Time did continue the same, for the Space of ten Weeks. By reason of which he is much injured in his Calling, Reputation and Business, and his Constitution, Health and Strength were, and still are, very much weaken'd and impaired; and his Body very much wounded, that his Life was in great danger; and other Wrongs and Injuries they to the said Alexander did, whereby the said Alexander is*

*greatly injured; and he brings his suit against the Defend-*
*ants for Damages of ten thousand Pounds.*

Cruden had calculated £10,000 to be suitable compensation
for false imprisonment for nine weeks and six days at £5 an
hour (an extravagant claim by any standards). This came to
£8280 and was rounded up to £10,000 by assessing the assault
and other damages at £1720.

Robert Wightman himself was not in court, and since he
was not directly accused in this case, did not appear at any
stage in the proceedings. Monro and Oswald both pleaded not
guilty to all the charges. Wright and Davis could hardly deny
that the plaintiff had been their prisoner, but justified it by
pleading that Cruden had been sent to Bethnal Green by
Robert Wightman, who had told them that he was mad and
that they were to take care of him. Cruden's counsel, Henry
Jenkin, then rose to make his opening address. Starting, on
his client's instructions, with 'an excellent speech against the
Evils of Private Madhouses', he told the jury that it was proper
for them to consider the following Questions: 'what Authority
had the Defendants to commit the Plaintiff?' and 'what way
could the Defendants justify their abusing the Plaintiff in the
manner complain'd of, particularly – and which greatly aggra-
vated the Defendants' guilt – since the Plaintiff was so abused
when in his right Senses?' Firing his biggest gun first, and in
order to establish right from the start that the plaintiff was
still 'in his right Senses', Jenkin showed the jury Cruden's
precious 'certificate of sanity', signed by those eminent physicians, Doctors Stuart, Stukeley and Innes. Watching Monro
closely as this document was being read out, Cruden saw him
puff out his cheeks and interpreted this as a clear sign of
discomfiture.

After this most satisfactory opening to the proceedings,
Jenkin called his first witness, a man 'of undoubted Character'

who had known the plaintiff since he had first arrived in England from Aberdeen.

*Mr Samuel Reynardson, one of the six Clerks in Chancery, made Oath that he had known the Plaintiff about fifteen years, and that he had been Tutor to Mr Coltman's only son at Southgate, his near relation. That the Plaintiff had behaved in the Family to Satisfaction. That the Plaintiff had been in his house on 8th March 1738, (about a fortnight before his Confinement at Bethnal Green), where the Plaintiff had behaved very sensibly. And that he had never taken him for a Madman.*

Reynardson was followed on the witness stand by another of Cruden's early employers, Thomas Fletcher of Ware in Hertfordshire, who declared 'that the Plaintiff had been in his employ for about a year, and that his Behaviour had been good and unexceptionable; that he had seen him frequently since, had employed him as a Bookseller, had visited him at Bethnal Green and found him perfectly in his senses, and that he thought there was no Occasion for his Confinement'.

Next to speak for Cruden was a man he described as being 'of Great Reputation in the World' whose word he thought would carry great weight in the court, the theological publisher Charles Rivington. Rivington testified 'that he had been concerned in the printing of Mr Cruden's Concordance to the Holy Bible, a book that was very well done; that he always looked upon Mr Cruden to be a wise, calm man, and that he had never seen him in any disorder'.

Witness followed witness; employers, friends, acquaintances, colleagues (and one kinsman) all swearing on oath that Alexander Cruden was not and never had been mad. The Sergeant-Major told the court of a conversation he had had with Dr Monro in which he had asked the doctor outright if

Cruden was a Lunatick, to which Monro had replied, 'No, he only has a fever on the nerves.' Matthew Wright's maid testified that her employer had said he would happily have set Cruden at liberty if only he would sign Wightman's letter. The Bethnal Green barber declared that he had shaved the plaintiff twice a week the whole time he was in Bethnal Green and that he had always found him in his right senses. William Simpson, Cruden's old friend from Aberdeen, swore that he had known the plaintiff for seventeen years and had never seen him other than 'perfectly in his senses and very reasonable'. In all Cruden's lawyer had subpoena'd nearly fifty witnesses to testify on Cruden's behalf. Not all, though, were heard. After some dozen or so had completed their testimony, suddenly and unaccountably 'the Court discovered an Inclination not to examine more Witnesses'.

Cruden was initially more perplexed than indignant about this unexpected development. After all, it seemed so obvious as hardly to need stating that once his sanity was proven the other charges laid against the defendants – of trespass, assault and false imprisonment – would have to be upheld; and there could be no doubt that his sanity had indeed been proven.

The mystery was soon solved. Lord Chief Justice Lee knew, as he had every right to know, the nature of the evidence that counsel for Monro and the other defendants was proposing to set before the court. By allowing Cruden's counsel to question thirteen of his witnesses, he considered he had given him a fair measure of the court's time. Now, quite reasonably in his view, he was keen for the case to move on. Lord Chief Justice Lee was a figure of awesome authority before whom, Cruden had noticed, the lawyers were 'as much afraid to speak as Schoolboys are before the most austere Schoolmaster'. When the judge said 'enough', that was it. Without any further prompting William Round, counsel for 'Monro & others', leapt to his feet and launched himself into his opening address.

His clients' defence against the charges brought by Cruden, he told the court, was quite simply that 'the Plaintiff had been in Disorder, and that they had acted out of Friendship for him'. But this was seemingly not what Lord Chief Justice Lee wanted to hear. Why, he demanded, did defence counsel not start with the letters? At that stage even Cruden did not know what letters 'the certain Person' was talking about.

*A certain Person in Court seem'd very fond of those three Letters, call'd for them and hugg'd them as a Treasure; whether this Person really thought them a sufficient Foundation to cast [condemn] the Plaintiff and to acquit his friend Monro, or what were his Thoughts and Ends in hugging them in such a Manner, his Conscience knows best.*

As soon as William Round began reading the letters, though, Cruden realised what was going on. Despite all the evidence to the contrary, despite everything that his witnesses had sworn on solemn oath, 'Monro & others' were intent on deriding his conduct and so demonstrating his derangement.

Even Cruden would admit that the first 'letter' made no sense. It consisted, in 'a few lines of the Plaintiff's writing', of some disjointed thoughts he had jotted down 'on waking from a disturbing dream about the Salvation of his friend Mr Bryan Payne'. It was dated 19 March 1738, the day after his hopes of married bliss with Mrs Payne had been dashed by the presence in her house in Piccadilly of John Oswald and William Crookshank – a painful experience which might easily have generated disturbing dreams. Pointing out that this note was clear proof that the defendants had caused his possessions to be rifled in search of evidence against him, Cruden would argue, very plausibly, that few dreams made much sense – even to those who were dreaming them.

The second letter – and this was a really dirty trick – was

a love letter from Cruden to Mrs Payne. He had apparently written it from Bethnal Green on 25 May 1738, just two days before he had 'happily projected' to make his escape from the madhouse, and therefore when his spirits had been at their very lowest ebb, but it too had been confiscated by Wightman. (Had it not been used as evidence in court, Cruden would never even have mentioned it, and sadly, apart from calling it a 'love letter', he gave no indication of what it said.) As if it was not enough to hear his dreams being brandished before the court, now his amours were being similarly flourished. Burning with embarrassment, Cruden nevertheless fought back valiantly.

*This Letter was an aggravation of the Defendants' Crimes, because they had impudently and illegally intercepted it, as they did a great many more. There was no particular part of it excepted against [objected to]; and if some might be apt to think it was a familiar Letter, it is to be remembered that it was not penn'd to be read in the Court of Common Pleas at Westminster Hall, but only by Mrs Payne, whom the Plaintiff studied to please.*

How low, he must have wondered, were the defendants prepared to stoop in order to escape their just deserts? The answer, it was almost instantly revealed, was considerably lower. The third letter would be the defendants' *coup de grâce*.

In the madhouse Cruden had written twice to his father in Aberdeen. These letters, along with most of his others, had of course been intercepted on Wightman's orders and had never reached their destination. Instead, Wightman had lifted Baillie William's address from his son's letter and had written him a letter of his own. This informed the old man (Baillie William was then well into his seventies) that his son Alexander 'had had an attack of mania', that he, Wightman, was taking care of him and that he had sent him for treatment to an institution. The letter to which the court was now introduced was Baillie William's reply to Robert Wightman.

It was short, but long enough to damn the plaintiff. In a shaky hand, Baillie William had thanked Wightman for everything he had done for his son and had confirmed that, yes, Alexander had been confined in Scotland 'under a Disorder' 'some eight or ten years previously', but that he had been well ever since. Cruden could sense the mood in court changing as the implications of this letter were absorbed; he heard the gasps of surprise, the voices rising in a crescendo of indignation: 'See! He has been mad for years! His own father has said so! Why are we wasting our time on a case brought by a madman?'

As the commotion spread to the gallery and threatened to get out of hand Lord Chief Justice Lee suggested the jury should withdraw. Cruden, in desperation, insisted that his attorney object to so blatant an attempt to curtail the proceedings. This, in turn, brought the fury of the judge down not on the head of the plaintiff but on that of the unfortunate attorney: 'His Lordship with great Zeal call'd for the Plaintiff's Attorney [in order] to punish him for bringing an Action against Monro, and also for laying the Damages at ten thousand Pounds.' Cruden was quick to vindicate his attorney. He claimed that the responsibility was entirely his, and requested permission to address the court himself.

With obvious reluctance, the judge gave his permission. Cruden thereupon plunged into a passionate, stammering speech insisting that he had indeed 'been exceedingly injured and barbarously abused, that no Verdict could make him believe that three and two made six, and that no man could prevent the scandalous Lies of selfish wicked Men'. He defended the claim for £10,000 damages, saying the sum could hardly be thought too great considering the harm the defendants had done to his personal and professional reputation, and he pointed out that 'had not Providence favour'd his wonderful Escape', he might still be under confinement – or even have died as a result of his injuries and ill-treatment. For the first and only time in his life, he also made reference to his 'uncommon treatment when a youth in Aberdeen'. 'In the year 1720,' he told the court, '[I was] in a treacherous Manner decoy'd into the publick prison at Aberdeen by the Advice of a conceited Man.' This nameless man he had later been 'inclinable to pursue to the utmost', a course which, 'out of Christian Consideration and respect for his Relations', he had eventually decided not to take. Even in his current desperation, this was all Cruden was willing to say. He could not defend himself further without betraying Elizabeth. The Blackwells' secret was still safe in his keeping.

Finally he protested that it was surely not proper legal procedure to quote the words of a man who could not be questioned further in court. Baillie William had died on 17 June, exactly a month before the case was convened and, although a man of great integrity, he had at the time he wrote the letter also been of great age, and his memory could not therefore be relied upon.

> It is to be observ'd that the Plaintiff's Father's Letter says that he was in disorder in Scotland 'about eight or ten years ago', whereas the Plaintiff arrived at Woolwich near London in the Phoenix of Aberdeen on April 2$^{nd}$ 1724, and hath never been out of England since that time – which is a few months more than fifteen years. This material Mistake would seem to be sufficient to make void his Father's Letter.

But even as he spoke Cruden knew that he was wasting his time. He slumped back into his seat reflecting bitterly that he might as well have been, as he put it, *surdis canere,* 'singing to the deaf'. His only hope now was that the rest of his character witnesses would be called.

*Immediately afterwards the Judge, contrary to the Plaintiff's Expectation, who did not think the Cause near an end and had many material witnesses still to call, began to sum up to the Jury the Evidence of the Examin'd Witnesses. It was proved that Wright had seized Cruden's letters; but his Lordship thought fit to excuse it to the jury saying 'What evil Intention could he have in that, seeing he told it to Sergeant Major Cruden the next day?' He also said to excuse the severe Blow near the eye given to the Plaintiff by Davis because 'Bless'd be God, the Eye is now well'. He then asserted two positions which seemed most shocking to the Injured Plaintiff; first, 'that if a Man have not a bad Intention, he is not to be blamed for sending a Person to a Madhouse', and second 'that in the present Case they could not be blamed for detaining the Plaintiff in his Confinement till he should sign a Release.'*

When Cruden stood up to protest at these 'strange' remarks he received a sharp reprimand from the judge, who threatened to commit him if he spoke one more word. But as the plaintiff was about to discover, Lord Chief Justice Lee had reserved his strangest remarks to the end.

*A certain Person in Court blamed the Plaintiff for making Monro a defendant, and said that it took off his Evidence. As to the injury done to the Plaintiff's character by being reputed Mad by their Management, he said 'That it was a common but a false Notion, for the wisest Men and best Geniuses were often most liable to that Disorder, and that it often proceeded from too much Religion or too much Reading'.*

*His Lordship then said positively and authoritatively to the Jury, 'You are to find for the Defendants.'*

The defendants were all acquitted. They were also granted their costs, which were laid against Cruden (although they seem to have been paid for him some time later by a nameless benefactor). To these insults was added a more lasting injury. The Reverend Thomas Blackwell, father of Alexander and Elizabeth, had died in 1728. Yet his malevolent influence had reached out over the years and the miles to touch a whole courtful of people who had never even heard of him, but who now believed, as Blackwell had always intended, that 'poor wee Alexander Cruden is out of his head, what a shame, and nothing he says can be taken seriously'.

# 9

# Too Much Religion

In due course and inevitably, Cruden would tell the world exactly what he thought about the proceedings in the Court of Common Pleas on that seventeenth day of July 1739. At the time, mindful of Lord Chief Justice Lee's threat to have him committed if he said one more word, he limited himself to just four. 'I trust in God,' he muttered, prompting the judge to snap back at him, 'I wish you had trusted more in God and had not come here.' On that distinctly testy note the court adjourned and Cruden's friends hauled him off to the Crown Tavern in Palace Yard to help him drown his sorrows. Here, loudly condemning the court's verdict, they agreed that the plaintiff had been 'bought and sold', that his treatment would have been illegal even if he had been insane, that his counsel was a coward, the jury had been nobbled and the entire proceedings had been rigged. But Cruden was too stunned to join in their protests. For twenty years he had been struggling to put the past behind him. His case against 'Monro & others' had been his final throw, and nothing his well-intentioned friends might say could alter the fact that he had failed. Instead of endorsing his sanity, his defeat in court had advertised his supposed insanity; instead of encouraging the regulation of private madhouses it had vindicated their keepers; and instead of securing him the regard of society it had invited only ridicule.

*After dining and tarrying for about two Hours, Mr C went home to his Chamber and that Evening writ by Post a letter to his valuable Friend Madam Coltman, and told her of his great Disappointment, but that he bore it patiently, was favour'd with inward Peace and Serenity of Mind, and that he submitted to the Will of God.*

For several weeks after the trial he lay low in his 'Chamber' (he was still lodging with the Sergeant-Major in Dutchy Lane*), praying not just for the humility to accept the verdict but for the wisdom to understand it. The court case had been intended to put everything right; how – and why – had it gone so horribly wrong?

With hindsight it is possible to see exactly why Cruden's case failed. As the judge had indicated, and as several other people would suggest to him both before and after the trial, his great mistake had been to include James Monro among the accused. Had he brought his action just against Matthew Wright, John Oswald and John Davis, he would almost certainly have won it. There could be no arguing with the fact that he had been imprisoned in a madhouse; he had produced more than enough witnesses to testify to his sanity, thus proving that his imprisonment had been wrongful; and, crucially, there would have been no reason for the judge or anyone else to protect Wright, Oswald or Davis from justice. James Monro was different.

---

* Now untraceable, but possibly south of the Thames near Stamford Wharf.

Since Cruden's Concordance had yet to make any great impact, its author was known principally as a proof-corrector. James Monro, on the other hand, was a mad-doctor; and mad-doctors were a rare and valuable species. It was inconceivable that the career of the most prestigious mad-doctor of them all should be ruined on the word of an ungrateful and insignificant patient. The moment Cruden's writ against the four defendants had been issued, the campaign to protect Monro had swung into action. The repeated delays and the constant switching of the case from court to court had been designed to discourage Cruden and persuade him to drop the charges altogether. When this plan had failed, the decision had been taken to reverse the order in which the cases were heard on the premise that if the case against Wightman had come to court first and succeeded (as well it might), it would then have been far more difficult to dismiss a subsequent case against Monro. Wightman, for his part, was prevailed upon to hand over the three fateful letters so that they could be used as evidence to clear Monro, and then to make himself scarce. This he did so effectively that he disappears from the scene altogether. Cruden's friends in the Crown Tavern had been right – the proceedings had been rigged, but in what those responsible for the rigging firmly believed was a good cause. Whether Lord Chief Justice Lee and Dr James Monro had been close friends, mere acquaintances or complete strangers, the outcome would have been the same; Cruden could not be allowed to win a case which would discredit the eminent Dr Monro.

Paradoxically, it was precisely because he knew James Monro was so influential that Cruden had insisted on including him in the action. From his guileless and unswervingly honest point of view, the fact that Monro was a man of education and high social standing made him the most culpable of all the defendants. Surely such a man had an even greater obligation to be conscientious in his duties and even less excuse for his maltreatment of the plaintiff than any of the other accused. 'The Plaintiff thinks he did Monro Justice in making him a Defendant, for he looks upon him as a capital Offender in this Scene of Iniquity. He doth not accuse him of want of Ability but of want of Integrity.'

Three years later James Monro would again face charges of false imprisonment, brought this time by a Bethlehem patient called Thomas Leigh. Again he would be exonerated. Monro's son John, on succeeding him as Chief Physician to Bedlam, would also be so accused and so exonerated, not once but twice. The dismissal of all these charges had as much to do with judicial reluctance to hold mad-doctors responsible for the iniquities perpetrated in madhouses as with the rights and wrongs of each individual case. Had one case been allowed to succeed, and had the floodgates thereby been opened, the few practitioners who were prepared to take on the unenviable task of caring for the insane might well have felt disinclined to carry on doing so. Mad-doctors were deemed worthy of official protection, at almost any cost.

In Cruden's case, though, it was not just a question of justice being forced to miscarry to save the reputation of a distinguished mad-doctor. Nor were Lord Chief Justice Lee's closing remarks to the plaintiff just gratuitous insults. The judge was genuinely relieved that Cruden had suffered no long-term ill from his imprisonment. Had it been otherwise he would have found it more difficult to resolve the case in favour of Monro. He could see that Cruden was surrounded by friends and well-wishers, so could reassure himself that the plaintiff's future would not be completely blighted by the adverse verdict. And he had done his best to comfort Cruden in his disappointment by reminding him that 'the wisest men and the best geniuses' were often liable to the same disorder. Had Lee's conscience still been troubling him after all these reassurances, Cruden himself by his very nature had unwittingly provided the perfect salve. In common with a great many of his contemporaries, including James Monro (and, as Cruden had already discovered, the Earl of Derby's lofty chamberlain Mr Clayton), the judge was deeply suspicious of 'too much religion'.

'Too much religion' was an incomprehensible notion to Scottish Presbyterians; they couldn't get enough of it. Not so for Anglicans. The savage excesses of the English Civil War had left them with a horror of religious extremism so acute it amounted almost to paranoia. Always uncomfortable with fervour, they regarded religion and passion as a dangerously volatile mixture. Parading religious beliefs in public, quoting too loudly from the Bible, putting too literal an interpretation on the Scriptures, or turning worship into some kind of dramatic performance, were interpreted as the early symptoms of extremism; those who indulged in such acts of zeal were labelled 'enthusiasts' and regarded with deep distrust. 'Leading Restoration Anglicans pictured a world that had been turned upside-down and a state that had literally lost its head, a civil society in which "enthusiasm" had become and remained a threatening politico-social force. According to such orthodox figures, enthusiasm was neither divinely nor diabolically inspired, but was a natural phenomenon, a dangerous madness, albeit one that could be prevented and, sometimes at least, cured.'[1]

As just such an orthodox Anglican, James Monro was all too ready to stigmatise religious enthusiasts as deranged. He would later get into trouble with John Wesley for viewing, and treating, Methodists as dangerous lunatics. Cruden, as a Calvinist proud of his convictions and not afraid to flourish them, and as a Biblical scholar whose literal approach to Revelation bordered on fundamentalism, was naturally suspect.

The two men, mad-doctor and 'prisoner', had met only

four times. At the first of these meetings Cruden had 'not thought it best to speak much' except to 'expostulate about his unjust confinement'. At the second meeting, the only one of the four which involved anything like a proper conversation, Cruden had told Monro that 'he awaited God's time for his deliverance' from the madhouse. Monro had seized on Cruden's statement as offering an easy diagnosis of his condition and had marked him down as an 'enthusiast'. The mad-doctor had even admitted as much in a conversation with Robert Wightman which was overheard by one of Cruden's friends and relayed to 'the prisoner' in Bethnal Green. 'The Prisoner was informed,' wrote Cruden in his diary, 'that Monro had said that the Prisoner was a man of Sense and Learning, but that he was a great Enthusiast.' Monro had then picked up Cruden's remark that 'he awaited God's time for his deliverance' and twisted it contemptuously into 'he believed that God would send an Angel from Heaven, or work some Miracle for his Deliverance'. Satisfied with his slick diagnosis, Monro had barely spoken to Cruden at their remaining two meetings, and Cruden had said nothing at all. With that one simple profession of his faith in God, Cruden had sealed his own fate. And Dr Monro and Lord Chief Justice Lee (who was also a High Church Anglican) could leave Westminster Hall confident that nobody would challenge the highly satisfactory outcome of a most unfortunate case.

Recent writers have accused Cruden of having a 'Job-like obsession with his own misfortunes' and 'a paranoid personality' – but as the wee man himself would ask those who questioned his persistence in trying to clear his name, 'How would you feel if this had happened to you?'

After the failure of his court case, Cruden's friends duly rallied round. He received quantities of letters, both from them and from strangers, full of indignation at the outcome. 'I must own I was not a little surpriz'd at a Verdict so different from what the World expected,' wrote one correspondent identified by Cruden merely as 'E.M.'; 'Your many Witnesses – who seem'd to be of unexceptionable Credit – unanimously proving your Sanity gave me the utmost Assurance of a Verdict in your Favour.' 'I could have wished your Trial had been taken down *verbatim* and published,' protested Henry Newcome, Master of a boarding school at Hackney, 'for it is a Scandal to the Legislative Power that so much Barbarity should be tolerated.' In similar vein, the Reverend Mr John Wilson of Dundee was certain that 'any Humane Person that heard your Treatment and Trial must bear the utmost Detestation to such Proceedings'. All this kind support eventually encouraged Cruden off his knees and back to his desk. Taking to heart the schoolmaster's suggestion, three months after the trial he published a forty-page account of the proceedings. It was dedicated to the King, George II, with a plea that 'Your Majesty may be graciously pleased to take such Methods as may be effectual to redress those great Evils and Injuries to which Your Majesty's Subjects are exposed by the present unrestrained Grievances of Private Madhouses.' His own case was lost, but the greater cause of social reform might yet be served.

Cruden's diary, which he had published three months *before* the trial under the title *The London Citizen Exceedingly Injured*, is a sprightly read. Meticulously chronological and minutely detailed, it cracks along at a lively pace, positively bristling with the author's certainty that all the wrongs it recounts will soon be righted. The tone of his *Account of a Trial*, published three months *after* the event, is very different. Disjointed, repetitive and fractious, it is the work not just of a disappointed man but of one for whom there is no longer any such thing as certainty. It is as if he was trying to construct by sheer weight of words an edifice to which he could cling in a world that had cast him adrift and did not even stay to watch him sink. His concern for the regulation of madhouses is swamped by his own sense of grievance. In court he had produced witnesses galore, including three physicians, to testify to his sanity; yet their testimony had been disregarded. Not a single witness, doctor or layman, had been called by the defence to testify to his insanity; yet he had lost his case. It seemed that the louder he shouted, the less he was heard; the more vehemently he protested his sanity, the madder he was thought to be; the harder he struggled to stay afloat, the deeper he sank.

Alexander Cruden was neither the first nor the last to be caught in this nightmare trap. As the anonymous writer to the *Gentleman's Magazine* in 1763 knew to his cost, 'if the patient persists in vindicating his reason, he is then deemed raving mad'. Thomas Tryon, a late seventeenth century Dissenter, decided that 'the world is just a great bedlam, where those that are more mad lock up those that are less', while dramatist Nathaniel Lee, who 'lost his reason through intemperance in 1684 and was confined in Bethlehem till 1689',[2] somehow managed to see the funny side of it: 'They said I was mad; and I said they were mad; damn them, they outvoted me.'[3] Cruden, too, had been outvoted, and his *Account of a Trial* shrieks of a frustration so intense that it threatened to suffocate him. Alternately pleading for understanding and raging at the world's refusal to understand, it makes painful reading. One can only hope that the act of writing it did something to ease the author's own pain; otherwise, it achieved nothing. Few people read it, and his case, which had briefly 'made a great Noise in the World', was quickly forgotten.

Cruden was now forty years old. His slight figure was as trim as ever, his clothes as sober and tidy and his manner as mild. Children did not point at him and stare; dogs did not bark at his approach. He might have lost a bit of weight, the strain of the past year might have sprinkled a little more grey in his hair or drawn a few more lines on his face, but otherwise he looked just as he had always looked – like a hard-working, law-abiding, unassuming and insignificant proof-corrector. The most eccentric thing he had done in his entire life – indeed almost the *only* eccentric thing – was to take a job as French Reader to the Earl of Derby knowing that he could not 'pronounce French exactly' – and that would surely better be described as over-optimistic, naïve, or just plain stupid. There are sheaves of other labels too that could be stuck on him. Certainly he was dedicated, meticulous and very stubborn. When it came to things he really cared about, like his Concordance, he was single-minded to the point of obsession. He was also too honest for the world in which he found himself; and his religious 'enthusiasm' made him something of a social misfit. Even taking all these things together, he had never done anything that could possibly be construed as mad. Yet the label, once applied, was indelible. To those who knew him only by later repute, Alexander Cruden *was* mad.

As if the condition were communicable, Cruden's irregular conduct – and there would be plenty of it in the years following the collapse of his court case – has been taken as a licence to be as cavalier with the details of his life as with his state of mind. His date of birth, for example, so easy to confirm in Aberdeen's parish records, is as often wrongly given as 1700 or even 1701 as it is rightly given as 1699. By common consent he is much more useful as a 'madman' than as the victim of a conspiracy the details of which no one could be bothered to fathom. He is more valued as an entertaining subject for social historians and a case-study for writers on psychological disorders than as the compiler of a uniquely valuable work of reference.

The notion of his madness has been so enthusiastically embraced that it has recently been stated that 'a herd of witnesses was mobilized [at the trial] and substantial quantities of evidence were introduced to prove that Cruden had indeed been insane'.[4] Yet the only account of the trial to go into any detail is Cruden's own, and he did not say anything of the sort. The judgement against him must have been based on *something*, the reasoning seems to go, so it can be safely assumed that 'a herd of witnesses' must have given 'substantial quantities of evidence' to prove that he had been insane.

Alexander Chalmers, Cruden's first biographer and the only one who actually met him, was never convinced that Cruden was mad. Personally acquainted with several people whose lives could still have been ruined if he explained what had really happened in Aberdeen, Chalmers felt obliged, right up till his own death in 1834, to keep quiet. He hinted at his doubts in such careful asides as '[Cruden] never appeared to be a lunatic in the eyes of his employers', 'it does not appear that he committed a single act which required the rigour of lunatic discipline', or, commenting on Cruden's diary, 'his being able to complain at all is no inconsiderable proof that confinement and harsh treatment were unnecessary'. Yet ever since Chalmers' first piece on Cruden was published in the 1789 *Biographia Britannica*, these hints have been brushed aside. The biographer's discretion has been dismissed as partiality, his mention of idiosyncrasies exaggerated, his insistence on normalities ignored.

The only known portrait of 'Alexander Cruden MA' well illustrates the point. Drawn from life in about 1760 by T. Fry, it apparently once hung in the Ashmolean Museum in Oxford and, though now lost, it inspired all the still extant portraits. The first of these, an engraving by W.C. Edwards, was printed in the second and many subsequent editions of Cruden's Concordance. It shows a distinguished, even good-looking, middle-aged man with gentle, pensive eyes and just the beginnings of a double chin. He could be a doctor, an academic or even a judge. In a later engraving ('T. Cook after R. [sic] Fry'), the double chin has gone, the face is much thinner, almost gaunt, and there are dark rings under the now large and mournful eyes. The most recent engraving, 'Derived by Rex Whistler from T. Cook's engraving after R. [sic] Fry' and commissioned as a frontispiece to Edith Olivier's *Eccentric Life of Alexander Cruden* published in 1934, carries the process to its inevitable conclusion. It is a travesty of the original, a wizened caricature of a perspiring, importunate and dangerous man. The eyes are enormous, popping from their sockets, staring rather than gazing, the flesh hangs in folds from the sunken cheeks, the nose has been sharpened to a point and the lips are pursed in an idiotic pout. Asked to depict a lunatic, Whistler had obliged. The 'demonisation' of Alexander Cruden MA was complete.

What Cruden was suffering from, and would continue to suffer from for a long time after his death, was not too much religion but too much stereotyping. Somehow, though, he had to learn to live with it. And somehow he still had to earn his living.

By February 1740 he was describing himself as 'Bookseller to her Late Majesty, over against the Blue-Coat Hospital in Newgate Street'. When this new venture did not prosper he went back to his old profession as a teacher. In December 1740 he wrote to the man he still regarded as one of his patrons, Sir Hans Sloane, to thank him for 'many kindnesses freely shewn to me', and to bring him up to date with his career:

*I have been since the beginning of July at Enfield, where I was very providentially engaged as Latin Usher* [teacher] *to Mr Blaide's Boarding School, which is a very considerable one of above fifty boarders . . . I desire to be at all times content and thankful for any business Providence provides for me . . . Enfield is a very pleasant place with good air, there are a great many people of fashion who live in it,*

*and it is said there are near fifty coaches in the parish . . .
I have had my health, blessed be God, very well.*[5]

It seems probable, since Enfield is just down the road from Southgate, that the 'Providence' that took Cruden to Mr Blaide's boarding school had been given a prod by the good Madam Coltman. She understood from long experience that in times of great stress her old friend was much happier away from the dirt and tumult of the city, and that responsible employment was the one thing above all others that would restore his shattered confidence. It was while he was living and working in Enfield that he received a commission that looked set to complete his rehabilitation. His former employer Mr Watson (who seems never to have had the slightest doubt about his sanity) asked him if he would be prepared to compile an index to John Milton's *Paradise Lost*.

Had the two men been contemporaries, Alexander Cruden would almost certainly have taken John Milton to task for denouncing Presbyterianism as a threat to religious freedom. But the pages of *Paradise Lost* were crammed full of just the kind of obscure Biblical references that were irresistible to Cruden. He comforted his conscience by telling it that the blind poet had been more critical of Episcopalianism than he had ever been of Presbyterianism, and accepted the task with relish.

*Paradise Lost* is not only very long – a total of twelve books averaging something like eight hundred lines each – it contains passages that are almost impossible for the layman to read, far less to mark, learn or inwardly digest:

> . . . *Nor content with such*
> *Audacious neighbourhood, the wisest heart*
> *Of Solomon he led by fraud to build*
> *His Temple right against the Temple of God*

*On that opprobrious Hill, and made his Grove*
*The pleasant Vally of Hinnom, Tophet thence*
*And black Gehenna call'd, the Type of Hell.*
*Next Chemos, th' obscene dread of Moabs Sons*
*From Aroer to Nebo, and the wild*
*Of Southmost Abarim; in Hesebon*
*And Horonaim, Seons Realm, beyond*
*The flowry Dale of Sibma clad with Vines,*
*And Eleale to th' Asphaltick Pool.*
*Peor his other Name, when he entic'd*
*Israel in Sittim on their march from Nile*
*To do him wanton rites, which cost them woe.*[6]

This is surely the stuff of every indexer's nightmares. But to the man who had compiled not just an index but a Complete Concordance to the Holy Bible (which, with passages such as: 'And Mizraim begat Ludim, and Anamim, and Lehabim, and Naphtuhim, and Pathrusim, and Casluhim (of whom came the Philistines) and Caphthorim, and Canaan begat Zidon his firstborn, and Heth the Jebusite also, and the Amorite, and the Girgashite, and the Hivite, and the Arkite, and the Sinite, and the Arvadite, and the Zemarite, and the Hamathite,'[7] can transcend anything Milton has to offer), *Paradise Lost* held no terrors.

References in an index to *Paradise Lost,* as in a Concordance to the Bible, are given not to page numbers, which change from one edition to another, but to Book and Line numbers (or Chapter and Verse), which remain constant in whatever format the work is printed. The same index can therefore be used in conjunction with any edition of the work, except, in the case of *Paradise Lost,* the first, in which the text had been presented in ten books rather than the later twelve. Hence the title of Cruden's *Verbal Index to Milton's Paradise Lost, Adapted to Every Edition But the First* which was published at the end of 1741 as a separate 248-page volume. Quickly recognised as exemplary, it led almost immediately to a commission for another index to *Paradise Lost*; not this time just an 'index of the words' but – an even more demanding undertaking – an 'index of the principal matters' dealt with in the poem (see plates section). This second index was to accompany a new and lavishly annotated edition of *Paradise Lost* being prepared by the Reverend Thomas Newton, soon to be made Bishop of Bristol; Newton's patron for the project was William Benson, Auditor for the Imprest and Surveyor-General of Works (in succession to Christopher Wren), who would later erect a monument to Milton in the Poets' Corner of Westminster Abbey.

It was at 'Auditor Benson's' specific request that Cruden was asked to provide the index. Newton himself seems to have been ambivalent about indexers, remarking in his Preface that 'The man who is at pains of making indexes is really to be pitied; but of their great utility there is no need to say anything, when several persons, who pass in the world for profound scholars, know little more of books than title pages and indexes, but never catch the spirit of an author, which is sure always to evaporate or die in such hands.' Whatever the intent of this swipe, Biographer Chalmers would describe Cruden's 'index to the principal matters' of *Paradise Lost* as 'an achievement second only in magnitude to the compilation of his Concordance'. The new edition of *Paradise Lost,* complete with a *Life of Milton* by Thomas Newton DD, *A Critique on Paradise Lost* by Rt Hon Joseph Addison and 'copious indexes' by this unacknowledged compiler, was published in 1749 to great critical acclaim.

It looked as if by keeping his head down and applying himself diligently to the tasks at which he excelled – compiling indexes and teaching – Cruden had managed to put his traumatic past behind him. Wightman had disappeared, Monro was forgotten, and nothing in the meagre documentation available suggests another brush with the madhouse-keepers. But things were not quite what they seemed.

'The subject [of the care of the insane],' as Dr Kathleen Jones pointed out in 1955, 'is not well documented. Private madhouses kept no records lest their defects should be discovered . . . Bethlem, the oldest and most famous of the lunatic hospitals, now has no records relating to any period before 1914. A conspiracy of silence covered the whole subject for many years.'[8] The 'conspiracy of silence' (which could probably more correctly be called a 'muddle') was broken in the years following the appointment of Bethlem's first professional archivist in 1967. Detailed records on inmates do not exist, but the hospital's Admission Registers do – and they reveal that on 17 December 1743 an 'Alexander Cruden of the parish of Enfield in the county of Middlesex'[9] was admitted to Bedlam.

There is no record of his condition at the time of his admission, nor any information as to who was responsible for having him admitted (or discharged eleven weeks later, on 3 March 1744) or why. But it must be presumed that this was indeed 'Concordance' Cruden. Maybe, in December 1743, he finally suffered the nervous breakdown that everyone supposed he had had in 1720. In December 1743 he was forty-four years old; by the age of forty-four you have become what you are going to become – and Alexander Cruden had become the man that everyone said was mad. It would hardly be surprising if the strain of living with this slur had become too much for him. But that is not the only possibility. 'Labelling someone mad,' according to Professor R.A. Houston, 'is a way of exercising power over them.'[10] And, he might have added, of rendering them powerless. Any Tom, Dick or Harry who took exception to (or who intentionally or unintentionally misinterpreted) anything that Cruden said or did had only to drop a word in the ear of the nearest constable and the lunatic would have been dragged right off back to the asylum. Cruden would have been powerless to prevent it. In the aftermath of the verdict of Lord Chief Justice Lee, no amount of arguing was going to convince anyone that Cruden was perfectly sane; and the fact that that verdict had been reached with the approval of the mighty Dr James Monro was enough to persuade any number of justices of the peace and other doctors to sign whatever certificates were necessary to have Cruden admitted. For all anyone knows, his stay in Bedlam in 1743–44 could have been just one in a string of occasions when a chance word or deed, or just a whim, gave someone somewhere an excuse to lock him up.*

Cruden himself never breathed a word about this episode; proof that although he was capable of making a very loud noise when he felt like it, he was capable of keeping silent too. And, not surprisingly, no one else mentioned it either. But then, no one ever did mention Cruden very much. Apart from when he was fighting for his reputation, or for some other cause close to his heart or his conscience, the dapper little Scotsman was inconspicuous to the point of invisibility. Luminaries of the age, like Defoe, Hogarth, Smollett, Pope, Johnson, Boswell, Fielding, Goldsmith, Gray, Gibbon, Sterne, 'formed part of an emergent culture industry, staking out self-identities as ... knowledge-mongers and opinion-makers'.[11] They spent a great deal of time making a great deal of noise about themselves and each other and dropped names like litter into their conversation or their journals or their works of art and literature. John Nichols' *Literary Anecdotes of the Eighteenth Century* runs to nine volumes of entertaining and sometimes scurrilous snippets of gossip about these and other 'men of letters'. But neither Nichols nor any other contemporary writer makes a single mention of Alexander

---

* But not in Bedlam, since his name does not appear again in the records.

Cruden; his name is not even dropped into a footnote. One can imagine him trotting unnoticed along the streets of London, intent on his Concordance or his *Verbal Index* or the text of Dr Guise's latest sermon and, like a blind man under a spotlight, oblivious to the brilliance of the 'knowledge-mongers and opinion-makers' and without the slightest desire to become part of their dazzling circle.

Almost as unobtrusively as Cruden had been living, meanwhile, his Concordance had been selling. The first printing of one thousand copies had moved only slowly, but word had gradually spread, from parsonage to manse to scholarly home, of this remarkable book that transformed the search for a reference, the preparation of a sermon or the pursuit of Biblical knowledge from a duty into a delight. Demand grew; a reprint of another thousand copies was followed by a second and then a third. A trickle of letters started reaching Cruden, from ministers of the Gospel and 'private Christians' alike, complimenting him on a work 'which must ever yield the greatest possible assistance to a Christian minister, being as necessary to him as a plane to the carpenter, or a plough to the husband-man'.[12] In one case that Cruden loved to quote, it 'taught the writer how to preach'. By the time he had completed his second index to *Paradise Lost* there was talk of a new and revised edition of his Concordance. This prospect was the ultimate tonic to his low spirits, and in the early 1750s he gave up his teaching post at Enfield and returned to London to lodge at the Golden Heart in Wild Court near Lincoln's Inn Fields.

It is impossible to discover what percentage (if any) of the proceeds from the First Edition of Cruden's Concordance reached Cruden himself. It was obviously not enough for him to live on because as soon as he was settled in Wild Court he went back to proof-correcting. By 1752 he was working on the proofs of a new edition of Spenser's *Faerie Queene* and starting to think about revisions for the Concordance. His future was looking more settled and more promising than at any time since he had presented a copy of his Concordance to Queen Caroline back in 1737. But just as then his peace of mind had been shattered by the death of Queen Caroline and the villainy of Robert Wightman, so now it was shattered by the arrival in his London lodgings of his next tormentor – his sister Isabella.

# 10

# The Hundredth Hair

The death of his father in June 1739, just before his case against 'Monro & others' had come to court, had offered Cruden the perfect opportunity to turn his back on what had been a calamitous year in London and return to Aberdeen. Had he won his case, he might well have been tempted to do just that. As his father's eldest surviving son, he had inherited the family home in the Gallowgate and, with his name cleared and his reputation established, he could have returned to his birthplace to console and support the grieving family of which he had now become the head. (Of his original ten siblings four had predeceased their father: George at the age of twenty-six, James at eighteen and William and Ann as infants. Two of the others had left home: Margaret, who had married, been widowed, married again and was now raising her four children near Stonehaven; and John, who had gone to seek his fortune as a planter in the Caribbean. The remaining four – his unmarried sisters Marjorie and Isabella and his two youngest brothers, the second William and David – were living at home with their mother.) But once Cruden had lost his case there was no longer any temptation to return; the homecoming which might have been welcomed by everyone concerned could now only be embarrassing to them all. He had therefore written to his father's lawyers saying that he would not be coming back.

Truth to tell, it was not just the reactions of his family that kept him away from Aberdeen. The city still held too many harrowing memories for him. It also still held too many Blackwells. Although the Reverend Thomas Blackwell had been dead for more than a decade, his eldest son Thomas, '*Ratio Profana*' and the *bête noire* of Cruden's student days, was very much alive, and was making almost as prestigious a name for himself in Aberdeen as had his father.

After the premature and much lamented death in 1723 of Cruden's brother George, Thomas Blackwell Junior had been appointed Professor of Greek at Marischal College in his place. Sixteen years on, Thomas Junior was still Professor of Greek at Marischal College, where 'the portly mien and dignified manner in which he stepped through the school impressed all the students with a deep sense of his professional importance'.[1] He had married a distant cousin, Barbara Black, had published a weighty tome of his own, *An Inquiry into the Life and Writings of Homer*, 1735 (which was thought to bear a suspicious resemblance to an earlier work on Homer by Lord Shaftesbury), and had become a skilful manipulator of University politics with his sights fixed on the soon-to-be-vacant position of University Principal.

There is no way of knowing whether Thomas Junior had played an active part in the conspiracy to have Cruden locked in the Tolbooth all those long years ago. Nor whether he had subsequently had any dealings with Robert Wightman. But he was the likeliest candidate for the paternity of his sister Elizabeth's incestuously conceived baby, and as the eldest son, future head of the family and professionally most distinguished, he had most to lose if Cruden had spoken out.

Certainly he would have known the whole disgraceful tale. It is easy to understand why Cruden was reluctant to give this successful and self-important man the satisfaction of seeing the victim of his family's persecution crawl shamefacedly back into Aberdeen as a legally confirmed madman. Less decent men than Cruden might have been tempted to use their knowledge of the skeleton lurking quietly in the Blackwell cupboard to balance the books, but the idea of using someone else's misfortunes to his own advantage would never have entered Cruden's head. Besides, he had no intention of betraying Elizabeth. So he had stayed away.

Alexander Blackwell, on the other hand, seems to have been anything but inhibited by the family secret. For a while after his release from Highgate Prison he had hung around Chelsea, relishing his liberty, basking in the success of Elizabeth's *Herbal* and living on its proceeds. But a man of such mercurial temperament and multifarious talents could not be idle for long. A medical student, a proof-corrector and then a printer, he now embarked on yet another new career as 'an agriculturalist specialising in the improvement of waste grounds'. It was not a very glamorous occupation for 'an indomitable adventurer', but perhaps he had been inspired by two years spent gazing at the waste grounds around Highgate Prison. Some rapid studies resulted in the publication of a treatise with the equally unglamorous title *A New Method of Improving Cold, Wet and Clayey Grounds*, which attracted the attention of James Brydges, 1st Duke of Chandos and one-time Paymaster General to the Duke of Marlborough. Chandos was currently improving his wife's family estate at Cannons in Stanmore (now Canons Park, one stop short of the northern terminus of the Jubilee Line). By the beginning of 1740 the Blackwells had moved from Chelsea to Stanmore and Alexander – or 'Dr Blackwell' as he had taken to calling himself – was advising the Duke on the layout and design of a new 480-acre park.

His employment with the Duke ended under a now-impenetrable cloud, but with a suitably silver lining. The Swedish Ambassador to London had visited Cannons, was impressed by Alexander's landscaping talents, and persuaded him to undertake a similar project in Sweden. So in 1742 Alexander parked Elizabeth in a small house near Covent Garden and sailed away, on his own, to Stockholm. There 'he was received in the kindest manner, was lodged in the house of the Prime Minister, and was allowed a pension'. After a year in Stockholm he was appointed Director of the Royal Model Farm at Ållestad in the district of Elfsborg from where he published two more treatises, *Rön om Humlegards plantering och bruk samt at fördrifva Mullvadar* ('Experiences in the laying out of Hop Gardens and how to extirpate Moles') and *Försök till Landbrukets förbättring i Sverige* ('An Essay on the improvement of Swedish Agriculture').

The Royal Model Farm did not prosper under Blackwell's directorship, and while the first of his learned works was greeted with a bemused silence, the second won ridicule from Swedish agriculturalists who suspected him of simply translating his English treatise into Swedish. Unlike his brother Thomas, Alexander was at least only plagiarising himself, but the Swedes were unimpressed. It was time for 'Doctor' Blackwell to switch careers again.

*The king of Sweden* [Frederick I] *happening to be taken dangerously ill, Blackwell was permitted to prescribe for him and had the good fortune to effect a cure. He was consequently appointed one of the King's physicians, although it does not appear that he ever took a degree in medicine. While enjoying all this good fortune, he was not forgetful of his wife, and she was on the point of sailing to join him at Stockholm when all his prospects, and life itself, were overwhelmed at one blow.*[2]

When the blow fell, Elizabeth Blackwell had been living on her own in London for five years – scant reward indeed for having worked so hard to pay off Alexander's debts. No doubt she was delighted with the improvement in her brother/husband's fortunes. But the good news was barely digested when the bad news followed. Alexander had been arrested and accused of treason.

Eighteenth century Swedish politics were just the sort of troubled waters in which a restless spirit like Alexander Blackwell could not forbear to fish. Formerly a major power in the Baltic, Sweden had suffered a humiliating defeat by a coalition of its neighbours (including Russia, Poland, Brandenburg-Prussia and Hanover) in the Great Northern War of 1700–21. At the insistence of the victorious Empress Elizabeth Petrovna of Russia, the childless Queen Ulrika Eleonora of Sweden had abdicated in favour of her husband Frederick (formerly Prince of Hesse), and the succession had then been settled on the Empress's favourite, Ulrika's nephew Adolph Frederick. With this peace settlement the authority of the Swedish monarchy all but evaporated, and for the next sixty years political power would lie with the Swedish Diet dominated by the Estate of Nobles. In 1738 the leader of the pro-French and anti-Russian 'Hat' party, Count Carl-Gustav Tessin, was elected Chairman of the Estate of Nobles. Naturally this was resented by the rival 'Cap' party,* whose foreign policy was inclined to be pro-English and whose social policy was dedicated to the reduction of noble privileges.

*Stockholm* [writes military historian T.A. Fischer] *was a dangerous place for a man of Blackwell's temper. It was*

---

* The parties were named for their respective headgear, hats for the nobles and caps for the commoners. The 'Caps' were sometimes also called the 'Night-caps'.

*ruled over by a weak king, torn by two hostile factions, the*
*Hats and the Caps, and political intrigue had undermined*
*all principles of morality. There was no slander, no bribery,*
*no crime from which the adherents of one party would*
*shrink, if the calumniation and destruction of the other*
*could thereby be promoted.*[3]

When Count Tessin (leader of the Hat party, Chairman of the
Estate of Nobles and the most ruthless of all intriguers) saw
Alexander Blackwell (to all intents and purposes an Englishman and therefore a presumed ally of the 'Caps') working his
way into the close confidence of King Frederick I, he moved
quickly to get rid of him. In March 1747 Blackwell was arrested
and accused of trying to influence the Swedish succession in
favour of the Duke of Cumberland (second son of George II).
When his trial finally came to court in May, it was held behind
closed doors. Only the verdict was made public – and Count
Tessin had made very sure there would only be one verdict.
As Elizabeth learnt to her horror in London, Alexander
Blackwell was found guilty of 'designing to alter the Swedish
constitution' and sentenced to 'be broken alive on the wheel,
and put to the death of a traitor'. Possibly because the Swedish
King Frederick I interceded on his behalf, or maybe because
the British government pleaded for clemency, the first part
of the punishment seems not to have been carried out. But
the second part stood. On 9 August 1747 'the unfortunate
Alexander Blackwell' was decapitated.

*On the scaffold he protested to the people his entire inno-*
*cence of the crimes laid to his charge, and, as the best proof*
*of what he stated, pointed out his utter want of all motive*
*for engaging in an attempt against the government. He*
*prayed with great devotion, but happening to lay his head*
*wrong upon the block, he remarked good-humouredly that,*

*as this was his first experiment, no wonder he required a little instruction.*[4]

Because the proceedings of the tribunal which had condemned Alexander Blackwell were sealed up by order of Count Tessin (and would remain locked away for nearly thirty years), all manner of rumours about the strange Scotsman who had joked at his own execution circulated round Stockholm. He had indeed been tortured, some said, hung by the hands from chains fixed to the ceiling of a subterranean cell at a height which allowed him just to touch the ground with one foot, and left there, naked and in agony, for days; he had confessed to everything, others said, admitting that he had been promised large sums of money to promote the Hanoverian succession in Sweden by arranging for Frederick I's pro-Russian successor-designate Adolph Frederick to be poisoned. There was talk, too, of an anonymous letter purporting to come from the Queen of Denmark (George II's daughter Louisa) suggesting Blackwell use his influence with King Frederick to make him adopt a more friendly attitude towards England and Denmark. The uncertainty about what had really gone on behind those closed doors, and about what Alexander Blackwell had or had not done, allowed the British government to limit its official reaction merely to recalling the British Ambassador in Sweden for a brief period of 'consultation' in London, and relations between the two countries remained on a relatively even keel. Not until Adolph Frederick's son Gustav III came to the throne of Sweden in 1771 were the papers relating to the tribunal deposited in the public archives in Stockholm, and not until nearly a century after the event were they unearthed and studied by Swedish historian Nils Arfvidsson. It is a measure of Count Tessin's talent for obfuscation that even such a diligent researcher as Arfvidsson had trouble unscrambling their contents.

*Ambition, imprudence, and a certain impetuousness of tem-per* [Arfvidsson finally decided] *caused Blackwell to be swallowed up in the vortex of party strife. More led than leading, he was finally sacrificed, less for minor political offences which he had actually committed than for his own* insouciance, *and the machiavellian designs of a person or persons whose interest imperatively required that his loose and sometimes flippant tongue should be silenced for ever. His trial proves that the unfortunate man was already doomed when arrested, and the hypocrisy of pedantically adhering to the letter of the law whilst its spirit was every-where broken makes this trial an instructive if also a very dismal page in our history.*[5]

So the black sheep of the Blackwell family was dead; Elizabeth Blackwell had lost her tempestuous companion and was now on her own. One of the sadnesses of the story of Alexander Cruden is that the only woman he ever really loved never knew the extent of his devotion. Even if she could never have reciprocated his feelings, the knowledge that someone, some-where, held her dear would surely have gladdened Elizabeth's heart; and his travails would surely have been much easier to endure had he known her heart was just a little glad.

Despite the fact that he had not seen any member of his immediate family for nearly thirty years, Cruden's own heart was far from glad when his sister Isabella landed on his door-step in Wild Court in the spring of 1753. From his later descrip-tion of her as 'conceited, light-headed and frivolous', it is clear that the siblings had little in common. Isabella, the youngest of his three surviving sisters, was still unmarried at the age of forty-four, and had been living at home in Aberdeen's Gallowgate with her sister Marjorie since the death of their mother in 1740. A bequest from her brother John, who had recently died in Jamaica, had at last allowed Isabella her independence. Now she had come to London in search of amusement, society and, if possible, a husband before it was too late.

Not surprisingly, after a lifetime of spinsterhood in Aberdeen, Isabella got a bit carried away by the excitement of living in London. No more surprisingly, Cruden found the gaddings of a middle-aged butterfly more than a little irksome in his dry and dusty world. He deplored her foolishness, her constant gossiping, her inappropriate friends; she in turn was infuriated by his sobriety and restraint. Their relationship was not improved when she responded to one of his homilies by demanding to know why she should listen to a madman. Doing his best to control his temper, Cruden decided that, as head of the family, it was his duty to find his sister a husband as quickly as possible.

Inevitably he deemed her first choice a gold-digger, and equally inevitably Isabella was reluctant to accept his alternative, a pious widower called Mr Wild. Luckily Mr Wild turned out to be prosperous as well as pious. Isabella came round to his suit, and on 27 August 1753, with a vast sigh of relief, Cruden 'acted as father' to give his sister away at her marriage. But by then she had worn his patience to breaking point, and within a couple of weeks of the wedding it snapped.

On the afternoon of 10 September 1753, while walking back along Southampton Row towards Wild Court after dining with friends, Cruden came across some soldiers fighting in the street. Fists and foul language were flying in all directions, and although he claimed that his intention had been to break up the mêlée, he suddenly found himself in the thick of it.

His intervention seems only to have exacerbated the situation; the fighting grew fiercer and the language plummeted to new depths of obscenity. Cruden snatched the shovel which was being brandished by one of the soldiers and struck out with it, accompanying each whack with an outraged exhortation, 'You must not swear.' By his own account, the middle-aged penpusher managed to hold his own with the scrapping soldiers 'for about an hour' during which time he 'gave and received several blows'. Then he dropped his weapon, flung after it a few well-chosen words on the evils of swearing in public, and walked the remaining couple of hundred yards to his lodging.

Word of the fracas followed him. When he opened the door of his room the next morning, he found it guarded by two sturdy men who had instructions not to let him leave. He spent the day alone 'praying and reading and writing', and in the evening his newly-wed sister Isabella arrived accompanied by Mrs Acott, the wife of his landlord. The ladies were shortly followed by the landlord himself, described by Cruden as 'perhaps as conceited a tailor as is between Hide-Park-Corner and Limehouse'. 'Without any directions from any body', Acott proceeded to tie Cruden up with strong ropes – a 'strange and mysterious providence' to which Cruden 'meekly submitted'. The assembled company then withdrew, to be replaced by the heavies of the night before with instructions to guard him closely.

Cruden would later discover that his sister and her allies spent the next few hours trying to persuade the proprietor of a private madhouse in Gloucester Street, one Michael Duffield, to admit him as a patient. 'Understanding that Alexander was to be the patient, Duffield said he would by no means receive him, for he had read his pamphlet written against Matthew Wright [of the Bethnal Green madhouse], and was afraid of being served in the same manner.' Although Duffield himself 'would have nothing to do with a man of Alexander's spirit and resolution', he suggested to Isabella that she try his nephew, Peter Inskip, who kept a private madhouse of his own in Chelsea. Inskip declared himself willing to take the risk.

*At five o'clock in the morning Peter Inskip, with Joseph Woodland* [one of his keepers] *came and violently seized Alexander in his bed, and clothed him with a Strait-Waistcoat, to which he made no resistance. Acott the tailor aided and abetted these* Myrmidons, *and took away his keys, watch and money, not leaving him one halfpenny in his pockets.*[6]

So once again Cruden had to submit to the indignity of being strapped into a strait-waistcoat and bundled down the stairs. As he clambered awkwardly onto the waiting coach with his arms tied tightly across his chest, Isabella told him reassuringly that he was merely being taken to 'country lodgings'. Cruden was not deceived. 'He knew too well that he was being carried to a madhouse and told her so with a directness which made her ashamed.'[7] The coach pulled away across the cobbles and after an uncomfortable journey of just over an hour Cruden was led, apparently unprotesting, into Peter Inskip's madhouse 'two doors beyond the Three Jolly Butchers in Little-Chelsea'.

It did not take him long to work out what had happened. While his chatterbox of a sister had been sharing his lodging in Wild Court, Mrs Acott had become one of her closest confidantes. Isabella had clearly told Mrs Acott that her brother had spent time in a madhouse, and when word of the brawl in Southampton Row had reached Mrs Acott, she had wasted no time in sending for Isabella. Between them, Cruden would later resignedly explain, his 'hot-headed landlady' and his 'light-headed sister' had decided that 'since he was a meek, peacable man, he would not have fought had he not been beside himself'.

There are two ways of interpreting Cruden's behaviour from this moment on. One would be to acknowledge that his confinement in a madhouse for the third – or even fourth – time, and this time on the instructions of his own sister, was the final straw; the relentless persecution had at last succeeded in pushing him over the edge and into that madness of which he had been accused since he was twenty years old; and that he would spend the rest of his days in a state of 'happy and harmless lunacy'.[8]

The other way is to recognise his confinement in a mad-house on the instructions of his own sister as a different kind of final straw. It was in effect the catalyst that liberated him from his incessant struggle to prove his sanity, that ripped off his blinkers and revealed to him the glorious truth that there was no longer any point in apologising, in struggling to con-form, in striving for approval and respect. Everyone, even his own sister, was convinced that he was mad; so from now on he could, and would, do exactly what he liked. The hundredth hair, to which he had been clinging so desperately for so long, was not worth the effort. Better simply to submit to the Will of God.

The Alexander Cruden who would eventually emerge from this catharsis would no longer be timid, unassuming or introspective; he would be generous, brave, angry and, if increasingly eccentric, also rather admirable. It didn't happen overnight, and the process would lead him into some bizarre behaviour indeed. But as Dr Johnson has one of his characters in *Rasselas* say: 'Perhaps, if we speak with rigorous exactness, no human mind is in its right state. There is no man whose imagination does not sometimes predominate over his reason, who can regulate his attention wholly by his will, and whose ideas will come and go at his command. No man will be found in whose mind airy notions do not sometimes tyrannise, and force him to hope or fear beyond the limits of sober prob-ability.'[9] For a while it seems that Cruden's imagination did 'predominate over his reason', but few could argue with his own explanation for it: 'Oppression,' he declared, quoting from Ecclesiastes 7.7, 'tends to make a wise man mad.'

Peter Inskip's madhouse in Chelsea was a marginally more civilised institution than Matthew Wright's in Bethnal Green, and by now Cruden knew what to expect. Although he was allowed to move freely round his room during the day, for the first four nights of his stay he was strapped into the strait-waistcoat, an experience which, with his new-found resolve, he endured 'in great calmness and tranquillity of spirit, being entirely resigned to Divine Providence'. It also gave him plenty of time to think. It was the Will of God that he should be here. The events that had led to his being here – his intervention in the drunken brawl and his objections to the profanities of the protagonists – must therefore also have been the Will of God. A happy thought struck him. Was God's purpose not that he resist a world that condemned him, but that he reform it? For thirty years he had been a corrector of proofs, eliminating errors, improving syntax. Could it be God's Will that he now become another kind of corrector – a corrector of morals?

There could be no doubting that the morals of the people of England were seriously in need of correction. In the late seventeenth century a whole string of 'Societies for the Reformation of Manners' had been founded in London and the provinces with just this objective in mind. The principles of these societies, according to historian Maureen Waller, 'appealed to thousands of small shopkeepers and skilled craftsmen, indignant at the loose morals of the upper classes and uneasy at the disorderly lewdness of the lower orders'. Their members were instructed to watch out for, and report back on, 'all those that shall impudently dare, in rebellion against the laws of God and man, to swear and curse, to profane the Lord's Day, or be guilty of the loathsome sin of drunkenness, also to search out the lurking holes of bawds, whores, and other filthy miscreants, in order to [procure] their conviction and punishment according to law'.[10]

Fifty years on, the Societies' only obvious achievement had been to antagonise both upper classes and lower orders alike – they had certainly had little noticeable effect on anyone's manners, or morals. Cruden had been living in and around London for nearly thirty of those years, and during that time had frequent encounters with all manner of drunks, blasphemers and 'filthy miscreants'. Yet if these encounters had bothered him, he had rarely mentioned it. He had certainly not joined any organised anti-vice campaign and, until his encounter with the soldiers in Southampton Row, his most likely reaction to any such encounter would have been to spend several hours on his knees praying for the souls of the sinners.

As he lay once again trussed like a chicken on his madhouse bed Cruden came to the conclusion that he had kept his head down for too long. His days of ignoring 'all those that dare to swear and curse, to profane the Lord's Day' and all those that were 'guilty of the sin of drunkenness; the bawds, whores, and other miscreants' were over. From now on he would actively seek out these miscreants, not with the object of 'procuring their conviction and punishment according to law', but in order to show them the error of their ways, to pray with them, to bring them closer to the Lord and thus procure their salvation. Had he followed his original calling and been ordained as a minister of the Gospel, this would all have been part and parcel of his pastoral duties. But since the machinations of the Reverend Thomas Blackwell had prevented him from following his original calling, the idea that he might somehow rediscover it was irresistible. From now on he would refer to himself – and think of himself – as 'Alexander the Corrector'.

Which is not to say he made no fuss in the madhouse. So awesome was his reputation, apparently, that Peter Inskip instructed two of his keepers to sleep in Cruden's room with him 'because he was feared to be strong'. For the same reason his strait-waistcoat was tied so tightly that he was 'tormented by the heat in this warm weather' and several times in the night 'he called out in his pain', whereupon the keepers swore at him, gave him a 'blow or two on the breast' and even put a pillow over his face to shut him up 'which might easily have smothered him'. A repeat performance the following night, including a punch in the mouth from one of the keepers which caused him to bleed all over the strait-waistcoat, led Cruden to demand of Peter Inskip that the man responsible, a boorish former ostler by the name of Richard Hare, be removed from his room and have no more to do with his care. When Inskip refused to comply with this request Cruden declared that 'he would neither eat nor drink anything but water till he was rid of the ostler'. His hunger strike lasted for four days.

*On Monday September 17th* [the third day of his fast], *the prisoner continued to drink water, and in the afternoon Inskip brought two keepers to assist him in pouring milk-porridge down his throat with a terrible iron instrument. He poured it down in such a passionate manner that the prisoner was oftner than once afraid he would have choked him, for it came out at his nose several times.*

It could have been worse. In the same statement to the 1815 Select Committee on Madhouses in which he would testify that the Bethnal Green madhouse was infested with bugs and rats, the White House apothecary would describe to the members of the committee how patients were forced to take food or medicine:

*I have known sundry instances where the mouth has been lacerated and the teeth forced out, and I have known patients suffocate. I recollect Mrs Hodges, wife of the vestry clerk at St Andrews Holborn, dying in this way. I do not suppose there is a keeper who has been in those houses for four or five years who has not had patients die under their hand in the act of forcing.*[11]

If Cruden was spared the worst kind of forcing, it was thanks to Mrs Inskip, the wife of the madhouse proprietor. There was something about Cruden – his gentleness? his piety? – to which women responded with sympathy and concern – so long, that is, as he kept his relationships with them on a strictly friendly basis. (When he started on 'love gallantry' they fled.) Mrs Inskip had taken to sitting in a corner of 'the Corrector's' room doing her stitching, had enjoyed several amiable conversations with him, and had found nothing at all in his behaviour to indicate that he was mad.

Distressed that Cruden was refusing to eat or drink anything but water, and hating to see him being force-fed, Mrs Inskip persuaded her husband 'with much difficulty' to take Hare off his case, whereupon, we learn, 'the Corrector dined very heartily on boiled mutton and plenty of turnips'. To prove just how much confidence she had in Cruden's sanity, after he had eaten his dinner Mrs Inskip asked him if he would care to push her eighteen-month-old daughter round the garden. 'He drew the child up and down the walk in her wheeled chair for a great while, till he was weary and very warm – which was evident proof that the Corrector was thought rational, for otherwise he would not have been entrusted with their darling.' Richard Hare, meanwhile, was planning his revenge.

Given the contemporary dearth of mad-doctors it was not an altogether strange coincidence that the physician attending Inskip's madhouse should be the eldest son of Cruden's former adversary Dr James Monro (who had died the previous year). Maybe because John Monro knew from his father's experience that it was not worth antagonising such a litigious patient, or maybe because he was a little less pleased with himself and a little more inclined to listen to his patients than was his father, doctor and patient found, probably to the surprise of each, that they got on very well. If the younger Monro's manner was gentler than his father's, though, his method of treating his patients was remarkably similar. After his first visit he left instructions that Cruden was to have twelve ounces of blood taken from him and then be dosed with some purging medicine.

*The prisoner was not displeased* [wrote Cruden], *for he knew that he could not get out of their clutches without taking some physick, and the sooner the better.*

On his second visit, two days after Cruden had given up his hunger strike, Monro ordered more of the same; Cruden was duly bled and the cut under his arm covered with the customary dressing. That night, when Inskip and Joseph Woodland were 'a little elevated and talking bawdy from having been at the Gun Tavern at Charing Cross', the vengeful Hare took advantage of their 'elevation' to retie Cruden's strait-waistcoat. But instead of crossing his arms over his chest and tying them behind his back, Hare stretched Cruden's arms out wide and tied them tightly to the bedposts. The dressing was thereby dislodged, the cut under his arm promptly reopened and he bled so copiously that when Inskip came to release him in the morning his shirt, his strait-waistcoat, his sheets, his pillow and half the bed were soaked in blood. 'It was only owing to the goodness of God that he had not bled to death.'

In fact this close shave worked in Cruden's favour, or, as he put it, 'God by his secret power and wisdom made it issue for his own glory and the Corrector's good.' The last thing Peter Inskip wanted was to have one of his patients die under his care, or lack of it. Hare was dismissed, the strait-waistcoat disappeared never to be seen again, and Inskip himself became a good deal more friendly in his dealings with Cruden.

John Monro was equally solicitous. He visited Cruden every few days and went out of his way to spend time with him and to try and work out what, if anything, was ailing him. Much as a nurse promises that 'this won't hurt' before delivering a painful jab with her needle, Monro assured Cruden that there was no humiliation in being locked in a madhouse. 'Do as you would be done by,' retorted Cruden *sotto voce*, clearly unconvinced. 'The Corrector was of the opinion that if the Doctor had been in Alexander's position he would know that the world generally judged it so.' Despite this small difference of opinion, on the whole Cruden thought Monro 'a very valuable gentleman, of good capacity and genteel behaviour'. His one fault was that he 'had not studied deep in divinity'. John Monro, for his part, was entertained by Cruden's account of what he called 'the battle of Southampton Row', perplexed by his description of himself as 'Alexander the Corrector' and inclined to regard his views on religion as a little eccentric. But the fact that he authorised Cruden's release from the Chelsea Madhouse after a stay of only seventeen days suggests that he found nothing the matter with him that warranted keeping him there.

His former landlady Mrs Acott refused, out of embarrassment or anxiety, to let Cruden return to his rooms in Wild Court, so Isabella had taken new lodgings at the Crown in Upper Moorfields for her brother to move into on his release. Her choice of location was either astonishingly tactless or intentionally cruel – the Crown was little more than a hundred yards from Bedlam. Cruden chose to interpret this as coincidence until a couple of days later, when the siblings having renewed their habitual bickering, Isabella told him to hold his tongue or she would send him back to the madhouse. This was too much for the new, emancipated, Cruden. He refused to say another word to Isabella, writing instead to one of her friends setting out the conditions on which brother and sister could be reconciled.

> *Out of compassion for my dear sister for whom I have a great love, none in the world being dearer to me than she is, I propose that she voluntarily submit to go to prison in Newgate for the space of forty-eight hours. I desire that she shall in every respect be well used and be attended by Mr Wild's niece . . . If she readily comply with this proposal, then love, harmony and peace will presently take place betwixt Isabella and her brother the Corrector. If this proposal be rejected, then a war at law may be expected to be declared; . . . moreover it will then be probable that Alexander shall lose a sister by discarding her for her obstinacy and impenitency.*

Cruden can scarcely have expected Isabella to accept this bizarre proposal – he was just making a point. 'It is a little comical,' he observed, 'that there should be so much trouble in getting this woman confined for forty-eight hours who by a word of her mouth confined the Corrector for seventeen days.' But he was still angry enough, and careless enough of consequence, to accuse her of wrongful imprisonment and take her to court when she turned him down.

Inevitably his second 'war at law' was as unsuccessful as his first. The defendants (Isabella, Inskip and Acott) were able to cite not only his confinement in Aberdeen but also his weeks in the madhouse in Bethnal Green as proof that they had been justified in locking him up. As before, the judge ordered the jury to find for the defendants, leaving Cruden to exclaim,

'Oh! Rare Logicians and Cloudy-headed Philosophers! If a person has been injured twice, is that a reason for injuring him a third time?'

But far from sending him into a decline, failure this time sent him trotting cheerfully back to his room at the Crown in Upper Moorfields, there to write – and publish – *An Account of the Chelsea 'academies' or private Places for the confinement of such as are supposed to be deprived of the exercise of their Reason.* With this sprightly document, far closer in style to his Bethnal Green diary than to his *Account of a Trial,* Alexander Cruden signed off his campaign to prove his sanity, acknowledging that he had failed, admitting that he was 'heartily tired with Law-Adventures' and 'committing his ways and concerns to God'. It was time to concentrate on his new calling – to become the corrector of the morals of the nation.

# 'That Which Men Call MADNESSE'*

The man in tracksuit and sandals who patrols Oxford Street
with a sandwich board urging lunchtime shoppers to become
'winners not sinners' by embracing the love of God provokes
a predictable reaction. To most of his intended audience he
is invisible. To the rest he is vaguely menacing because, surely,
he must be a little mad. Cruden, always the kindest of men,
would never have called anyone (except himself) a sinner. It
would have been too cruel. Besides, that was a judgement only
God could make. The Corrector's intention – and he would
stick to it – was merely to point out to those who uttered
profanities or who did not observe the Sabbath with sufficient
solemnity that they were breaking God's Law, and to encour-
age them to change their ways. He had a whole lifetime of
knowing that it was hard to get a hearing of any sort if you
were both invisible *and* thought to be mad. So, in the same

---

* 'To have stronger and more vehement passions for any thing, than is
ordinarily seen in others, is that which men call MADNESSE.' Thomas
Hobbes, *Leviathan*, 1651.

spirit and for the same reasons that he had sought the Royal Warrant to lend weight to his Concordance, he set off in search of official recognition to lend weight to his campaign.

He started by trying to get himself appointed the official 'Corrector of the People'. The ancient Romans, he knew from his studies in Aberdeen, had just such an office: 'Their censors or correctors of the people,' he explained, 'were reckoned prime Magistrates ... as the consuls were too much taken up about other matters to be at leisure to look near enough into the behaviour of the people, a person of good character was elected to the office of censor ... a great part of his business was to inspect and correct the Manners of the People.'

He printed up for distribution to the great and the good several dozen copies of *The Adventures of Alexander the Corrector*, which in addition to telling the tale of his visit to the Chelsea madhouse, outlined his plans for correcting the morals of the nation. Encouraged by glowing memories of his 1737 visit to St James's Palace when he had presented the first copy of his Concordance to Queen Caroline of Anspach, he turned up once again at the palace with a copy of his *Adventures* to be presented to her husband, the by now seventy-one-year-old King George II.

*April 2nd 1754. The Corrector went to St James Palace and waited on the lord-of-the-bedchamber-in-waiting, Earl Poulett. This noble lord civilly received the pamphlet from the Corrector, but told him that he never permitted any pamphlet to be presented to the King without first reading it.*

Cruden hung around the palace all day waiting for Earl Poulett to come off duty, only to be told by the Earl when he did appear that he had not had a chance to read the pamphlet and that he should 'wait until next day for his final answer'.

Far from being discouraged, Cruden celebrated the fact that the Earl had spoken to him so kindly and had 'not run away from the Corrector as others were afterwards apt to do' (although he admitted wryly that this was probably because, being 'goutish in his feet', the Earl was unable to run). After three more calls on Earl Poulett, and three more refusals on the part of the goutish Earl to commit himself over the pamphlet, Cruden decided on a different route to royal attention: 'he writ a letter to the king and, inclosing the pamphlet of the *Adventures*, delivered it to the page-of-the-back-stairs, who took care of it'.

He also sent copies of his *Adventures* to every Duke, Princess, 'Vice-countess', Bishop and Archbishop he could think of, and he visited St James's Palace every day for a fortnight ('except on the two days that are devoted to God') looking for some sign that the King had received the copy that had been smuggled up the back stairs and was at least thinking about appointing him official Corrector of the People. By joining the crowds who were permitted to assemble in one of the antechambers to watch His Majesty process to his daily levée in the audience chamber he actually saw the King every day. But the elderly monarch never so much as glanced in his direction. Once Cruden even gained access to the audience chamber itself where he watched the King confer a knighthood on one William Burnaby Esq, 'formerly captain of the *Litchfield* ship of war'. The solemn ceremony inevitably gave him another idea. A knighthood would be good. Not, perhaps, quite as good as an official 'Corrector-ship', but sufficiently impressive to serve his ends. 'Sir Alexander Cruden'. People would surely listen to 'Sir Alexander Cruden'.

*The Corrector wrote to Lord Hyndeford, lord-in-waiting this week, asking him to lay before His Majesty the reasons for his desiring the honour of Knighthood to be conferred*

*upon him. When he later called at his house, Lord Hynde-*
*ford told the Corrector that it was not his business to apply*
*for knighthoods, and that application should be made to*
*the Secretaries of State. So the Corrector wrote to Lord*
*Holderness, Secretary of State for the northern provinces*
*. . . but his lordship left word with one of his servants that*
*the Corrector was to apply to the Treasury. The Corrector*
*was at pains to go to the Treasury and one of the clerks*
*was so civil as to read the case as it had been presented to*
*Lord Holderness; his answer was that the proper method*
*was to apply to the Lord Chancellor . . .*[1]

Travelling either on foot or by boat up and down the Thames,
Cruden covered many miles every day scurrying between his
lodgings, the offices of various secretaries of state, the resi-
dences of various dignitaries and the Court of St James, where
he collared every noble whose face he recognised or whose
influence he hoped might further his cause. These elevated
persons soon became as irritated by Cruden's persistence as
he was irritated by their refusal to take him seriously. But for
once it was Cruden's patience that ran out first.

*Some nobles heard the Corrector and spoke in a kind*
*friendly manner, but some others were so uncomplaisant*
*and disobliging that they would not hear what the Corrector*
*had to say. There is also a criminal practice too much in*
*fashion, namely the giving of orders to servants to speak*
*falsely, and to say that their masters are not at home when*
*they are. He is truly noble who is truly good. Those among*
*the nobles that are debauched persons, and ruin women,*
*and indulge themselves in sensual lusts and other crimes,*
*deserve to be stript of their nominal nobility that their bad*
*example may not infect dependents or inferiors.*[2]

Thus cured of his formerly unquestioning respect for the nobility, Cruden came to the conclusion that if that was what nobles were like, he no longer wished to be admitted to their select company. He would prefer to achieve the required status among his own kind.

> *April 17th. The Corrector perceiving that he was not like to succeed in obtaining the honour of knighthood; and the election for the representatives of the City of London in parliament coming on the 30th inst., it was full time to declare his resolution to offer himself a candidate.*
>
> *April 18th. The Corrector now suspended his going to court and wrote an Appendix to his Adventures containing the motives of his being a candidate for the City of London and caused copies of it to be dispersed in the coffee-houses near the Royal Exchange.*

The Members of Parliament for the City of London were elected by the sheriffs, aldermen and liverymen of the city from among their own number. Cruden qualified as a candidate by virtue of the fact that he was still a liveryman of the Stationers' Company. The election took place at an extended ceremony in the Guildhall before a large crowd of aldermen and liverymen and started with the nomination of candidates. Cruden was understandably anxious that he would not find the necessary two liverymen prepared to nominate him. 'Two seemed to agree,' he reported, 'but when the giving up of their names was required, they flinched and declined.' After an embarrassing pause when it looked as if he would be forced to withdraw before the voting even started, the two Sheriffs of the City of London, Alderman Chitty and Alderman Blakiston, came to his rescue by 'unexpectedly resolving to put up the Corrector as candidate even without nomination'. This decision prompted 'much hollowing and clapping of hands'.

Sensing as much mockery as genuine enthusiasm for his candidacy in this noisy reaction, and realising that all the other candidates were either aldermen or knights, Cruden withdrew his name from the list before the crucial vote. But there had been no malice in the applause. The atmosphere in the hall remained good-humoured and friendly, and he consoled himself with the thought that though he might not have won the hands of many of his fellows, he had certainly won their hearts. Further consolation came from a kindly 'gentleman at law' who told Cruden that he had been 'too late in declaring himself a candidate, and that if he had been a candidate six weeks before he might have had success'. Although it was now unlikely that he would ever become 'Sir Alexander Cruden' or 'Alexander Cruden MP', but would just have to remain plain 'Alexander the Corrector', Cruden assured the gentleman at law that he was very 'chearful and contented, and not at all affected at the loss of his election'. Indeed, he added, 'the behaviour of the Sheriffs and the Aldermen is to be honourably and gratefully acknowledged, for there was a great difference between the sociable and kind behaviour of the aldermen and the sly and unkind behaviour of *some persons in the western end of town* [i.e. the Court of St James]'.

As Cruden has been accused of snobbery for describing John Davis, the Under-Keeper at Bethnal Green, as a 'ruffian' and a 'yeoman', and the former ostler Richard Hare as 'boorish' and 'an ignorant country clown', so there was a strong element of snobbery in the refusal of those members of the establishment to whom he had applied for support even to consider giving him a leg-up into their exalted world. For all its intellectual 'enlightenment', eighteenth century London society was ferociously hierarchical; it might have had 'a place for every man', but it expected every man to stay firmly in his place. A Guildhall full of 'citizens and liverymen of the City of London' was Cruden's 'place'; here he was among his social equals, his peers, men who were naturally inclined to be sympathetic towards one of their number who, mad or not, had obviously been through the mill. Those 'unkind persons in the western end of town', on the other hand, had seized on his supposed madness as a good excuse to slam the door in his face. Academics were sympathetic towards the author of the incomparable Concordance too, as were most churchmen. Confronted by Cruden at the levée at St James's Palace, one Bishop had told him he thought his Concordance the most useful book he had come across in years, before declining to support his campaign to become official Corrector.

In the early summer of 1755 Cruden decided that since he had now accumulated enough reserves to enable him to hand in his notice at the printing office, it was time to take his mission to 'correct the morals of the nation' out of the capital and onto the road. His first stop was Oxford, and here, at the university, his welcome quickly dispelled any lingering regrets he may have had about his own lack of status. Fellows and students alike greeted him with great respect. He dined twice with the librarian of the Bodleian. The Vice-Chancellor professed himself delighted to make the acquaintance of the author of *Cruden's Complete Concordance,* and invited him to attend a 'commemoration' in the Sheldonian Theatre as his guest of honour, where he 'received a respectful loud clap' when introduced to the assembled company. Maybe a knighthood wasn't necessary after all.

On hearing of Cruden's intention to 'put a stop to profane swearing and Sabbath breaking', the Vice-Chancellor wished him well, although he obviously doubted his chances of success. 'He told the Corrector that he would be a greater Conqueror than Alexander the Great if he succeeded in these things.' Nothing daunted, Cruden spent the next three weeks trudging the length and breadth of the university town, handing out leaflets and trying to get his message across to anyone who would listen.

> *Alexander behaved with great meekness on his mission, making friends with both ladies and gentlemen, and begging them so humbly not to break the Sabbath by walking* [i.e. promenading, not simply going somewhere] *on that day, that many of the young men at least abstained from walking near the University Church. The dons did not think him mad. They respected his mission, and liked him for carrying it out.*[3]

So pleased was he with the success of his month-long visit to Oxford that Cruden then moved on to Cambridge, announcing his arrival by circulating a pamphlet entitled 'Alexander the Corrector wisheth grace, mercy and peace to the inhabitants of Cambridge'. In Cambridge too he was given a warm welcome, and was invited to dine with the Fellows of Emmanuel College. It was here that he made the acquaintance of the Reverend Dr J. Nevile, writer of an oft-misquoted letter to the Reverend Dr Cox Macro, chaplain to George II. 'We have here at present,' wrote Nevile to Macro on 18 July 1755, 'a very extraordinary man, Mr Cruden, the author of a very excellent book, *The Concordance to the Bible*. The poor man (I pity him heartily) is supposed not to be quite in his right mind.' (The 'supposed to be' is invariably omitted, thereby enlisting Nevile in the ranks of those who testified to Cruden's insanity.)

After another dinner, this time at the home of Jacob Butler (described by the *DNB* as 'an old and eccentric lawyer'), one of the guests, who had obviously heard about Cruden's fruitless quest for a knighthood, devised a charade which involved 'the Corrector' being ceremoniously 'knighted' by a gaggle of giggling girls, a cruel joke to which Cruden submitted with his customary good humour. Butler, like Nevile, was of the opinion that 'the Corrector might as well attempt to make the stream run backward as to reform ye people', and, curious to see how he fared, insisted on accompanying Cruden on the following Sunday when he set out to 'correct' the numerous inhabitants of the town who broke the Sabbath by strolling in Clare Hall Walks. But Cruden seemed able to charm those he was attempting to correct. Almost everyone to whom he spoke gave him a friendly hearing, and to his great delight the crowds in Clare Hall Walks did soon disperse. Nevile, though, detected another reason for this.

> *They had not been upon ye walks long, before most of ye company dispersed, which ye Corrector observing, concluded that it must be owing to his Admonitions, but others ascribed it to a very different Cause – to an unlucky accident of a Shower which drove ye ladies and their swains away much sooner than was common.*

Cruden, of course, saw the shower as divine endorsement. According to Nevile, Jacob Butler also took him to the red-light district of Cambridge so that he might 'correct' the denizens of 'some of ye Bawdy Houses at Barnwell'. This was a great success. 'He did more service in a quarter of an hour than most of us preachers would do in a twelvemonth, for he talked to one of ye naughty Ones in so solemn a manner and with such an Air of Gravity that he brought her at last to her Tears.'

By now well into his stride, Cruden went from Cambridge to Windsor, where he was welcomed by the Provost and Headmaster of Eton College as well as by the Dean and Canons of Windsor Chapel. His attempts to persuade the crowds who strolled the terrace of Windsor Castle on Sunday evenings that they were breaking the Sabbath, however, were undermined by one of the canons who insisted on strolling along with them in his clerical gown, telling Cruden that he had no objection to 'the irreligious practice of walking on Sabbath evenings'. Sunninghill was a disappointment too: when Cruden suggested to a portly clergyman he saw playing cards at an assembly 'that it was not becoming one who had the care of souls to be so employed', the clergyman told him in a loud voice that he was 'an impudent fellow'. 'In all his peregrinations as Corrector,' Cruden would recall, 'he was never so ill-used as by this opulent and public card-player.' It seems that not all clergymen took kindly to Cruden trespassing on their patch.

By this time his peregrinations as Corrector were nearly over. After a last stop at Tunbridge Wells, he was forced by lack of funds to return to London and to work. Once again 'he rendered himself useful in every employment where the talents of a scholar and the scrupulous eye of a corrector were requisite'. During this time, according to his biographer Alexander Chalmers, 'several editions of the Greek and Roman classics were published with great accuracy under his inspection'.

In Chalmers' eyes, taking to the highways of England trying to correct the morals of the people was the maddest thing Cruden ever did. 'In such attempts,' declared Chalmers, 'consisted the whole of Mr Cruden's real or supposed lunacy.' But it was not the only 'airy notion' that forced Cruden to hope 'beyond the limits of sober probability' during this unquiet time – nor was it his only luckless campaign.

In the interval between his release from the Chelsea madhouse and his departure for Oxford, Cruden made a third, equally ill-fated, attempt to find himself a wife. From October 1753 until November 1754 'we find him solicitous of the hand of Miss Elizabeth Abney, daughter to Sir Thomas Abney of Newington'. He had never met, and indeed never would meet, Elizabeth Abney. He had seen her from a distance, knew her father by repute as a former Lord Mayor of London with 'a hearty zeal for the Protestant interest', and decided to put to the test the possibility that 'divine Providence hath predestinated this valuable and excellent Lady to be his prudent wife as a blessing from the Lord'.

Cruden's courtship of Miss Abney (who, since her father had died in 1722 at the age of eighty-two, could not have been in the first flush of youth) took the form of an endless stream of letters. 'Alexander hopes to be favoured soon with the honour and pleasure of waiting upon the precious Lady,' he wrote, 'and communicating some things not to be written with pen and ink.' And again: 'The Author of the Concordance proposes soon to have the honour and happiness of waiting on the dear lady at her own house, where he hopes that the judicious Lady will personally acquaint him with her thoughts and sentiments about this great affair.' For two months he bombarded her with letters, to none of which he received any response. On 15 December he wrote 'to assure her of her lover's resolution to visit her', and two days later arrived on her doorstep in Stoke Newington (then a village to the north of London).

*The Corrector being put into a room, sent his name by the Lady's maid, and it seems a council was called to determine this grand affair; for there appeared to be as great a consternation as if Alexander had suddenly invaded [Stoke Newington] with ten thousand men with the intention of carrying the Lady and her vassals into captivity. It may be supposed that the Lady's maid was afraid to return to the Corrector with an answer, for one of the footmen appeared with the answer that the Lady would not be spoke with. The Corrector mildly received the answer, and left his respects with the Lady, and returned home with meekness and calmness of spirits.*

He went back to his lodgings in Upper Moorfields and turned to his Bible for comfort, but his reading was interrupted by a knock at the door and the entrance of Miss Abney's steward with 'the disagreeable message not to write any more to the Lady, and returning the letters that had been sent'.

'Being ambitious to obey her orders' (besides being fully occupied by his campaign for a knighthood and a seat in Parliament), Cruden left Miss Abney alone for five months. But in May he again started writing to her, 'letters which', he was sure, 'could offend no body'. Miss Abney continued to return them unopened. One Sunday morning he waited outside the church near her home that he knew she was in the habit of attending to watch her leave, which, warned of his attendance, she did 'with the velocity of a bird upon the wing or like an arrow out of a bow'. And when she left Stoke Newington for a prolonged summer tour of the West Country, he wrote prayers on pieces of paper – 'prayer-bullets', he called them – and sent them round all the churches in Bath, Bristol and Exeter in the hope that she might hear one of them being read out at morning service.

Twice more he attempted to visit her at her home in Stoke Newington. The first time he was refused entry, but the second time he managed to charm 'Mrs Rachel the cook' into 'conducting him kindly into the parlour of the great house'. Miss Abney, who seems to have been extraordinarily patient with her admirer, once again refused to see him and once again sent her steward to ask him to leave. While showing him to the door, the steward, who was not so good-natured, accused Cruden of being more interested in the lady's fortune than the lady herself. This insulting suggestion cut him to the quick – but it did the trick.

*On November 14<sup>th</sup> 1754 the Corrector wrote to the dear Lady to remind her that there is no law in England against* *a lover waiting upon his beloved Lady. When the lover behaves in a calm and mild manner and submits to the Lady's commands, there is no injury done, nor no law violated. He told her also that he would strive to submit to the severe mortification of being denied the great personal blessing of being favoured with the dear lady.*

It would be unduly harsh to describe Cruden as a 'stalker'. He intended Miss Abney no harm, and he finally accepted his dismissal with as much dignity and grace as he could muster. When he published an account of this unhappy courtship (which he did because 'he supposes that his readers, whether ladies or gentlemen, will be pleased to enjoy some "love-adventures", and if they be a little extraordinary it is to be remembered that it is generally said the Corrector is an extraordinary man') he preserved Miss Abney's anonymity, referring to her by the 'emblematical name' of 'Mrs Whitaker', and he ended his account with an assurance to his readers that he had told the story 'in an humoursom way, for the Corrector hath always said he would have the dear Lady fairly and honourably or not at all'. But there is no getting away from the fact that he made a terrible nuisance, and a considerable fool, of himself by so persistently pressing his suit on the 'beloved lady' when it was so clearly unwelcome. If most of the sympathy is due to Miss Abney, though, a smidgen might be reserved for Cruden himself. He was fifty-six years old and unresigned to bachelorhood. Yet, longing to be married, he had no idea how to go about developing the sort of relationship with a woman that could have led to marriage. His first two 'love-adventures', with Elizabeth Blackwell and with Mrs Payne, had ended in disaster; the third, with Elizabeth Abney, had petered out in ignominy; only his new-found confidence enabled him to rise above the disappointment.

It would have been easy for Cruden, after such a long succession of failures and rebuffs, to slide gently into oblivion. He could have ended his days as a sad, disillusioned wretch, dressed in the eighteenth century equivalent of a dirty mac, wandering the streets of London searching for a friendly ear into which to pour his ramblings about knighthoods and Correctors and the Will of God. He did no such thing. When he said he was prepared to submit to the Will of God, he really meant it. If God did not intend him to succeed in his 'love-adventures', then so be it. And if it was God's Will that he should 'suffer afflictions' along the way, it was only because the Almighty was preparing His servant for better things to come. So he bided his time, correcting proofs and firing off occasional pamphlets on subjects dear to his heart, such as the pernicious influence of Jacobites (which 'trouble-makers' he blamed for everything from high taxes to British involvement in the 1702–13 War of the Spanish Succession), or the reasons for the huge earthquakes that destroyed much of Lisbon in 1755. (The 'inhabitants of Great-Britain', he warned, 'should take heed'; similar earthquakes might occur very much nearer home unless 'the loud calls from Divine Providence for a speedy and thorow reformation' were heard.) He bided his time – and God did not disappoint. In 1758 the decision, long-mooted, was finally taken to proceed with a new and extensively revised edition of Cruden's Concordance.

The Second Edition of his Concordance was the saving of Alexander Cruden. It was as if his path had suddenly been illuminated by a bright light and at last he could see where he was going. There would be no more pamphlets, no more quests for status, no more 'love-gallantry' and no more 'Adventures of Alexander the Corrector' (although he would still and always think of himself as 'the Corrector'). He had more important things to do.

> *Our author* [recalled Alexander Chalmers] *was at this time corrector of the press to the* Public Advertiser, *a paper then printed by Mr Woodfall Senior, and his fatigues were rather severe. The business of the printing office was rarely over before one o'clock in the morning, when the paper was put to press, and by six in the morning he might always be found turning over his Bible, and adding, amending and improving his Concordance with the most scrupulous attention.*

Cruden had always known that 'notwithstanding the great pains taken in the *First*, there was room for considerable improvements' to his precious Concordance, and here was his chance to make them. He changed the layout, 'filling up the lines to make the text fuller, which could not so well be done in the manuscript copy as in the printed'; he 'made the text more distinct in many places by the leading words being distinguished in *Italic characters*'; he improved the *Significations* of many words, added more detail to the '*historical accounts* of some eminent persons', and 'other things that need not be particularly mentioned'.[4] He spent two years going through every word on every page – taking time out to comply with his publisher's request that he sit for his portrait – and then, as before, he supervised the typesetting, correcting, printing and binding until he was satisfied that the end result was worthy of its subject. The portrait, Fry's original drawing of 'Alexander Cruden MA' that would later hang in Oxford's Ashmolean Museum, was engraved and printed as the frontispiece. The 1888 *DNB* describes it as giving its subject 'a very winning countenance'.

As before, Cruden had one copy specially bound for his dedicatee, this time the young King George III, who had succeeded to the throne on the death of his grandfather the previous year. On 21 December 1761 he donned a fresh cravat, his newest wig and his best coat and breeches and went to St James's Palace to present it, in person, to the King.

> *It happened by a singular coincidence* [would write the Reverend Jonas Dennis in 1820] *that [the Second Edition of] Cruden's Concordance to the Bible was published about the same time that Laurence Sterne published some works which were justly considered as having a tendency injurious to morality. Both Cruden and Sterne were presented at court on the same day. To the former* [Cruden] *the King paid the most marked attention, taking him by the hand and thanking him for the service he had done to the cause of religion. When the latter* [Sterne] *was presented, the King made so slight a bow that the disappointed author told the noble lord by whom he was presented that he was confident the king could not have distinctly heard his name. On his name being again announced, the King replied to the nobleman 'My Lord you have told me so already.'*[5]

Such eloquent proof of 'His Majesty's great regard for those who promoted the Christian religion' would have been reward enough for Cruden. To be shown such preference by such a king over so well-known (if so controversial) an author as Laurence Sterne was almost overwhelming. When the King was then 'graciously pleased to order him a hundred pounds' (a favour he signally failed to bestow on Sterne), Cruden's cup of happiness filled to overflowing. These few moments in the Audience Chamber of St James's Palace made up for all the slights and mockery, all the frustrations and disappointments, all the afflictions of what had surely been a 'sorely afflicted' life. And as if the honour of being spoken to so warmly by the King himself was not enough, the award of £100 from the royal purse (which money, this time, *was* forthcoming), when added to the £500 he had been paid by his publisher John Knapton for the Second Edition of the Concordance, meant that he was financially secure for the first time in his life.

## 12

# A Matter of Life and Death

Being an Aberdonian and a careful man, Cruden let neither his delight nor his unaccustomed wealth go to his head. His only extravagance was to move into slightly more comfortable lodgings in Ivy Lane, conveniently close to the printing office of the *Public Advertiser* in Paternoster Row.* Here he continued to spend his nights correcting proofs of the newspaper for Mr Woodfall and his days working on commissions from other publishers, including 'the last genuine edition of Hervey's *Commentary on the Bible*, in five folio volumes' which was 'printed entirely under his inspection'. The rest of his time, according to Alexander Chalmers, he spent in 'performing acts of benevolence to his fellow-creatures'.

Cruden had never lacked friends and was ever held in more affection than contempt. But the success of his Concordance, his more relaxed demeanour and, if not his celebrity, at least

---

* And just a few doors down from the Ivy Lane Club, formed twelve years previously by Dr Johnson 'with a view to enjoy literary discussion, and amuse his evening hours' (Boswell).

his wider renown, had brought him a flood of new acquaintances and admirers. It was a casual conversation with one of
these new contacts that plunged him into his most dramatic
act of benevolence.

Albert Innes was an official Prosecutor in the Court of the
Lord Mayor. One Friday evening in August 1763, when Cruden
was dining with Innes, his host told him the sad story of a
case that had come before the Lord Mayor's Court some
months before and in which he, as Prosecutor, had had to
play a most regrettable role. It concerned a nineteen-year-old
seaman by the name of Richard Potter, a native of the Isle of
Wight, who had been duped by an unscrupulous fellow seaman
into committing a capital offence.

Potter's ship the *St Janeiro*, 'a Spanish man of war taken at
*Havannah*', had foundered off Ramsgate and, although Potter
had been rescued, everything he owned in the world had gone
down with the ship. He had been provided with dry clothes
and sent to London to collect the pay that was due to him,
but no sooner had he pocketed his £3.14s.6d. than he had been
set upon in the street, hit over the head with a stick 'which
blow was so severe that the mark of it will always remain near
the crown of his head', and robbed of every penny of his
earnings. Potter, said Innes, was a stranger in London and was
easily deceived. When another seaman by the name of John
Garvin, 'a Dublin-man off the *Burford* ship of war', bought
him a 'pot of beer and a dram' and offered to pay him for
performing a small commission, Potter was only too glad of
the chance to make good at least some of his losses. Garvin
told Potter that one of his messmates on the *Burford* had
been forced to leave town and had asked Garvin to collect his
prize-money of thirty-five shillings on his behalf. If Potter
would collect the money he, Garvin, would pay him half a
guinea for his pains. Garvin then took Potter to the office in
Fenchurch Street where the prize-money was paid and told

him he would wait for him in a nearby alehouse. The outcome, as described by Cruden, was wholly predictable.

*Potter went into the office, said that his name was Andrew Maggee of the* Burford, *and made a cross for that name; but no money was received, for he was asked the name of the Captain of the* Burford *and he knew it not. Mr Dixon, the agent for the* Burford, *said that he was a rogue and he would have him hanged. Potter directly and humbly confessed that his name was Richard Potter; he trembled very much and was very sorry for what he had done; he begged forgiveness, and said he had never done any such thing before; but no ear was given to him.*[1]

A constable was sent for and Potter was dragged away to the Poultry Compter (the 'extremely dirty' jail near the Grocers' Hall where prisoners committed by the Lord Mayor were held before going for trial). Four days later he was brought before the Lord Mayor at the Mansion House. The Lord Mayor ordered him to be sent to Newgate, and he had been held in that notorious prison in irons for ten weeks until his trial at the Old Bailey in July. (The unscrupulous Garvin, needless to say, had 'made off', never to be seen again.) At the Old Bailey the prize-book containing the incriminating cross had been produced as evidence and Albert Innes had been called, as the Lord Mayor's Prosecutor, to testify that it was indeed Potter who had 'put his mark to receive Maggee's money'. Potter's defence was that he had been put up to the fraud by Garvin, that he had been 'in liquor', and that he had never actually taken possession of Maggee's money. The jury was unmoved. It had 'brought him in guilty', and he had been sentenced to death.

Although there was no denying that the boy had attempted to commit a crime, even the prosecuting Albert Innes thought that the sentence of death was too severe a punishment for one who was far from being 'an hardned old offender'. Indeed Innes was visibly distressed to have been 'the instrument of a poor ignorant creature's losing his life in a case that is deserving the greatest compassion'. It was eight weeks since the sentence had been passed, during which time Potter had been held in 'double-irons' in the cells of Newgate. Now all hope of reprieve must be abandoned. For that very morning, Innes told Cruden, the 'dead warrant' for Potter had been issued; in five days' time, on the Wednesday of the following week, Richard Potter would go to the gallows.

Shocked and saddened by this woeful tale, Cruden spent the weekend 'thoughtful and prayerful' and increasingly determined to use his endeavours 'to save this poor sailor, though unknown and unseen by me'. On the Monday morning he hurried to Albert Innes's office near Tower Hill where, willingly and at Cruden's dictation ('for neither I nor many of superior qualities can write letters so well as Mr Innes'), the Prosecutor wrote a letter to the Under-Secretary of State in the Earl of Halifax's Office, 'humbly begging that he would be pleased to lay the case of Richard Potter before the Secretary of State Lord Halifax, that he may be pleased to apply to His Majesty to turn the sentence into transportation'. Cruden tucked the letter into his pocket and set off on a frantic chase about London at a speed which is matched only by the breakneck pace of his account of it. This, significantly, and in contrast to everything he had written for years, is the very model of straightforward reportage. No more referring to himself in the third person, no more flowery excursions into irrelevance, no more 'Mr C' this or 'the Corrector' that; just urgency, clarity and determination.

*Upon receiving this letter I thought that I was now engaged about a matter of life and death, and I went with speed to the Old Swan steps and called for oars, and landed at Whitehall Stairs and went through St James's Park to the Secretary's office near St James's Palace and asked for my good and honoured friend Mr Weston, under-secretary, but I was told that he was one hundred and fifty miles off.*

Cruden had no horse or carriage of his own. He travelled about London on foot or, since the Thames served as the city's main highway, by boat. The river thronged with vessels: cargo boats and passenger boats, fishing smacks and pilot cutters, barques and jolly-boats and flat-bottomed lighters, timbers creaking, sails billowing and chains rattling as they strove to catch the tide or dodge the current or gain a favoured mooring. Darting about in this hazardous mêlée like beetles on a pond full of ducks, watermen plied the river in their diminutive single- or double-oared rowing boats, picking up and dropping passengers at the numerous 'steps' or 'stairs' along the river-bank which served as bus stops. Cruden's endeavours to help Richard Potter would bring the watermen good trade.

Fortunately the clerk at the Under-Secretary's office, Mr Larpent, recognised Cruden from having seen him present the Second Edition of his Concordance to King George III. Being anxious to help, Larpent suggested he take the letter to the Recorder.

*I left the Secretary's office and set out again for Whitehall Stairs and went down the river and landed at the Three Cranes in Queen Street and went to Guildhall to enquire where I might find the Recorder. I was directed to his chambers in the Temple, but stopped a little at my lodging in Ivy Lane to read a passage of Scripture, which mightily encouraged me to proceed; after a prayer I set out for the Temple. [The Recorder declined any assistance] which was a great discouragement, but my conscience directed me onward; therefore I went directly to Temple Stairs and took oars back to Whitehall Stairs and thence back across St James's Park to the under-secretary's office where I delivered the letter to Mr Larpent, who said it would certainly be delivered to the Earl of Halifax in person. I left the event to Providence and returned home to Ivy Lane.*

This was all before lunch. Today anyone challenged to cover as much of London in one morning on foot and by public transport would be in a state of collapse long before they got back to Ivy Lane. But Cruden was not finished. He dined at his lodging and spent the afternoon 'correcting two sheets of a work postponed in the morning'. Then he set off once more, this time to Newgate 'to inquire what sort of a man poor Potter was'. On being reassured that 'Potter was a well-behaved young man', he finally called it a day. 'I went home for the rest of the evening, and thought and prayed for the poor prisoner.'

By six o'clock next morning Cruden was on the move again, first to write a covering letter to the Earl of Halifax explaining who he was and why he was so desirous of obtaining a reprieve for Richard Potter, and then to call on Mr Roe, the chaplain at Newgate Prison, 'to hear what he would say concerning the poor prisoner'. When he presented himself at the chaplain's Newgate lodging, however, he was told that Mr Roe did not live there but a couple of miles away in the village of Islington. So it was off to Islington, where the chaplain 'spoke with great compassion of poor Potter, who he says he is a poor ignorant young man who has behaved humbly and quietly, and it would be a thousand pities not to save him'. Fortified by this testimony to his protégé's good character, Cruden headed south again to Blackfriars, then up the river to Whitehall, across the leafy meadow of St James's Park, past the dairymaids dispensing fresh milk from their tethered cows, and back to the Secretary's office near St James's Palace to give Mr Larpent his covering letter and to find out when and how he was planning to get the letters to the Earl of Halifax. Mr Larpent greeted him 'most obligingly' and approved of Cruden's covering letter. He said that Mr Innes's letter had already been delivered to the Earl and suggested that Cruden should go to George Street and give his own letter to the Earl himself.

> *I directly went to George Street and told the servants that I wanted to see my Lord Halifax upon an affair of life and death. They answered that I could not see him, for his Lordship was very busy and had the business of both Secretaries to do, the other Secretary the Earl of Egremont being dead two days before. One of the upper servants said that if I had a letter he would deliver it to his Lordship, so I gave him the letter and was desired to go into a parlour and wait.*

After so many years of being ignored or rebuffed by persons of rank, Cruden had fully expected to be shown the door. As it was he resigned himself to sitting in the parlour all day and then being told that the great one had left for an appointment elsewhere and would therefore be unable to see him. When he was politely informed, after a wait of just fifteen minutes, that the Earl was ready to receive him, he could not but reflect on how things had changed. But he was too intent on his errand of mercy to dwell on the unexpected honour.

> *The Earl of Halifax is a very pleasant looking gentleman, and he kindly said to me 'I have got Mr Innes's letter here, and also your letter, and I shall be with the King about an hour hence, and will represent the case to His Majesty'. I*

*pleaded that it was just a reprieve that was at present*
*desired, but His Lordship warned that 'when things come*
*so far, we seldom make a change.'*

Now all Cruden could do was wait. The hanging was due to
take place the following morning; time was running out. Too
anxious to concentrate on his proofs, he spent the afternoon
visiting friends and in the evening went back to Newgate to
see if any word of a reprieve had come through. 'None being
come, I was much discouraged and thought that all my labour
was lost.' After a prayerful evening and a sleepless night, he
rose again at six and as soon as he had breakfasted went to
Mr Say's counting-house opposite the prison. Here, from the
upstairs window, he would be able to see the prisoners being
loaded into the carts that would take them to the gallows at
Tyburn, and get at least a glimpse of the man he had striven
so hard to save.

*There were three put into the first cart, and two were put*
*into the second, and the report being that there was no*
*other prisoner to come, though there were six in the dead*
*warrant, I jumped down from the window and went briskly*
*through the mob to Newgate, where I heard the joyful news*
*that a reprieve had come for Potter last night after eleven*
*o'clock.*

This triumph was just the beginning. The reprieve was only
for a fortnight, and Cruden knew that if he did not manage
to have that period extended he would have done Potter no
favours at all, 'for he would then have to go twice through
the fears of death'. Before he tackled that problem, though,
he thought it proper to pay his protégé a visit. And that meant
going inside Newgate Prison itself.

Cruden's conscience was sorely troubled in the matter of places of detention. He had never forgotten his shameful behaviour in the madhouse at Bethnal Green when he had objected to remaining in the 'publick parlour' with the lunatic inmates. At his court case in Westminster Hall against 'Monro & others' he had made an impassioned plea for the reform and licensing of private madhouses, but had been too distraught, after losing the case, to press his campaign. When his sister Isabella had rented rooms for him just a stone's throw from Bedlam, the memory had come back to haunt him. But his second incarceration at Chelsea (not to mention that mysterious experience of Bedlam to which he would never even whisper a reference) had revived his horror of public places of detention; he had been unable to set voluntary foot inside one since.

Newgate was a prison, not a madhouse; but according to a 1755 Common Council report to the Corporation of London, conditions inside it were if anything worse. Newgate, said the report, was 'overcrowded with victims of public justice, under the complicated distresses of poverty, nastiness and disease'.[2] Four years previously the novelist Henry Fielding had described it as 'a seminary of vice and a sewer of nastiness';[3] and in 1767 Sir Stephen Jansen, one-time Lord Mayor of the City of London, would call the prison 'an abominable sink of beastliness and corruption'.[4] Clearly in 1763 nothing had changed. A former prisoner identified only as 'BL' described conditions in Newgate first-hand, reserving his harshest condemnation for the wing holding female prisoners waiting to be transported.

*They suffer themselves to lie far worse than swine, and, to speak the truth, the Augean Stable would bear no comparison to it, for they are almost poisoned by their own filth, and their conversation is one continued course of swearing, cursing and debauchery, insomuch as it passes*

*all description and belief. It is with no small concern that
I am obliged to observe that the women in every part of
the prison are exceedingly worse than the worst of the men,
not only in respect to nastiness and indecency of living, but
more especially as to their conversation, which to their great
shame is so profane and wicked as hell itself can be.*[5]

The similarities between prison and madhouse were far more
striking than the differences. Cruden had to force himself to
step through the gates and into the 'sewer of nastiness and
disease'. Step through he did, though, and he would take the
same step through the same gates every day for months.

Although in theory Newgate was supposed to house around
two hundred prisoners, 'the idea governing the capacity of all
prisons in those days was that they should be filled to the
uttermost corner – literally until the jailers could find no space
for further prisoners'.[6] Cruden was confronted, as he must
have known he would be, with scenes that whisked him straight
back to Aberdeen Tolbooth forty years before: a foul-smelling,
foul-mouthed mess of festering humanity, jammed into cells,
crouching in corners or milling about the dirt-strewn court-
yard, the air thick with cries and curses and harsh consumptive
coughing – sights and sounds that must have sent shivers of
icy recognition flitting down his spine.

From the depths of this 'abominable sink of beastliness'
one of the jailers produced Richard Potter for Cruden's inspection. 'A tall young man, of agreeable countenance', he was
said by the jailer to be 'one of the most harmless and peaceable
prisoners he could ever remember'. Potter was still trembling
from the shock of such a narrow brush with death but
responded willingly to his benefactor's suggestion that the first
thing they should do was pray together. Brushing aside the
young sailor's awkward efforts to thank him, Cruden gave him
some money so he could augment the meagre prison rations

of 'a penny loaf a day and water', reassured him that he would do everything in his power to get the reprieve extended, and promised to return the following day.

Once back in his lodgings he wrote an open letter to the newspapers telling the story of Potter's 'crime' and begging anyone who read it to petition for his pardon. He rushed the letter round to the printer of *Lloyd's Evening Post* for inclusion in that day's edition and in six other papers the following morning. Over the next few days he wrote prayers for Potter's salvation and delivered them to churches around the city to be read out during services. He sought out two acquaintances from the Isle of Wight and asked them to visit their 'townsman' in jail. He attended prayers in the prison chapel with Mr Roe and asked the chaplain if a way could not be found to move the chapel from its inconvenient place on the upper floor to save the prisoners 'struggling up so many stairs with their chains rattling'. And every day he spent time talking and praying with Potter, who was 'still in his cell with heavy irons on both his legs'.

Initially only concerned for Potter, Cruden soon started to notice other prisoners – 'a decent-looking woman who had been convicted some months before of stealing a coat and a pair of breeches to the value of Nineteen Shillings, who had now been delivered of a male-child and who brought the infant to the chapel to be churched', a fifteen-year-old boy who had been sentenced to be transported for seven years for 'taking a handkerchief out of a man's pocket on the Strand – value sixpence', and an older man under sentence of death 'for the robbery of a hat on Tower Hill'. Every time he went into Newgate he heard more stories of misery and injustice, and every time he returned to his lodging in Ivy Lane he went down on his knees and prayed for the souls of the wretched prisoners inside.

On 30 August, being 'deeply concerned for Richard [Potter],

as one that must be executed on the 7$^{th}$ September if his reprieve is not extended, and whose countenance is still the picture of death', Cruden wrote to Mr Larpent begging for news, and went up the river to the Secretary's office to deliver the letter in person.

> *The Clerk was so kind as to show me the Gazeteer of this day where it was said that there came an order written by the excellent Earl of Halifax to the Sheriffs 'that Richard Potter was to be reprieved during His Majesty's pleasure'. He then showed me a second order, newly arrived, wherein it was said that His Majesty orders and appoints the Sheriffs of London to transport Richard Potter to His Majesty's Colonies in America, where he is to remain for fourteen years.*

According to Alexander Chalmers, to have a death sentence commuted to transportation was almost unheard of. It was 'a thing so extremely improbable that [Cruden's efforts] would, no doubt, have been accounted the maddest act of his life, had he not by repeated applications actually succeeded'. According to Cruden, it was certainly one of the most satisfying acts of his life and, having shared his joy with Mr Larpent, he headed back to the prison to break the news to Potter, stopping briefly on the way to buy him a present. He knew that transport ships were few and far between, and that Potter would have to stay in Newgate, possibly for months, until he could be put on a ship to America, so 'I bought him *Dilworth's Spelling Book*, that the poor prisoner might learn to read.'

That same day he showed his gratitude to the Secretary of State by sending him a copy of the Second Edition of his Concordance. He inscribed it with an elegant Latin dedication dripping with superlatives:

*Nobilissimo, consultissimo, Excellentissimoque Viro, Georgio Montague Dunk, Comiti de Halifax . . . Hoc Dictionarium Christianum Scripturarum sacrarum Concordantia in signum ingentis observantiae et verae gratitudinis propter insignem benevolentiam tuam in ausculando supplicationibus meis ardentibus, et Richardum Potter a mortis poena liberando, humillime offertur . . .*
*Londini, Ivy-Lane, Idibus*
*Septembris, Anno Aerae Christianae MDCCLXIII*

Now that his main objective had been achieved, Cruden could relax. But by this time he was so involved with Newgate and its inmates that he continued to visit it as frequently as ever. As well as teaching Richard Potter to read and write, 'he taught him the principles of religion and made a convert of a poor wretch who had scarcely ever heard of a God, except when his name was taken in vain'. He gave money to Potter and to other prisoners for food and medicine and bedding, he collected cast-off clothes from his friends and distributed them amongst those in greatest need, and he read to them from the Bible, prayed with them and preached to them. He also complained to the prison authorities and anyone else who would listen about lack of hygiene, lack of fresh air, overcrowding, and the severity of the sentences. 'I am not convinced that the Christian Religion allows the taking away of life for stealing or robbing people of a small sum of money.' Inevitably, he also condemned the swearing and non-observance of the Sabbath. He was spending so much time in Newgate that he was barely able to fulfil his obligations elsewhere: 'I was straitened for time this day,' he wrote on 7 October, 'and a printer calling on me this morning, I had promised the proof-sheet for about two o'clock and was obliged to finish correcting it in the Hall of Newgate.' Even when Potter fell seriously ill, Cruden continued to visit him, at no small risk to his own health.

Lack of hygiene and gross overcrowding meant that the prison was subject to frequent outbreaks of typhus. This 'jail-fever' was so contagious that according to the 1755 Common Council report to the Corporation of London, 'the prisoners carry the scourge into the Sessions House, where it is often contracted by those about the court. On one occasion the Judges, the Recorder, the Lord Mayor and others having business in the Court to the number of over fifty, succumbed to the disease; its ravages within the jail itself are frightful'. Cruden was not convinced that Potter was suffering from typhus, but he took precautions anyway. To stave off infection, on the advice of the apothecary he held either a stick of cinnamon or some 'rapee-leaf tobacco' in his mouth during his visits,* and took snuff, 'which is a novelty to me'.

*I saw the prisoner this morning and was told that he had had a bad night, and had been in great pain, and had little or no sleep. He was in the dark dungeon of the middle ward, a very disagreeable place, and the turnkey agreed to move him to the upper hall, where there is more air and fewer prisoners. I assisted in moving his things, and he being very weak was moved with difficulty. I then went directly to the apothecary on Snow Hill and desired him to visit [Potter], but the apothecary was so frightened of the jail-distemper that he declined going.*

So Cruden bought 'tincture of *Volatile Guaiacum*' and other 'physick' from the 'timorous' apothecary and himself dosed Potter. He carried bowls of broth and mint tea into the prison and fed the invalid tiny mouthfuls with a spoon, 'but he was so very ill that he could not keep it on his stomach'. He sponged his face and changed his bedding, he said prayers for

---

* In 1665 Samuel Pepys had likewise chewed tobacco to fend off the plague.

his recovery, and then he went home and washed his own head and feet with hot water and changed his linen and all his clothes, 'for the apothecary said that the distemper had been often catched by peoples clothes'. He badgered the prison servants into mending a broken ventilator, complaining that 'it has not been working for many weeks past, which is a great omission, it being of great use to draw out the infectious air', and he complained to the City of London authorities about everything else.

> *It is to be lamented that this prison of Newgate is so unwhol-som and dangerous a place* [he wrote]. *Might not the Sheriffs find out some method of remedying this evil, at least in some measure? They give Judges and Magistrates several dinners both on Week-days and Sabbath days, who then set an indifferent example by drinking a great part of the afternoon: might not that money be better laid out in cleansing and repairing Newgate and for the benefit of the poor prisoners?*

By the time Potter had recovered enough to leave his bed, eleven other prisoners in the upper hall had fallen sick 'of the jail-distemper', and one, a twenty-five-year-old man from Enfield 'whose accusation was for stealing some clothes', had died of smallpox. In the face of his daily exposure to this noxious miasma of sickness and disease, Cruden calmly 'considered the cxxi$^{st}$ Psalm, and *trusted that the Lord would be my keeper, and preserve me both in soul and body*'. Which He did.

Buoyed by the success of having twice saved Potter's life, and confident that 'the Grace of God has touched his heart', Cruden looked for other bodies and other souls to rescue. He wrote to 'the noble Earl of Halifax' again, this time pleading for a reprieve for Thomas Madge, a prisoner 'of weak intellectual faculties' who had been sentenced to hang for stealing twenty shillings. These pleas were unsuccessful, and Cruden had to settle for accompanying Madge to Tyburn and promising that he would arrange, and pay for, a proper burial for his body. He continued to hand out books and tracts and leaflets in the prison, but he knew in his heart that as soon as his back was turned they were being sold by the prisoners and the money spent in drinking. He even, briefly, considered reviving his old ambition to be ordained as a minister of the Gospel, 'but it did not take place: it seems Providence designed otherwise'.

That he could be philosophical about his failure to effect any real improvement in conditions either in private madhouses or in prisons is a measure of just how much Cruden had mellowed. Besides, not everyone was convinced that he had completely failed. His might only have been one small voice protesting against 'the taking away of life for stealing or robbing people of a small sum of money', but when added to others saying the same, it did not go unheard. Statistics show that 'whereas in the late 1780s about 50 per cent of those convicted in capital cases in London and Middlesex were hanged, by 1808 the figure had dropped to a little over 10 per cent'.[7] Similarly, Alexander Chalmers awarded Cruden much of the credit for the fact that 'the abuses of private madhouses soon became so notorious and shameful to the character of the nation as to attract the attention of the legislature and those receptacles were at length subjected to new laws'. As for prison conditions, William Youngman would point out in 1840 that the blame for Cruden's lack of success lay not in his unconventional approach but in its being premature.

*The state of the prison at that period, and the total want of discipline which then prevailed, rendered his efforts at reformation abortive. A philanthropist of the present day has cultivated this barren waste with greater success. Uniting female tenderness with the loftiest principles of*

*Christian enthusiasm, and aided by the countenance of the*
*wise and good in the higher classes of society, Mrs* [Eliza-
beth] *Fry has been able to accomplish what was denied to*
[Alexander] *Cruden and* [John] *Howard.*\*8

Though none of his other campaigns would give him as much
satisfaction or be as dramatically successful as that to save the
life of Richard Potter, Cruden was not tempted to rest on his
laurels. Now aged sixty-five, he took ferociously against John
Wilkes, the outspoken journalist and politician who dared to
attack not just the government but the King himself in his
weekly journal the *North Briton*. Such disloyalty to the Crown
(and to the government in which his friend the Earl of Halifax
was Secretary of State) was anathema to Cruden. When in
1764 Wilkes was expelled from the House of Commons for
libels contained in issue N°. 45 of his *North Briton*, his sup-
porters chalked the number '45' on walls all over London in
protest at his expulsion; Cruden promptly mounted his own
counter-protest, carrying a wet sponge around in his pocket
and washing off the offending graffiti wherever he found it.†

He continued to 'labour for the wants of the passing day'
and to use the proceeds of those labours to help others. In
one case he funded a destitute family until their suicidal father
found work whereby he could support them. In another he
rescued 'one of those daughters of infamy who nightly prowl
through the streets of the metropolis, and who laid hold of

---

\* Prison reformer (1726–90), for whom the Howard League for Penal
Reform is named.
† At the age of twenty-two Wilkes had married the daughter of Dr Richard
Mead, patron of Elizabeth Blackwell's *Herbal* and close friend of Dr James
Monro – yet another example of how small a world was eighteenth century
London. Since Miss Mead was ten years his senior and no beauty, Wilkes
was said to have married her for her (or her father's) money. The marriage
did not last.

his arm with the familiarity of her wretched profession' by taking her on as his servant. In this station she remained with him until his death. 'Such actions,' wrote Samuel Blackburn in his preface to the Tenth Edition of Cruden's Concordance, 'shed on the memory of Alexander Cruden a glory more pure and lasting than that obtained by the conqueror of nations.'

At last, it seems, Alexander Cruden was at peace with himself and with the world. In 1769, having overseen the publication of the Third Edition of his Concordance (for which he received £300 and 'twenty copies printed on fine paper'), he decided that the time had finally come for him to return, after an absence of forty-five years, to Aberdeen.

# 13

# Much Personal Respect

On 31 May 1769 Alexander Cruden celebrated his seventieth birthday. Perhaps it was the realisation that he had reached his Biblically allotted span of 'three score years and ten' that gave him the notion to return to the place of his birth just once before he died. Perhaps he had been longing to return for years but only now felt sufficiently confident of his reputation and at peace with the world to do so. He must have realised that by now very few of the major players in the drama that had led to his leaving were still alive to remind him of its pain.

Even if there had been nothing to link them, Cruden would have heard about the dramatic death of his old schoolfellow Alexander Blackwell in Stockholm in 1747. Hangings might have been so numerous in those days as to pass almost without comment, but news of the execution for treason in a foreign capital of such a 'well-bred, accomplished gentleman' had certainly featured in the London newspapers of which Cruden was such an avid reader.

He would have known, too, that Elizabeth Blackwell, his

first and only love, had died in London in 1758. Just before Alexander's execution in 1747, Elizabeth had sold all the remaining rights to her *Curious Herbal* to London bookseller John Nourse. He had then sold them on to a German publisher, and between 1752 and 1773 a revised version, with a hundred additional plates drawn and engraved by N.F. Eisenberger, was published in five volumes by Christoph Jacob Trew of Nuremberg under the title *Herbarium Blackwellianum*.[1] The cause of Elizabeth's death is not known, and no trace of her grave remains. But it was located, at her own request, in the churchyard of Chelsea Old Church close to that of her patron Sir Hans Sloane. The latter's monument still survives in the greatly reduced graveyard, and records that Sloane, 'in the year of our lord 1753 the 92nd of his age, without the least pain of body, and with a conscious serenity of mind, ended a virtuous and beneficent life'.

The insufferable Thomas Blackwell Junior was also dead. Cruden's childhood tormentor and latterly Principal of Marischal College had apparently 'brought on a consumptive habit by great abstemiousness and died at Edinburgh on his way to London, 8th March 1757, in his 56th year'.[2] Ironically, if Thomas was indeed the father of his sister Elizabeth's baby, Christiana, he and his wife Barbara had no children. Barbara would survive her husband by more than thirty years, and when she eventually died in 1793 she left several generous bequests to Marischal College, including the funding of the University's first Chair of Chemistry. This bequest contained one stipulation of interest: 'I do hereby Name and Appoint,' reads the notice of her endowment, 'Doctor George French to be Professor of Chemistry in the Marischal College of Aberdeen during all the days of his life ... and ordain that the said Doctor George French ... be paid the sum of Fourty pound sterling yearly.'

The only surviving member of the Blackwell family of any significance to Alexander Cruden was Christiana. In 1749, at the age of twenty-eight, the Reverend Thomas Blackwell's youngest 'daughter' had married John French, a successful Aberdeen lawyer. The couple had had at least three children, two of whom had died in childhood, and John French himself had died in 1759. It was their surviving son, George, who at the stipulation of his 'aunt' Barbara Blackwell would become the first Professor of Chemistry at Marischal College in 1793. Either George French was so outstanding a chemist that he was the only possible nominee for the prestigious new post, or Barbara Blackwell was providing with extraordinary generosity for her husband's grandson.

Cruden's own family had been similarly depleted by the passing years. By 1769 all six of his brothers and two of his four sisters were deceased. Only Isabella (the now Mrs Wild who had been responsible for sending him to the Chelsea Madhouse) and Marjorie survived, the former living near Langley in Buckinghamshire, and the latter, as she had done all her life, in the Cruden family home in Aberdeen's Gallowgate.

What Marjorie thought of her brother's return after forty-five years is not known, but according to Alexander Chalmers his welcome from the city fathers was warm and appreciative; the lectures he gave in the Town Hall, 'some in Latin, some in English', were well attended, and 'the simplicity and worth of his character procured him much personal respect'. It was at one of these lectures that the ten-year-old Chalmers met the man whose life he would one day chronicle with such sympathy. Writing fifty years later, Chalmers could 'still remember with pleasure the tender regard and winning manners by which Mr Cruden endeavoured to allure children to read their Bibles and Catechisms'.

Cruden stayed in Aberdeen for a year, during which time, 'among other endeavours to reform his townsmen, he had the Fourth Commandment, "*Remember the sabbath day, to keep it holy.*" (*Exod.20.8*), printed in the form of a hand-bill and distributed it to all persons, without distinction, whom he met in the streets on Sunday. For young people he always had his pockets full of religious tracts, and some of considerable price, which he bestowed freely on such as promised to read them.' It looks to have been a happy year, perhaps the happiest Cruden had ever passed in the city of his birth, for at the end of it he summoned his lawyers and wrote his Last Will and Testament. With two exceptions – a bequest of 'ten pounds in trust to ... the Church of Christ of which the Reverend Mr John Stafford is Pastor in New Broad Street at London' and one of £30 to his sister Isabella in England – he left everything he owned to citizens and institutions of Aberdeen.

Most of his money and the house in the Gallowgate he left to his sister Marjorie, 'with this reservation or limitation that my sister Isabella Cruden or Wild may have a right to possess an apartment in the said house during her natural life'. He left small legacies to the three sons and one daughter of his only married sister the late Margaret and the only daughter of his youngest brother the late David. And he bequeathed £100 'to fund a bursary to a student in the Marischal College of Aberdeen where I was educated'. The conditions attached to this bursary were wonderfully predictable: 'The person who shall enjoy it may be thirteen years old, a native of Aberdeen or of that county or within twenty reputed miles of that town ... and a sober youth [who has] the Westminster Assembly's shorter catechism by heart, a considerable knowledge of the fundamental principles of the Christian religion and a competent knowledge of the Latin language.'*

As for the Concordance, 'All the profits and benefits ...

---

* The Cruden bursary continued to fund scholars at Marischal College well into the twentieth century. In 1934 it was merged with another; both have since expired from lack of funds.

from every future impression' were given in trust to the Town Council of Aberdeen 'to purchase the following books and give them to seriously disposed persons or families in the town or county of Aberdeen or within twenty reputed miles of that town'. There followed a lengthy list of religious titles ranging from 'Bibles bound with the Scotch Psalms' and 'the Westminster Assembly's Confession of Faith' to 'Guthrie's *Trial of a Saving Interest in Christ*', 'Allen's *Alarm to the Unconverted*' and 'Henry on *The Pleasure of Religion*'. All were 'to be well bound in good sheep leather'. Likewise he requested that 'the six copies of the Concordance I am intitled to on every impression may be well bound and given by my executors to the pious and orthodox Ministers or Preachers of the Gospel in the Synod of Aberdeen'.

These specifics were followed, towards the end of the document, by the clause which largely prompted this book. A final, lengthy, catch-all paragraph includes the breathless sentence: '. . . and I give and bequeath ten pounds to the Magistrates and Town Council of Aberdeen my executors to be laid out in coals and other things for fire for the poor families and indigent persons in Aberdeen or the suburbs and *I give and bequeath ten pounds to Christiana Blackwell daughter of the pious and great minister of the gospel Mr Thomas Blackwell late of Aberdeen or her heirs* and I give and bequeath to the Magistrates and Town Council of Aberdeen in trust my executors twenty pounds to be applied as follows' namely to purchase within a year after my decease thirty Bibles . . .'.

Once he was satisfied that his worldly goods had been suitably distributed among the near, the dear and the deserving, and once the Will had been drawn up and signed (which it was on 10 April 1770), Cruden said his final farewells to Aberdeen. 'The end of his career,' intones Alexander Chalmers, 'was now at hand.'

> *He returned to London and took lodgings in Camden Street,*
> *Islington . . . No illness or decay indicated his approaching*
> *dissolution. He had suffered from a slight attack of asthma,*
> *but retired to rest on his last evening as usual. In the*
> *morning the maid rang the bell to summon him to break-*
> *fast. No answer was returned; and she entered his bed-room,*
> *but he was not there. She proceeded to his closet, and found*
> *him dead, in the attitude of prayer, kneeling against a*
> *chair. Alexander Cruden died on November 1ˢᵗ 1770.*

Chalmers first wrote about Cruden's death less than twenty years after it happened. It is instructive to compare his version of the event with one written more than two hundred years later.

> *Unswervingly zealous to the end, he was found on his knees*
> *in the closet he had transformed into an altar, his corpse*
> *melodramatically frozen in the wholly characteristic act of*
> *praying.*[3]

In a later memoir, Chalmers would pen his regret that 'the memory of a man to whom the religious world lies under very great obligations' was already being distorted by 'traditionary misrepresentations'. The process has continued without mercy ever since.

So how much did Cruden know about Elizabeth Blackwell and her baby? Either because he was too discreet, or because he found it too painful, he had never made mention of her, Principal Blackwell or anyone else who had been involved in the unhappy episode until, at the very end of his life, he buried that revealing bequest in his Last Will and Testament. Christiana Blackwell had been three years old when Cruden had left Aberdeen; during those three years he had either been in prison or otherwise out of circulation. It is most unlikely that he ever met her. Why, then, would he leave money to her in his Will? It can only have been because he at least knew *about* her.

The last surviving member of an affluent family, widow of one successful man and mother of another, Christiana French (*née* Blackwell) can hardly have been in straitened financial circumstances. It was not a case of a benevolent old man coming to the rescue of an impoverished widow. There must have been hundreds of far more impoverished widows in Aberdeen in 1769. So why was Christiana's the only personal bequest to anyone outside Alexander Cruden's immediate family? Even if, during those last months he spent in Aberdeen, they did eventually meet, it would be too much of a coincidence for the by now venerable and serene seventy-year-old to have formed so close a relationship with the forty-eight-year-old widow as to feel inclined to remember her, above all others, in his Will.

The weight of probability, therefore, is that he did know about Elizabeth and her baby. Probably he also knew who the baby's father was. There seem to be only two possible reasons why he would mention in his Will the person who had been that baby. One is that it was a peace offering, a message to let her know that he had, at the end of his life, forgiven the family for the wrong they had done him and that he harboured no grudge against them for everything he had suffered. Or maybe, because he knew the truth would never be revealed by anyone else, there was another purpose behind the legacy in his Will to 'Christiana Blackwell, daughter of the Reverend Thomas Blackwell, minister of the gospel of Aberdeen'. Maybe – surely, even – he left it as the most discreet of all possible clues, hoping that someone, somewhere, sometime, would notice it, pursue it, and ask again whether Alexander Cruden had ever really been mad at all.

# Epilogue

On 17 November 1770 the Reverend Dr J. Watson of Hatton Garden in London wrote a letter to 'the Hon'ble George Shand Esq Lord Provost of Aberdeen'. The letter, which survives in the Aberdeen City Archives, reads as follows:

*My Lord*

*Yesterday afternoon I was favoured with yours of the 8ᵗʰ inst and also with a letter from Mrs Wild and Mrs [Mistress] Cruden of the same date. I would have returned answer last night but could not have access to the bank for inspection so that I might answer your question with that degree of precision you no doubt expect.*

*This morning I went to the bank and to Stationers' Hall and do find that the late Mr Cruden's sums of £500 and £160 stand upon the books as they are set forth in his will. Besides the above mentioned sums, I understand from Mr Maitland [?] after Mr Cruden came hither from Aberdeen he lodged £14 in their house, which remains there still. There is also a balance of about a dozen or 14 pounds in the hands of Mr Kieth [sic] the bookseller, and £5.5 in Mr Oliver's hand.*

*It seems, according to the best of my information, he had only a few shillings in his pocket, when he went from Mr Oliver's to Islington on the Monday before his death, and on the Tuesday he sent three shillings and sixpence to the Angel Inn to pay for his lodging. I have not heard of any claim upon his estate since his death, and I believe if he owed anything at the time of his death, it must be very trifling, for he used to be punctual.*

*The interment is ordered according to your Lop's [Lordship's] and the Ladies' directions to be in the burying ground belonging to my meeting, and we have fixed upon Monday next for that purpose. I intend to write to Mrs Cruden and Mrs Wild in a post or two after the funeral and if anything further concerning the affairs of our deceased friend should come to my knowledge, you may depend upon notice from*

*My Lord, your Lop's most obedient humble servant*
*J Watson.*

Adding together the various sums mentioned in this letter, and give or take the 'few shillings' he might have had in his pocket, it seems that Cruden was worth about £700 when he died – the equivalent of some £40,000 today, and a not inconsiderable sum. But it would also seem from this letter that Cruden's sisters, Isabella and Marjorie, wasted no time in writing to Dr Watson to find out whether this was really all their brother had left, or whether there might not be even more money lurking somewhere in London. These ungrateful ladies certainly disregarded their brother's request that his body should be buried in the graveyard of St Nicholas Kirk in Aberdeen 'where my pious father and his family are interred'. Instead, according to the *Dictionary of National Biography*, 'Alexander Cruden was buried in the burial-ground of a dissenting congregation [presumably Dr Watson's] in Deadman's Place, Southwark, which now [1888] appears to be included in the brewery of Messrs Barclay & Perkins.'

\*     \*     \*

Many apparently promising sources of information on Elizabeth Blackwell turned out to deal not with her but with her more famous namesake. The *other* Elizabeth Blackwell (1821–1910) was born in Bristol, emigrated to America with her family at the age of eleven and went on to become the first woman to qualify as a doctor in the United States, graduating MD from Geneva College, New York State, in 1849. An outstanding medical pioneer who, amongst other achievements, founded the New York Infirmary for Women and Children and was instrumental in setting up the Infirmary's Medical College, this Elizabeth Blackwell is commemorated in the names of several American high schools and colleges, as well as in exhibitions, awards, scholarships, etc. throughout the United States. The two women are not infrequently blended into a single person, Cruden's Elizabeth Blackwell being described in a current catalogue as the 'Scottish doctor and author'. One writer has gone even further and turned Cruden's Elizabeth Blackwell into an amalgam of three women, stating that after producing her *Herbal*, 'she went on to study obstetrics with William Smellie . . . and she became a wealthy and successful general practitioner' (*Hypatia's Heritage* by Margaret Alic). The confusion here seems to have arisen from the coincidences of there being a 'Mrs Blackwell' (first name unknown) practising as a midwife in London in the 1740s and of William Smellie also being a Scot. Known facts in the life of Cruden's Elizabeth Blackwell preclude the possibility of her being the 'Mrs Blackwell' who worked with William Smellie.

Warburton's White House in Bethnal Green was not finally closed down until 1921.

At a ceremony in Islington in 196(5?) the future Poet Laureate Sir John Betjeman unveiled a brass plaque set into the wall above the entrance to No. 45 Camden Passage. Beside a profile in relief of a distinguished, even good-looking, middle-aged man, the legend reads:

> *Alexander Cruden (1699–1770)*
> *Humanist, scholar and intellectual, born Aberdeen,*
> *educated Marischal College, came to London 1719 as*
> *tutor, appointed bookseller to Queen Caroline in 1737,*
> *compiled the Concordance to the Bible, died here in*
> *Camden Passage Nov 1ˢᵗ.*
> *'Whom neither infamy nor neglect could debase'.*

By the time of his death in 1770 Cruden's Concordance had run to three editions, all of which he had edited himself. The hundred years following his death saw the publication of thirty-two more editions. The nineteenth century saw forty-four editions; the twentieth century a further twenty editions. It has appeared in 'Complete' editions, in 'Useful', 'Popular', 'Handy', 'Portable', 'Compact', 'Students' and 'Cleartype' editions. The shortest, abridged, version runs to five hundred pages, the fullest version to over a thousand. It has been reprinted times without number, most recently in America in 1999 as part of a spectacular 'Bible of the Bimillennium'. It has never, in more than 250 years, been out of print.

# Notes

CHAPTER 1: A Singular Addiction

1 William Kennedy, *Annals of Aberdeen from the Reign of King William the Lion to the End of the Year 1818* (1818).
2 Ibid.
3 Alexander Keith, *A Thousand Years of Aberdeen* (Aberdeen, 1972).
4 Edith Olivier, *The Eccentric Life of Alexander Cruden* (London, 1934).
5 E. Malcolm, 'Women and Madness in Ireland, 1600–1850' (1991).

CHAPTER 2: The South Part of this Island

1 P.M. Handover, *Printing in England* (1960).

CHAPTER 3: Monsieur Whatever-You-Please

1 Bodleian Library, Rawlinson MSS c.793.
2 James Boswell, *The Life of Samuel Johnson* (1791).
3 Olivier, op. cit.

CHAPTER 4: Oh, for an 'Orlando'!

1 Bruce Madge, 'Elizabeth Blackwell: The Forgotten Herbalist' (2001).
2 Alexander Chalmers, *General Biographical Dictionary: Containing*

an *Historical and Critical Account of the Lives and Writings
of the Most Eminent Persons in Every Nation; Particularly the
British and Irish; From the Earliest Accounts to the Present
Time* (Aberdeen, 1812–17).

3 Roger L. Emerson, *Professors, Patronage and Politics: Aberdeen
University in the Eighteenth Century* (1992).

4 Andrew Blaikie, *Illegitimacy, Sex and Society: North-East
Scotland 1750–1900* (Oxford, 1993).


CHAPTER 5: No Ordinary Queen

1 G.M. Trevelyan, *England Under Queen Anne* (London, 1945).

2 Laurence Worms, 'The Book Trade at the Royal Exchange', in
Ann Saunders (ed.), *The Royal Exchange* (London
Topographical Society publication no.152, 1997).

3 BL MSS Sloane 4056 f.341.

4 Chalmers, op. cit.

5 Wilfrid Blunt and William T. Stearn, *The Art of Botanical
Illlustration* (London, 1950).

6 Liza Picard, *Dr Johnson's London: Life in London 1740–1770*
(London, 2000).

7 Chalmers, op. cit.

8 Ibid.

9 Ian Norrie (ed.), *Publishing and Bookselling: A History from the
Earliest Times to the Present Day* (after Frank Mumby),
(London, 1982).


CHAPTER 6: Receptacles of Misery

1 R.A. Houston, *Madness and Society in Eighteenth Century
Scotland* (Oxford University Press, 2000).

2 12 Anne, c.23.

3 Andrew Scull, *Museums of Madness* (1979).

4 Ibid.

5 Roy Porter, *Mind Forg'd Manacles: A History of Madness in
England from the Restoration to the Regency* (London, 1987).

6 William Pargeter, *Observations on Maniacal Disorders* (1792).

7 Andrew Scull, Charlotte Mackenzie and Nicholas Hervey,
    *Masters of Bedlam: The Transformation of the Mad-Doctoring
    Trade* (Princeton, 1996).
8 William Cullen, *First Lines of the Practice of Physic* (1796).
9 Scull, Mackenzie and Hervey, op. cit.
10 Jonathan Andrews and Andrew Scull, *Undertaker of the Mind:
    John Monro and Mad-Doctoring in Eighteenth Century
    England* (Berkeley, 2001).
11 John Mitford, *A Description of the Crimes and Horrors in the
    Interior of Warburton's Private Madhouses* (London, 1825).


CHAPTER 7: A Hundred Hairs to Hang by

1 *The Gentleman's Magazine*, no. 33 (1763), pp.25–6.
2 John Wesley, *Journal*, 1777; quoted in B. Weinreb and
    C. Hibbert (eds), *The London Encyclopaedia* (1983).
3 Bethnal Green parish records.
4 Picard, op. cit.


CHAPTER 8: *Coup de Grâce*

1 Quoted in Madge, op. cit.
2 James Bruce, *Lives of Eminent Men of Aberdeen* (Aberdeen, 1841).
3 Chalmers, op. cit.
4 Blanche Henrey, *British Botanical and Horticultural Literature
    Before 1800* (London, 1975).
5 Quoted in Andrews and Scull, op. cit.
6 Quoted in Madge, op. cit.
7 James Coutts, *A History of the University of Glasgow from its
    Foundation in 1451 to 1909* (Glasgow, 1909).
8 Quoted in Porter, op. cit.


CHAPTER 9: Too Much Religion

1 Andrews and Scull, op. cit.
2 *Concise Dictionary of National Biography.*
3 Quoted in Porter, op. cit.

4 Andrews and Scull, op. cit.

5 BL MSS Sloane 4056 f.341.

6 John Milton, *Paradise Lost*, I, 399–414.

7 1 Chronicles 1, 11–16.

8 Kathleen Jones, *Lunacy, Law and Conscience 1744–1845: The Social History of the Care of the Insane* (London, 1955).

9 Bethlem Royal Hospital Archives.

10 Houston, op. cit.

11 Roy Porter, *Enlightenment: Britain and the Creation of the Modern World* (London, 2000).

12 Preterist Archive.

CHAPTER 10: The Hundredth Hair

1 Chalmers, op. cit.

2 Ibid.

3 T.A. Fischer, *The Scots in Sweden* (Edinburgh, 1907).

4 Chalmers, op. cit.

5 Nils Arfvidsson, essay entitled 'Blackwellska Rättegången' in the periodical *Frey* (1846, quoted in Fischer, op. cit.).

6 Alexander Cruden, *The Adventures of Alexander the Corrector* (1754).

7 Olivier, op. cit.

8 William Youngman.

9 The philosopher Imlac in *Rasselas* (1759).

10 Maureen Waller, *1700: Scenes from London Life* (London, 2000).

11 Quoted in Jones, op. cit.

CHAPTER 11: 'That which Men call MADNESSE'

1 *The Adventures of Alexander the Corrector*, Part III.

2 Ibid.

3 Olivier, op. cit.

4 Preface to the Second Edition of Cruden's Concordance.

5 Reverend Jonas Dennis, *A Key to the Regalia* (1820).

CHAPTER 12: A Matter of Life and Death

1 Alexander Cruden, *The History of Richard Potter* (1763).
2 W. Eden Hooper, *History of Newgate and the Old Bailey* (London, 1935).
3 Henry Fielding, *An Inquiry into the Causes of the Late increase of Robbers . . .* (1751).
4 Hooper, op. cit.
5 Quoted in ibid.
6 Michael Ignatieff, *A Just Measure of Pain: The Penitentiary in the Industrial Revolution 1750–1850* (London, 1978).
7 Ibid.
8 'Memoir of Alexander Cruden', Preface to Eleventh Edition of Cruden's Concordance.


CHAPTER 13: Much Personal Respect

1 Madge, op. cit.
2 Selections from the records of Marischal College in P.J. Anderson, *Fasti Academiae Mariscallanae Aberdonensis* (1889).
3 Andrews and Scull, op. cit.

# Bibliography

Anderson, Peter J. (ed.), *Fasti Academiae Mariscallanae Aberdonensis*, Aberdeen 1889

Andrews, Jonathan (and Briggs, Porter, Tucker and Waddington), *The History of Bethlem*, London 1997

Andrews, Jonathan and Scull, Andrew, *Undertaker of the Mind: John Monro and Mad-Doctoring in Eighteenth Century England*, University of California Press 2001

*The Bath Journal*, 14 September 1747

Battie, William, *A Treatise on Madness and John Monro's Remarks on Dr Battie's Treatise* (reprint of 1758 edn), London 1961

*Biographia Britannica*, London 1789

Blackmore, Richard, *A Treatise of the Spleen and Vapours*, London 1725

Blaikie, A., *Illegitimacy, Sex and Society: North-East Scotland 1750–1900*, Oxford 1993

Blunt, Wilfrid and Stearn, William T., *The Art of Botanical Illustration*, London 1950

Bobrick, Benson, *The Making of the English Bible*, London 2001

Boswell, James, *The Life of Samuel Johnson*, 1791 (Penguin reprint 1986)

Bristow, Edward J., *Vice and Vigilance: Purity Movements in Britain since 1700*, Dublin 1977

Brown, P. Hume, *Early Travellers in Scotland*, Edinburgh 1891 (facsimile reprint Edinburgh 1978)

Browne, W.A.F., *What Asylums Were, Are, and Ought to Be*, Edinburgh 1837

Bruce, James, *Lives of Eminent Men of Aberdeen*, Aberdeen 1832, 1841

Bruckshaw, S., *One More Proof of the Iniquitous Abuse of Private Madhouses*, London 1774

Chalmers, Alexander, *General Biographical Dictionary* (32 vols), Aberdeen 1812–17

Chambers, Robert, *A Biographical Dictionary of Eminent Scotsmen*, Glasgow 1835

Conolly, John, *An Inquiry Concerning the Indications of Insanity*, London 1830

Coutts, James, *A History of the University of Glasgow from its Foundation in 1451 to 1909*, Glasgow 1909

Cruden, Alexander, *The London Citizen Exceedingly Injured*, London 1739

Cruden, Alexander, *An Account of a Trial*, London 1739

Cruden, Alexander, *The Adventures of Alexander the Corrector*, London 1754

Cruden, Alexander, *The History of Richard Potter*, London 1763

Cullen, William, *First Lines of the Practice of Physic* (4 vols), Edinburgh 1796

Defoe, Daniel, *A Review of the State of the English Nation*, London 1710

Defoe, Daniel, *Augusta Triumphans*, London 1728

Dennis, Jonas, *A Key to the Regalia*, London 1820

Dennison, E.P., Ditchburn, D. and Lynch, M. (eds), *Aberdeen Before 1800*, Tuckwell Press and Aberdeen City Council, Aberdeen 2002

Emerson, Roger L., *Professors, Patronage and Politics: Aberdeen University in the Eighteenth Century*, Aberdeen University Press 1992

Fischer, T.A., *The Scots in Sweden*, Edinburgh 1907

Foucault, M., *Madness and Civilisation: A History of Insanity in the Age of Reason*, London 1967

*Gentleman's Magazine*, September 1747, pp.424–6

# Bibliography

*Gentleman's Magazine*, 33, 1763, pp.25–6, 'A Case Humbly Offered to the Consideration of Parliament'

George, M.D., *London Life in the Eighteenth Century*, London 1952

Gordon, S. and Cocks, T.B., *A People's Conscience*, London 1952

Hallett, Mark, *Hogarth*, London 2000

Handover, P.M., *Printing in England*, London 1960

Henrey, Blanche, *British Botanical and Horticultural Literature Before 1800*, London 1975

Hooper, W. Eden, *History of Newgate and the Old Bailey*, London 1935

Houston, R.A., *Social Change in the Age of Enlightenment, Edinburgh 1660–1760*, Oxford 1994

Houston, R.A., *Madness and Society in Eighteenth Century Scotland*, Oxford 2000

Howard, John, *State of the Prisons*, London 1777

Howe, Ellic (ed.), *The London Compositor*, London 1947

Hunter, R. and MacAlpine, I. (eds), *Three Hundred Years of Psychiatry 1535–1860*, London 1963

Ignatieff, Michael, *A Just Measure of Pain: The Penitentiary in the Industrial Revolution 1750–1850*, London 1978

Ingram, Allan (ed.), *Patterns of Madness in the Eighteenth Century*, Liverpool 1998

Jones, Kathleen, *Lunacy, Law and Conscience 1744–1845: The Social History of the Care of the Insane*, London 1955

Keith, Alexander, *A Thousand Years of Aberdeen*, Aberdeen 1972

Kennedy, William, *Annals of Aberdeen from the reign of King William the Lion to the end of the year 1818* (2 vols), London 1818

'The Lucubrations of Alexander the Corrector', *Northern Gazette* (No.26), Aberdeen 1787

MacDonald, Michael, *Mystical Bedlam: Madness, Anxiety and Healing in Seventeenth Century England*, Cambridge 1981

Madge, Bruce, 'Elizabeth Blackwell: The Forgotten Herbalist?', *Health Libraries Review* 18, pp.144–52, 2001

Malcolm, E., 'Women and Madness in Ireland 1600–1850', in MacCurtain, M. and O'Dowd, M. (eds), *Women in Early Modern Ireland*, Edinburgh 1991

Marshall, Emma, *The Story of John Marbeck*, London 1887

Masters, A., *Bedlam*, London 1972

Mitford, John, *A Description of the Crimes and Horrors in the Interior of Warburton's Private Madhouses etc.* Parts 1 and 2, London 1825

Munro, Alex M. (ill. G. Gordon Burr), *Old Landmarks of Aberdeen*, Aberdeen 1886

Nichols, John, *Literary Anecdotes of the Eighteenth Century* (9 vols), London 1812–16

Nicol, Rev. Anderson, *St Nicholas Parish Church, Aberdeen*, Aberdeen 1980

Norrie, Ian (ed.), *Publishing and Bookselling: A History from the Earliest Times to the Present Day* (after Frank Mumby), London 1982

Olivier, Edith, *The Eccentric Life of Alexander Cruden*, London 1934

Orem, William, *Old Aberdeen*, Aberdeen 1750

Pargeter, W., *Observations on Maniacal Disorders*, Reading 1792

Parry-Jones, W.L., *The Trade in Lunacy*, London 1971

Paternoster, R., *The Madhouse System*, London 1841

Paterson, Dale, *The Literature of Madness*, PhD thesis, Stanford University Press 1977

Paterson, Dale, *A Mad People's History of Madness*, University of Pittsburgh Press 1982

Payton, John, *From Camden Passage with Love*, Lewes 1992

Perceval, J.T., *A Narrative of the Treatment Received by a Gentleman during a state of Mental Derangement*, London 1838

Picard, Liza, *Dr Johnson's London: Life in London 1740–1770*, London 2000

Piggott, S., *William Stukeley*, Oxford 1950

Plomer, H., *Biographical Dictionary of Booksellers (1726–75)*, London 1850

Porter, Roy, *Mind Forg'd Manacles: A History of Madness in England from the Restoration to the Regency*, London 1987

Porter, Roy, *A Social History of Madness*, London 1987, 1996

Porter, Roy, *Enlightenment: Britain and the Creation of the Modern World*, London 2000

# Bibliography

Reed, Talbot, *A History of the Old English Letter Foundries* (revised and enlarged by A.F. Johnson), London 1952

*The Retrospective Review*, Vol. X, p.20, 1824

Risse, Guenter B., *Hospital Life in Enlightenment Scotland*, Cambridge 1986

Robbie, William, *Aberdeen, its Traditions and History* (3 vols), Aberdeen 1893

Rogers, J.W., *A Statement of the Cruelties and Frauds which are practised in Mad-houses*, London 1816

Saunders, Ann (ed.), *The Royal Exchange*, London Topographical Society pub. no.152, 1997

'Scoto-Britannicus', *The Scottish Biographical Dictionary*, Edinburgh 1822

Scott, Hew, *Fasti Ecclesiae Scoticanae*, Edinburgh 1915–50

*Scottish Notes and Queries* (first series), Aberdeen 1890

Scull, Andrew, *Museums of Madness*, London 1979

Scull, Andrew, *The Most Solitary of Afflictions: Madness and Society in Britain 1700–1900*, Yale University Press 1993

Scull, Andrew (with C. Mackenzie and N. Hervey), *Masters of Bedlam: The Transformation of the Mad-Doctoring Trade*, Princeton University Press 1996

Smollett, Tobias, *The Adventures of Sir Launcelot Greaves*, London 1762 (1925)

Stark, John, *Biographia Scotica*, Edinburgh 1805

Tomalin, Claire, *Samuel Pepys: An Unequalled Self*, London 2002

Trevelyan, G.M., *England Under Queen Anne*, London 1945

Waller, Maureen, *1700: Scenes from London Life*, London 2000

Whytt, Robert, *Observations on the nature, causes and cures of the disorders which have been called nervous, hypochondriac or hysterical*, Edinburgh 1765

Wyness, F.A., 'A Curious Herbal – the Unusual and Romantic Story of Elizabeth Blackwell', *Scotsman*, 11 November 1961

# Index

Aberdeen 1–2, 8–10, 14, 19, 27, 53, 58, 71, 161, 173, 182, 236

Aberdeen Grammar School 3, 4, 6, 8, 12, 25

Aberdeen Tolbooth 3, 14, 17, 18, 19, 21, 24, 28, 41, 54, 66, 69, 89, 95, 228

Aberdeen Town Council 2, 8, 10, 11, 241

Abney, Elizabeth 211–14

Abney, Sir Thomas 211, 212

*Account of the Chelsea Academies, An* (Cruden) 201

*Account of a Trial, An* (Cruden) 170, 171, 201

Acott, Mr 191

Acott, Mrs 191, 192, 199

Act for Regulating Private Madhouses (1774) 100

Adams, Dr 48

Addison, Rt Hon Joseph 177

Adolph Frederick, King of Sweden 186, 188

*Adventures of Alexander the Corrector, The* (Cruden) 203, 204, 215

*Adventures of Sir Launcelot*

*Greaves, The* (Smollett) 103–4, 108, 117

Aldgate, London 95, 134, 136

Alexander VI, Pope 5

*Anatomy of Melancholy, The* (Burton) 18, 96, 106

Andrews, Jonathan 114

Anne, Queen 9, 39

Apothecaries, Society of 79, 146

Arfvidsson, Nils 188–9

Ball, Mr 38, 46

Barnard, Sir John, Lord Mayor of London 137–9, 141–2

Bedlam *see* Bethlehem Royal Hospital

Benson, William, Auditor for the Imprest 177

Bethlehem Royal Hospital, London 97, 104–5, 113–14, 123, 128, 167, 171, 178, 179, 199, 227

Bethnal Green, London 95, 101, 105, 109, 116, 121, 132, 134, 142, 151, 159, 200

Betjeman, John 247

Bettesworth, A. 84

Bible 4, 7, 8, 13, 20, 29, 30, 31, 34, 80, 86, 176
Bible & Anchor, London 74
*Biographia Britannica* 15, 173
Blachrie, Elizabeth 60, 61, 62
Blachrie, William 60
Blackburn, Reverend Samuel xvii, 236
Blackmore, Sir Richard 107
Blackwell, Alexander 25, 26, 56–63, 67, 70–2, 77, 81, 144–6, 148, 163, 184–9, 237
Blackwell, Barbara (*née* Black) 183, 238, 239
Blackwell, Charles, 63
Blackwell, Christian (*née* Johnston) 12, 57, 62, 147
Blackwell, Christiana 55, 56, 57, 66, 238–9, 241, 242–3
Blackwell, Dr Elizabeth 247
Blackwell, Elizabeth 56–63, 65, 66, 67, 69, 70–2, 77, 78–81, 84, 144–8, 161, 163, 183, 186, 187, 189, 214, 237–8, 242, 247
Blackwell, George 63
Blackwell, Reverend Thomas 11, 14, 22, 25, 55, 56, 57, 60, 64–5, 66–9, 163, 183, 195, 241, 242
Blackwell, Thomas, the younger 14, 56, 62, 63–4, 68, 183, 185, 238
Blackwell, William and Blanche Christian 77
Blaide's Boarding School, Enfield 174
Blakiston, Alderman 206
'Blind Bench' 122, 124
Blunt, Wilfrid 148

Bodleian Library, Oxford 41, 208
Boswell, James 48, 179
Boulanger, Mme 42
Bourignon, Antoinette 13fn
Bruce, James 58, 59, 60, 70, 77, 78, 145
Brydges, James, 1st Duke of Chandos 184
Bull, Frederick 129, 140, 141
Bull, Kelsey 129, 140
*Burford* (ship)220–1
Burnaby, William 204
Burton, Robert 18, 96
Butler, Jacob 209, 210
Byron, George [Lord] 4

Calamy, Reverend Dr Edmund 22, 26, 69
Calvinists 2, 7, 168
Cambridge 209
Camden Passage, London 247
Cannons, Stanmore 184–5
Caroline of Anspach, Queen 75, 85, 87–8, 95, 181, 203
Chalmers, Alexander 15, 16, 18, 20, 31, 33, 34, 52, 53, 54, 59–60, 62, 63, 69, 71, 78, 81, 173, 177, 211, 216, 219, 230, 234, 239, 241–2
Chalmers, James 15, 52, 53
Charles VI, Holy Roman Emperor 75
Chelsea Old Church, London 238
Chelsea Physic Garden, London 79, 80, 146
Chesterfield, Earl of 48
Chitty, Alderman 206

Clarke, J. 84
Clay, F. 84
Clayton, Mr 37, 38–9, 45, 46, 168
Coltman, Henry 22, 23, 148, 156
Coltman, 'Madam' 24, 144, 148, 165, 175
Coltman Junior 22, 23, 24, 38, 148, 156
*Commentary on the Bible* (Hervey) 219
Common Council report to the Corporation of London (1755) 227, 232
Comyns, Lord 143
Connolly, John 49
Cook, T. 173, 174
Court of Common Pleas, London 152–3, 159, 164
Court of King's Bench, London 99, 152, 154
Covent Garden, London 185
Crookshank, William 90, 158
Cruden, Alexander: birth, 2; education, 3–8, 11, 13, 14; falls in love, 14, 15, 16; in Tolbooth, 14, 17, 19; leaves Aberdeen, 21; as tutor, 22–5; returns to London, 25, 26; works on Concordance, 28, 47–9, 80–4; as French Reader, 35–42; meets Elizabeth Blackwell, 53–4; Bookseller to Queen Caroline, 77; First Edition of Concordance published, 85; woos Mrs Payne, 88–91; abducted by Wightman, 94; in Bethnal Green madhouse,

101–32; escapes, 132; loses court case, 163; indexes *Paradise Lost*, 175–7; Battle of Southampton Row, 190–1; in Chelsea madhouse, 192–9; 'the Corrector', 195, 201–4, 208–11; campaign to become knight, 204–5; campaign to become MP, 206; courtship of Elizabeth Abney, 211–14; campaign to save Richard Potter, 220–33; in Newgate Prison 226–34; returns to Aberdeen, 237; death, 242
Cruden, Sergeant-Major Alexander 110, 116, 124, 128, 129, 139, 144, 148, 156, 162, 165
Cruden, Ann 182
Cruden, David 182, 240
Cruden, George 3, 5, 8, 11, 12, 66–7, 69, 182
Cruden, Isabella 181, 182, 189, 190, 191, 192, 199, 200, 227, 239, 240, 246
Cruden, Isobel (*née* Pyper) 2, 11, 189
Cruden, James 182
Cruden, John 182, 189
Cruden, Margaret 182, 240
Cruden, Marjorie 182, 189, 239, 240, 246
Cruden, Baillie William 2, 8, 10, 11, 12, 14, 159–60, 161
Cruden, William 57, 182
Cruden Bursary 240
Cruden's Concordance 14, 16, 29–34, 40, 41, 47–9, 50, 69, 80, 81–4, 141, 156, 180, 208, 240–1, 248; Second Edition

Cruden's Concordance – *cont.*
50, 173, 215–18, 223, 230, 248;
Third Edition 236; Eighth
Edition 52; Tenth Edition
236
Cullen, William 57, 107
*Curious Herbal, A* (Blackwell)
62, 78–81, 84, 85, 144–7, 184,
235fn, 238

Davidson, J. 84
Davis, John 95, 101, 102, 108,
110, 111, 112, 116, 122–3, 125,
126, 128, 129, 135, 136, 149, 155,
162, 165, 207
*Decline and Fall of the Roman
Empire, The* (Gibbon) 82–3
Defoe, Daniel 2, 99, 119, 179
Dennis, Reverend Jonas 217
Derby, Lord *see* Stanley, James,
10th Earl of Derby
*Dictionary of National
Biography* 56–7, 58, 216, 136
*Dictionary of the English
Language* (Johnson) 29,
47–9, 84, 146
Duffield, Michael 191
Dunton, John 73

*Eccentric Life of Alexander
Cruden, The* (Olivier) 174
Edinburgh College of
Physicians 107
Edwards, W.C. 173
Egremont, Earl of 225
Eisenberger, N.F. 238
Elizabeth Petrovna, Empress of
Russia 186
Elphinstone, Bishop William 5

Emmanuel College, Cambridge
209
Enfield 174, 175, 180
English Civil War (1642–48) 168
Episcopalians 9, 175
Eton College 210

*Faerie Queene, The* (Spenser)
180
Fallowes, Thomas 101
*Fasti Academiae Mariscallanae
Aberdonensis* (ed.
Anderson)63
Fielding, Henry 179, 227
Fischer, T.A. 186
Fletcher, Thomas 156
Ford, R. 84
Fordyce family 61
Franck, Richard 1
Frederick I, King of Sweden
185, 186, 187, 188
Frederick, Mr 37, 38, 41, 42, 45
French, George 238, 239
French, John 239
Fry, Elizabeth 235
Fry, T. 173, 174, 216

Garvin, John 220, 221
*General Biographical Dictionary*
(Chalmers) 59
*Gentleman's Magazine* 25,
125–6, 171
George I, King 2, 11
George II, King 75, 170, 187,
188, 203, 204, 209
George III, King 216, 223
Gibbon, Edward 82–3
Glasgow 5, 12, 147
Glasgow University 62, 147

Grant, Mr 92–3, 94, 137–8
Grant, Mrs 91, 92–3, 94
Great Northern War (1700–21)
     186
Great St Helen's Church,
     London 35, 42
Grocers' Hall, London 136,
     141–2, 221
Guildhall, London 206, 207
Guildhall Sheriff's Court,
     London 152
Guise, Reverend Dr 35, 42, 88,
     122–3
Gustav III, King of Sweden 188

Halifax, 2nd Earl of, Secretary
     of State 222, 224, 225–6, 230,
     233, 235
Halnaker, Sussex 35, 37–9,
     40–1, 49
Handover, P.M. 82
Hare, Richard 196, 197, 198, 199,
     207
*Herbarium Blackwellianum*
     (Blackwell) 238
Hett, R. 84
Highgate Prison, London 72,
     77, 80, 145–6, 184
Hitch, Charles 84
Hogarth, William 27, 73, 178
Holderness, Lord 205
House of Commons Enquiry
     (1763) 100
House of Commons Select
     Committee on Madhouses
     (1815) 113, 196
Houston, Professor R.A. 18,
     178
Howard, John 235

Huguenot refugees 42
Hyndeford, Lord 204–5

illegitimacy 64–6
incest 64, 65
Innes, Albert 220, 221, 222, 225
Innes, Dr Robert 143, 155
insanity 96–8, 106
Inskip, Mrs 197
Inskip, Peter 191, 194, 196, 198,
     199
Irish, David 101
Isle of Man 24
Isle of Wight 220, 229
Islington, London 224, 242, 247
Ivy Lane, London 219, 223, 224,
     229

Jacobites 9, 10, 215; Rising (1715)
     9, 10, 12
James IV, King 5
James VI & I, King 8
Jansen, Sir Stephen 227
Jenkin, Henry 152, 155
Jerome, Saint 33
Johnson, Dr Samuel 47, 48, 52,
     84, 179, 193, 219fn
Johnston, Christian *see*
     Blackwell, Christian
Johnston, Professor John 62,
     147
Jones, Dr Kathleen 178

Keith, Alexander 9
Keith, George, 5th Earl
     Marischal 6
Keith, George, 10th Earl
     Marischal 9, 10, 11
Kennedy, William 64

King's College, Aberdeen 5, 6
Knapton, John 84, 218
Knapton, P. 84
Knowsley, nr Liverpool 39, 40, 42, 44–5

Larpent, Mr 223, 224, 225, 230
Lee, Nathaniel 171
Lee, Lord Chief Justice Sir William 152–4, 157, 158, 160, 162–3, 164–7, 169, 179
Leiden, Holland 26, 71
Leigh, Thomas 167
Lisbon earthquake (1755) 215
*Literary Anecdotes of the Eighteenth Century* (Nichols) 72, 179
Little Britain, London 26, 35, 47, 52
Liverpool 45–6
*Lives of Eminent Men of Aberdeen* (Bruce) 58, 60, 70, 145
*Lloyd's Evening Post* 229
London, Job 104, 107, 112, 115, 137
*London Citizen Exceedingly Injured, The* (Cruden) 101, 170
Longman, T. 84
Louisa, Queen of Denmark 188
lunatic asylums 17, 19, 97, 98–101, 104–6, 112–13, 170

Macro, Reverend Dr Cox 209
Maddox, Reverend Dr 35, 36, 46
Madge, Thomas 233–4
madhouses *see* lunatic asylums

Maggee, Andrew 221
Mar, Earl of 9, 10
Marbeck, John 33–4
Marischal College, Aberdeen 3, 5, 8, 11, 12, 13, 22, 23, 15, 56, 68, 183, 238, 239
Mary, Queen 33–4
Matthews, Robert 74
Mead, Dr Richard 79, 80, 81, 146, 235fn
Midwinter, D. 84
Mile End Road, London 95, 133
Milton, John 175, 176, 177
Mitford, John 119
Monro, Edward Thomas 104, 114
Monro, Henry 105
Monro, Dr James 104, 105, 110, 112, 113, 116, 118, 122–3, 124, 129, 138, 146, 149, 152, 153–5, 160, 165–9, 177, 179, 198, 235fn
Monro, Dr John 104, 113, 167, 198, 199
Monro, Thomas 104, 113, 114
Morgan, Jacob 139, 141
Morgan, Sarah 139, 141

Nathan, Rabbi Mordecai 33
Nevile, Reverend Dr J. 209, 210
Newcome, Henry 170
Newgate Prison, London 200, 221, 222, 224, 226
Newton, Reverend Thomas 177
Nichols, John 72, 179
*North Briton* (periodical) 235
Nourse, John 146, 238

Old Bailey, London 221
Olivier, Edith 174

Oswald, John 84, 90, 110, 122–3, 149, 155, 158, 165
Oxford 208–9

Paisley 12
*Paradise Lost* (Milton) 175, 176, 177, 180
Pargeter, William 100, 106
Parry-Jones, Professor W. 101
Paternoster Row, London 73, 219
Payne, Bryan 89, 158
Payne, Mrs 89, 90, 91, 92, 120, 131, 158, 159, 214
Pellett, Dr Thomas 146
Pemberton, J. and J. 84
*Phoenix* (ship) 21, 22, 161
Polwhele, Reverend Richard 145
Potter, Richard 220–33, 235
Poulett, Earl 203–4
Poultry Compter, London 221
Presbyterians 4, 6, 168, 175
*Public Advertiser* 216

*Rake's Progress, A* (Hogarth) 27
Rand, Isaac 79, 80, 146
Reynardson, Samuel 156
Rivington, Charles 84, 156
Rivington, John 84
Robert the Bruce 9
Robinson, John 115
Roe, Reverend Mr 224, 229
Rogers, Dr 'Gout-Oil' 130, 138, 140, 142, 150
Rose & Crown, London 26
Round, William 152, 157
Royal College of Physicians 81
Royal Exchange, London 52, 53, 69, 73–4, 75, 79, 84, 206

Royal Model Farm, Ållestad, Sweden 185
Royal Society 75, 78

St Charo, Hugo de 33
St James's Palace, London 86–7, 88, 95, 203, 204, 208, 217, 223
St James's Park, London 27, 223, 224
*St Janeiro* (ship) 220
St Luke's Hospital and Asylum, London 105
St Nicholas Kirk, Aberdeen 3, 12, 25, 57, 66, 246
St Paul's Cathedral, London 53, 73, 95
Scott, John 84, 102–3, 127
Scull, Andrew 105, 114
Shand, George, Lord Provost of Aberdeen 245
Sheriffmuir, Battle of (1715) 10
Simpson, William 22, 140, 157
Sloane, Sir Hans 75, 77, 78–9, 80, 86, 146, 174, 238
Smithfield, London 26, 53
Smollett, Tobias 103, 108, 117, 179
Society for the Propagation of Christian Knowledge 84
Society for the Reformation of Manners 194
Soho, London 42
Southampton Row, London 190, 192, 195, 199
Southgate 22, 23, 132, 144, 174
Spring Gardens, London 94

Stanley, James, 10th Earl of
  Derby 35, 37, 39–40, 42–3, 45,
  49, 168, 172
Stationers' Company 74, 76,
  137, 206
Stearn, William T. 148
Sterne, Laurence 179, 217
Stewart, James Francis Edward,
  the Old Pretender 9, 10
Stockholm, Sweden 185, 188
Stoke Newington, London 211,
  212
Stuart, Dr Alexander 143, 146,
  155
Stukeley, Dr William 143,
  155
Sunninghill 211
Swan Walk, London 79

Tessin, Count Carl-Gustav 186,
  187, 188
Trevelyan, George 44, 48
Trew, Christoph Jacob 238
Tryon, Thomas 171
Tunbridge Wells, Kent 211
Tyburn, London 226, 234
Tyndale, William 7

Ulrika Eleonora, Queen of
  Sweden 186
Union of the Crowns (1603) 8
Upper Moorfields, London 199,
  213

(Vagrancy) Act (1714) 97, 98

Walpole, Sir Robert 75, 76
Warburton, Thomas 101, 105,
  109, 113, 247

Warburton's 'Red House',
  London 109fn
Warburton's 'White House',
  London 109fn, 113; *see also*
  Wright's Private Madhouse
Ward, A. 84
Ward, Constable 134, 137
Ware, R. 84
Ware, Hertfordshire 24, 156
Watson, Mr, printer 26, 36, 40,
  47, 175
Watson, Reverend Dr J. 245
Wesley, John 168
Westminster Hall, London 152,
  169, 227
Weston, Mr 223
Whistler, Rex 174
'Whitaker, Mrs' 214
'White House' *see* Wright's
  Private Madhouse
Whitechapel, London 27, 95, 133
White's Alley, London 90, 92,
  94
Whitwell, Mr 45
Wightman, Robert 91–3, 94,
  101, 102, 109, 110, 112, 115, 118,
  120–2, 123, 125, 128, 129,
  137–9, 142, 143, 149, 152, 155,
  159–60, 166, 169, 177, 181, 183
Wild, Mr 190
Wild Court, London 180, 190,
  199
Wilkes, John 235
Wilkins, Mr 26
Windsor Castle 210
Windsor Chapel 33, 210
Wood, J. 84
Woodfall, Mr 216, 219
Woodland, Joseph 192, 198

Worms, Laurence 73–4
Worshipful Company of
 Grocers 137
Wren, Sir Christopher 53, 177
Wright, Matthew 101, 109, 111,
 117, 122, 127, 128, 129, 136, 137,
 152, 155, 157, 162, 165, 191

Wright's Private Madhouse 95,
 109, 113, 123, 132, 150, 194, 196,
 227, 247
Wyness, Fenton 60

Youngman, Reverend William
 xvii, 18, 28, 54, 62, 234